Adolescence and Death

Charles A. Corr, Ph.D., is Professor in the School of Humanities, Southern Illinois University at Edwardsville, and a member of the Board of Directors of Hospice of Madison County in Granite City, Illinois. Previous volumes which he has coauthored or coedited include: *Death Education: An Annotated Resource Guide* (Volume I: 1980; Volume II: 1985); *Hospice Care: Principles and Practice* (1983); *Helping Children Cope with Death: Guidelines and Resources* (2nd edition: 1984); *Childhood and Death* (1984); and *Hospice Approaches to Pediatric Care* (1985).

Joan N. McNeil, Ph.D., is Assistant Professor in the Department of Human Development and Family Studies, Kansas State University, Manhattan, Kansas. Author of *People: Patterns and Puzzles*, a workbook for human development students, and articles on family communication about death, Professor McNeil also has served as President of the Forum for Death Education and Counseling from 1982 to 1984 and edited its national *Newsletter*.

Adolescence and Death

Charles A. Corr, Ph.D.
Joan N. McNeil, Ph.D.

Editors

SPRINGER PUBLISHING COMPANY
New York

Springer Publishing Company, Inc.
536 Broadway
New York, NY 10012

86 87 88 89 90 / 5 4 3 2 1

Library of Congress Cataloging-in-Publication Data
Main entry under title:

Adolescence and death.

   Includes bibliographies and index.
   1. Youth and death.   2. Bereavement in youth—
Psychological aspects.   3. Youth—Suicidal behavior.
I. Corr, Charles A.   II. McNeil, Joan N.
BF724.3.D43A36   1986   155.9′37   85-31713
ISBN 0-8261-4930-8

Printed in the United States of America

For the Corr, Sistrunk, and McNeil kids
—our adolescents, past and present

Contents

Contributors

David W. Adams, M.S.W, C.S.W., is Director, Social Work Services, McMaster University Medical Centre Division, Chedoke-McMaster Hospitals, and Associate Professor, Department of Psychiatry, McMaster University, Hamilton, Ontario.

Rheba Adolph, M.S.W., is a social worker at the Adult Mental Health Clinic, North York General Hospital, Toronto, Ontario.

Thomas Attig, Ph.D., is Professor and Chairperson of the Department of Philosophy, Bowling Green State University, Bowling Green, Ohio.

Dorothy A. Austin, Th.D., is Lecturer on Psychology in the Department of Psychiatry, Harvard University, and at The Cambridge Hospital, Cambridge, Massachusetts.

Carol Ann Barnickol, M.A.S.W, is a consultant for Sudden Infant Death Syndrome Resources, Inc., St. Louis, Missouri.

Alan L. Berman, Ph.D., is Professor of Psychology, American University; past President of the American Association of Suicidology (1984–1985); and in private practice at the Washington Psychological Center, Washington, D.C.

Suzanne Calvin, M.R.E., is Editor, *Rocky Mountain United Methodist Reporter*, Denver, Colorado.

Eleanor J. Deveau, B.Sc.N., is Project Associate for Special Studies in Pediatrics, Social Work Services, McMaster University Medical Centre Division, Chedoke-McMaster Hospitals, Hamilton, Ontario.

Stephen J. Fleming, Ph.D., is Associate Professor, Department of Psychology, Atkinson College, York University, Toronto, Ontario.

Helen Fuller, M.S.W., is Executive Director, Sudden Infant Death Syndrome Resources, Inc., St. Louis, Missouri.

Audrey K. Gordon, M.A., A.M., is Research Associate in Community Health Sciences, School of Public Health, University of Illinois at Chicago Health Sciences Center, Chicago, Illinois.

B. Gail Joralemon, M.Div., is an ordained clergywoman in the United Church of Christ, and Executive Director, Abortion and Pregnancy Testing Clinic, Albuquerque, New Mexico.

Robert Kastenbaum, Ph.D., is Editor of *The International Journal of Aging and Human Development* and of *Omega: Journal of Death and Dying*, as well as Professor and Director, Adult Development and Aging Program, College of Public Programs, Arizona State University, Tempe, Arizona.

Elizabeth P. Lamers, M.A., is a reading specialist and educational consultant in Malibu, California.

John E. Mack, M.D., is Professor of Psychiatry at Harvard University and at The Cambridge Hospital, Cambridge, Massachusetts.

Richard A. Pacholski, Ph.D., is Professor and Chairperson, Department of English, Millikin University, Decatur, Illinois.

Nina Ribak Rosenthal, Ph.D., is Professor of Education, California State University, Stanislaus, Turlock, California.

Joan Rifkin Sellers, M.S.S.W., L.C.S.W., is a substance abuse consultant in private practice in Beverly Hills, California.

Beth Shinners, M.S.W., is a partner in Professional Health Associates, and a professional advisor to the Compassionate Friends chapters in St. Louis, Missouri. Her contributions to Chapter 8 are based on five years' work as Pediatric Medical Social Worker in the Neonatal Intensive Care Unit, Children's Hospital at Washington University Medical Center, St. Louis, Missouri.

Inez M. Smith, M.A., is a counselor at Northglenn High School, Adams County School District #12, Denver, Colorado.

Sharon M. Valente, R.N., M.N., C.S., F.A.A.N., is Adjunct Assistant Professor, Department of Nursing, University of Southern California, a clinical specialist in mental health in private practice, Los Angeles, California, and a Fellow of the American Academy of Nursing.

Preface

Much has been written about adolescence, and—especially recently—a good deal has been written about dying, death, and bereavement. But very little has been written about the issues involved in the conjunction of these phenomena—with the notable exception of adolescent suicide. This book sets out to remedy that important deficiency by exploring the full spectrum of topics that have to do with adolescence and death. The aims are: to define some of the primary contours of the field; to determine the present state of our knowledge about this pressing subject; to identify areas in which there is a need for additional study and research; and—perhaps most important of all—to provide helpful guidelines for assisting adolescents presently struggling with the difficult issues of dying, death, and bereavement.

When we first undertook this project, we realized that it posed certain problems. Interactions between adolescence and death present a shifting set of relationships kept in flux by alterations in the two primary variables. Consider the fact that adolescence as a distinct period in the life span is a fairly recent invention. It did not exist throughout much of our own history and still may not exist in certain societies. Adolescence seems to have come into being with the realization that the passing of childhood did not automatically entail the advent of adulthood. In other words, adolescence is the product of a certain set of circumstances (among which is increased average life expectancy) wherein society acknowledges a kind of interval between childhood and young adulthood. But that interval itself is changing: on the one hand, childhood is in some ways prolonged and in others precociously transformed into adolescence; on the other hand, adolescence itself is extended into what otherwise might have been thought of as the early adult years.

At the same time, social experiences with dying, death, and bereavement have also been changing: average life expectancy has increased; overall mortality rates have declined and have become significantly more stable; the principal causes of death have changed from communicable to degenerative diseases; dying has in many ways become subject to institutionalization, professionalization, and specialization; many bereavement rituals have been abandoned; and the prospect of mass death in a nuclear holocaust has come to overshadow us all. We are living not with a static phenomenon, but with the changing face of death. Our portrait of adolescence and death must be painted in a way that respects all of these ongoing transformations.

With this state of affairs, a number of limitations became obvious. The cross-cultural comparisons that might have attracted us were clearly beyond our scope. Even within our own society, it has been necessary to focus primarily on the mainstream of adolescent experience. More to the point, it soon became evident that no single individual could be expected to have detailed and accurate knowledge of a subject as complex as adolescence and death. We turned, therefore, to a number of experts in particular areas, asking each to address a specific set of issues. With the assistance of these contributors, each chapter in this book has been specifically designed both to explore an important subject in its own right and to contribute in a significant way to the overall discussion. We are pleased and grateful that so many busy people worked so cooperatively with us to achieve these goals. The result is that readers are free to read the book straight through as a whole or to turn directly to individual chapters as their interests or needs require.

In addition to those who wrote chapters for this book, we owe a debt of gratitude to many who helped us along the way. This project grew out of our experiences in teaching courses on Death and Dying, our shared interests in hospice care and in issues relating to children and death, and stimulating contacts made through the Forum for Death Education and Counseling. Administrators and colleagues at our respective institutions—Southern Illinois University at Edwardsville and Kansas State University—supported our work. Our families encouraged our efforts and helped when things did not always go smoothly.

Bringing this book into being has been an exciting and instructive adventure for us. We trust that those who consult or use it will share our sense of discovery and will appreciate our respect for things yet to be learned.

Charles A. Corr, Ph.D.
Joan N. McNeil, Ph.D.

PART I
Adolescents and Death: Contemporary Interactions

When it comes to matters of death, dying, and bereavement, adolescents in our society are often treated in conflicting ways. From the standpoints of theory and research, for example, developmental psychologists are likely to be heard telling us that children do not achieve a mature concept of death until around the ages of 10 or 12. That would seem to suggest that adolescents are essentially to be contrasted with younger children and treated on a par with adults. But in practice, adolescents are often screened or sheltered—insofar as that is possible—from "real life" involvement in death-related matters. They may not be taken to visit a dying relative, their feelings of grief are often minimized, and their views are not likely to be sought by those concerned about nuclear warfare.

Which is it to be? Are adolescents children or adults? If adolescents are children, then perhaps adults can safely dismiss themes of separation, loss, and death that loom so large in their music and peer-group environment. But how can such children then be sent to fight and die for their country? If adolescents are adults, why then is it so striking when one of them commits suicide or chooses abortion to end an unwanted pregnancy?

There is, of course, a third possibility: namely, that adolescents are neither children nor adults. In this view, adolescents are young people living through a distinct time in the life span. No longer merely children and not yet quite fully adults, adolescents are individuals with their own characteristic needs, problems, and tasks. Surely this third perspective is most nearly correct. Our endeavor in this book will be to test its validity by searching out what is distinctive in adolescent encounters with death. Is it their thoughts and feelings about death, the things that are likely to happen in these years, the ways in which adolescents frequently or even occasionally behave, the limits of their resources, the values and concerns—or perhaps all of these together—that will be most significant in the world of adolescents coping with death?

In quite different and yet fundamentally compatible ways, Robert Kastenbaum and Audrey Gordon take up these issues in Chapter 1 and Chapter 2, respectively. Kastenbaum brings wit and insight to bear on familiar preconceptions as to what it is like to be an adolescent encountering death. He incorporates a rare appreciation of the fundamental humanity of the adolescent. Gordon suggests that adolescence may be better understood as consisting of more than just a single period in life, and illustrates both this point and many of the special features of the adolescent experience by describing a range of situations in which adolescents are called upon to cope with the implications of death.

The next two chapters in Part I examine more closely two specific aspects of the world inhabited by adolescents. The first of these is music. While television, film, and sports might also be selected, music is perhaps the most immediate and certainly the most pervasive feature in the world of contemporary adolescence. Thomas Attig's extraordinarily detailed survey in Chapter 3 reveals just how multifaceted death themes are in adolescent music. This music is an ongoing phenomenon whose historical evolution cannot be captured in a single analysis, as Attig recognizes. But it is also an important idiom through which access can be obtained and dialogue promoted for those willing to become familiar with a rather specialized adolescent vernacular.

Finally, in Chapter 4, Dorothy Austin and John Mack offer significant insight into what it means to be an adolescent in the nuclear era. Nuclear weapons, megadeath, and the possible extinction of humankind at our very own hands are new facts that have come into the world only since 1945. Not confined to adolescents alone, they remind us again of Kastenbaum's point about the essential humanity shared by adolescents with the rest of us. Nevertheless, even as we recognize that death themes are not confined solely to the music of adolescents, it is useful to maintain a tension between what is common and what is unique. This is accomplished by Austin and Mack through their careful emphasis on the adolescent perspective and the adolescent voice in the nuclear discussion. It is important to pay attention to the positive conclusion of Chapter 4: fears of extinction and anxiety related to nuclear weapons are important concerns for at least some adolescents, but they can be managed in constructive ways through psychological empowerment and thoughtful intervention by adults.

1

Death in the World of Adolescence

Robert Kastenbaum

Straight thinking about either adolescence or death has proven difficult enough. Taken separately, each theme has given rise to a bewildering variety of interpretations. Caution is appropriate, then, in considering adolescence and death together. The temptation is to select those bits and pieces of information that lend themselves to an ego-syntonic construction rather than to examine all the facts and acknowledge all the limitations of our knowledge and understanding. Take, for example, the following illustrations: would these have a place in your theory of adolescence and death?

SOME UNFORTUNATE EXAMPLES

From Research

"Storm and stress" are inherent in the adolescent experience, of course, as we have known for more than a century. Unfortunately,

> . . . young adolescents [are] thought to be at highest risk for adolescent turmoil. Our study fails to support the proposal that young people are generally tumultuous at this age. The reports of self-image in our data are generally positive, and they increase over the years studied. (Abramowitz, Petersen, & Schulenberg, 1984, p. 25).

Nevertheless, we can place reliance in the ability of our trained professionals to evaluate adolescents with objectivity and accuracy:

The misconceptions that mental health professionals hold about the normal adolescent form clear and consistent patterns. . . . professionals perceived normal adolescents as being more defensive, more sensitive, and more tense under normal circumstances than the young people described themselves as being. Professionals believed that teens are more resentful of criticism and that their feelings are more easily hurt than the young people themselves reported . . . [and] as being less relaxed both under usual circumstances and under pressure than normal adolescents stated. (Hartlage, Howard, & Ostrov, 1984, pp. 34–35).

Other findings of the above study indicated that mental health professionals were more on target in predicting the attitudes of parents than adolescents—a clue, perhaps, to the way in which society often constructs its views of the adolescent experience.

Sad to say, the moral fiber of our nation continues to come unravelled, as is all too well illustrated by youth's abandonment of traditional values. Just look at what was found in a study that compared adolescent attitudes in the same community for 1924 and 1977:

There is no trace of the disintegration of traditional social values [in "Middletown"] that is commonly described by observers who rely on their own intuitions. . . . The young people in 1977 are as strongly imbued with religion, patriotism, and the Protestant ethic as their grandparents were at the same age . . . [but] also more tolerant of those who disagree with them, or who hold other values. (Caplow & Bahr, 1979, p. 17)

The idealism, social immaturity, and fluctuating passions of the adolescent create a distinctive psychic vulnerability in which heightened awareness of death figures prominently. This we know from much informed opinion over the years. Therefore, systematic research on adolescence gives much attention to thoughts, feelings, and actions related to death:

The *Handbook of Adolescent Psychology* (Adelson, 1980) and *Review of Human Development* (Field, Huston, Quay, Troll, & Finley, 1982) are major current reference books offering more than twelve hundred pages of knowledge. The total number of references to death in both volumes is zero. Is death really that trivial a subject, or our knowledge of death in childhood and adolescence really that complete? (Kastenbaum, 1985, pp. 630–631)

From Everyday Life

Reaching puberty is a transfiguring event, producing a new self that asserts its emerging biological imperatives and psychosocial demands. One woman reflects upon this time from more than 50 years distance:

We didn't make that much of a do about it in those days. To tell you the absolute truth, I never thought of myself as an adolescent or a teenager or any such. I was just, well, myself, and part of the family. I was the oldest of the girls and I'd always had responsibilities. I suppose I thought of myself as almost a grownup for a long time. . . . Oh, no! [laughing] I don't think "hanging out" had been invented yet—not for girls, anyhow. I remember that it became more important for me to "look nice" so the boys would take notice—but, then, not too much notice either! . . . The farm was everything and the family was everything and I was just one part of it. And there was so much to do practically all the time. . . . I didn't have to think that much about growing up; that just sort of took care of itself.

This was but one woman's reminiscence, taped as part of my conversations with residents of an Arizona adult community. A roomful of women ranging in age from the early twenties to the late thirties could be expected to bring a different perspective to memories of their adolescence during a conference break-out session. Notice with what pride and satisfaction they describe the experience of being a modern teenager with all the newer privileges and liberties:

I was the loneliest person in the world.

That's exactly the way I felt most of the time. I could never get in the "in-group." I always felt I was on the outside [in high school]. I felt at home only at home.

Well, I had it made. I made cheerleader every year right from the start. Everybody look at me! See how wonderful I am! But don't you believe it. I felt out of it even when I was into it. I didn't think anybody really liked me for myself and there was always that doubt. I had to keep smiling and laughing and jumping up and down and maybe I could fool myself into thinking I was really somebody and really having fun. Thank God I don't have to go through all that again!

[From several voices] Amen.

I guess I didn't have as much trouble as what I've been hearing. I had a few close friends from elementary school and we stayed together pretty well. My mother made me believe there was plenty of time for everything I wanted. I didn't have to do it all right away. When I screwed up or something went wrong, it was no big deal at home. I must have had very understanding parents: I still do.

The confrontation with death in adolescence—in actuality or in prospect—overwhelms the fragile defensive structures at this time of life, often leading to extreme reactions. Consider the following report from a young man working as an aide in a nursing home:

> He looked like he was sleeping so soundly that I left his bed to make up for last. I had saved up some jokes I thought he would like. We would always tell each other jokes. But he was dead. I didn't know what to do. I mean, I knew what to do, the procedure, but I didn't know how to feel. I was so used to taking care of him and joking and now his body was cold and kinda bluish/purple. . . . I had one other aide help me get his body ready. Ready for what, huh? It felt weird just to be doing things to his body and not really talking with him or anything. So I did. . . . I told him the jokes, anyway. I think I did that to make everything seem normal, even though it wasn't. The woman who was working with me thought at first it was weird for me to be talking to him and telling him jokes, but then, she said, "Maybe his ghost is listening and will have a few laughs in the next life." And then she said something sort of weird, that the air was heavy in here. With death. So we opened a window so his spirit could fly away—even though we didn't believe in any of that stuff. . . . Yes, the air felt lighter when we did that. I just can't describe how weird it feels to find somebody dead; wow, it makes you quiver down the spine. Still you have to go ahead and carry out the procedures, don't you, and then go on with your own life as though nothing really happened—but it did. Weird!

The same young man gets himself around on a motorcycle. His macho defiance of fate is no doubt a typical adolescent strategy for distancing one's self from the possibility of personal death:

> I think about it almost every time I put on my helmet. Something could happen. I could be creamed and spend the rest of my life in a wheelchair, or even not have any rest of my life to spend. I like my cycle; I always wanted one. But, say, Dad, I saw this neat Ford yesterday. It's an old roadster and I could get it cheap. . . . Oh, about twenty-four. . . . Yeah, thousand.

A student preparing herself to be a social worker admits how the inexplicable mystery of death has preyed constantly on her mind since early adolescence:

> First my dog died. I should have said "our" dog, but he really was mine. Then grandma died. Then I thought: well, anybody can die. I guess I had been expecting everybody I love to live forever. But death is as natural as can be. Can't get more natural than that! I don't like to think about death but it's not because it's so strange and hard to understand. It's just because it's so sad and permanent and there's not much we can do about it.

Death Imagined

All the facets of adolescence presented above are rather unpromising from the standpoint of supporting a satisfying conceptual image. They reek too much of "normality." There are some failures in our appreciation of the realm of death as well. The basic fact that "dead is dead" often has failed to satisfy the need for meaning, leading to a thriving market for belief systems that construct meanings around the bare fact of mortality (Ariès, 1981; Choron, 1963; Gatch, 1969; Kastenbaum, 1981). Two examples may suffice. Observe first how Maeterlinck tried to prepare us for standing *Before the Great Silence* (1936):

> Now, "nothing," whether a thing or a state, cannot exist without ceasing to be "nothing." If nothingness had ever existed, if it could ever exist anywhere, it would have invaded everything, since there is not room, simultaneously, in the universe, for being and for not being. (p. 60)

Philosophical efforts of this genre are almost guaranteed to fail. It is not a question of whether Maeterlinck was wrong or right, but rather a question of how much nourishment, comfort, or inspiration society can derive in the face of death from an intellectual, analytical approach. "Not much!" is the usual verdict. Although a few individuals might respond to such obsessive dialectics, society at large generally gives little heed. We seek a sense of confidence at the edge of the void, not ruminations and doubts:

> You had a lot of time to yourself while you were standing watch at night, three or four hours in the dark all to yourself. What else are you going to think abo it, man? Your fucking friend got blown off. He died on you. You try to make some kind of sense out of it, to come to terms with it at a new level. Not at the old level where you exist with him. Now you have to exist without him. Why? Wherefores? What does it mean. . . . When death comes into your head, you don't have the strength to push it aside. You're just so fucking tired. Nineteen-year-old bodies with thirty-five-year-old minds. (Baker, 1982, p. 130)

In a much harsher way, the Vietnam War brought both death and questions about death to the immediate attention of the participants (many of whom were youths). The "dead is dead" factor was all too clearly established—but where was the meaning? Part of the despair experienced as the war continued centered on its perceived lack of purpose and the absence of any acceptable shared meanings that could explain or justify death. The inability to answer the questions "Why should we die? Why should we kill?" represents a crucial limitation of the belief systems that had contributed to participation in the Vietnam War in the first place. The young soldier wondering why his friend had been blown away was not exhibiting a peculiarly adolescent state of mind, but rather, again, generic human despair in the presence of death and the absence of meaning.

Unwelcome Examples

The instances sketched here would not be welcome in most theoretical orientations toward adolescence and death. Whether culled from formal research or picked up in the course of daily life, these examples fail to support some of our most cherished notions. Adolescents are depicted in rather too normal a manner. Even their encounters with death have more of a generically human rather than a distinctively adolescent character. The constructions of adolescence and of death that have enjoyed the greatest popularity and influence tend to be of a dramatic nature. The "storm and stress" view has already been mentioned, a conception that depicts adolescents as hypersensitive idealists who are torn apart by passion and much in need of the steadying influence only their seasoned elders can provide. The hero of Goethe's *The Sorrows of Young Werther* (1774/1949) served long and well as a classic example of youth in turmoil. Some may still believe that large numbers of sensitive young Germans followed his example of lovelorn suicide, an early example of the contagion theory. As far as I know, however, there has been no supportive evidence that this literary suicide actually was followed by a substantial real-life epidemic. It does make a good story, however, and this seems to be a prime requirement for any account of adolescence if it is to catch the imagination of public and professionals alike.

An authentic account of the relationships between adolescence and death will require breadth of observation, including the mundane as well as the spectacular, individual differences as well as generalities, and, above all, a keen sense of balance. What is related to the universal phenomena of pubescence must be balanced against what is specific to the "coming-of-age" process in particular societies at a particular time. What is specific to being adolescent must be balanced against what is specific to being a male or female, being under greater or lesser pressure for worldly success, and having adequate or inadequate access to sociocultural resources. Seldom do we contribute to the understanding of a phenomenon by attributing it to "adolescence" (or to "old age" for that matter). With these cautions in mind, we can at least identify a few of the issues most in need of clarification.

SOME UNRESOLVED QUESTIONS

"I Die, Therefore I Am"

This variation on Descartes can be proposed as one characteristic theme of adolescent cognition. Universal? Probably not. The *only* way that adolescents think about death? Certainly not. Nevertheless, this theme deserves attention for what it might tell us about the process of reconstructing the world in adolescence. Consider some of the contributing factors:

1. *By the time we have reached adolescence we have also come into possession of advanced cognitive abilities.* In the language of Piaget (1958), we are now able to engage in "formal operations" rather than limit our thinking to the "concrete" level. We can take ideas apart and put them back together again in new ways, examine possibilities as well as present realities, and build entire systems of thought. Piaget's emphasis on development and maturation has sometimes been misinterpreted as a denial of environmental influence. It is difficult to understand this error when Piaget (1958) has repeatedly acknowledged that

> the formal structures are neither innate *a priori* forms of intelligence which are inscribed in advance in the nervous system, nor are they collective representations which exist ready-made outside and above the individual. Instead, they are forms of equilibrium which gradually settle on the system of exchanges between individuals and the physical milieu and on the system of exchanges between individuals themselves. (p. 338)

We should expect adolescents, then, to review and revise the ideas and assumptions brought forward from childhood. This reconstruction of the world is likely to be carried out both in thought and action. Trying out a different life style can serve a quasi-philosophical function intended to answer the question: "Who is this self, and in what kind of world?" In diaries and poetry intended for no other eyes or in long, meandering conversations with a best friend, adolescents try to find the words and images for a more adequate and more personal construction of the world.

2. *Recognition of not-being is an inherent part of the reconstruction process.* Here there is some reason for questioning the Piagetian approach with its emphasis on growth, consistency, integration, and endurance. The child must develop the ability to ignore what is transient and mutable, and attend instead to what is invariant and persistent. This bias introduces a serious distortion. "Reality" is comprised of the transient as well

as the enduring, the variant as well as the invariant. It is just as important for the child to learn "all gone!" from the melting of an ice cream cone or the flushing of a toilet, as it is to recognize that a pint of water is still a pint of water whether poured into a tall or a short container (Kastenbaum, 1973). We learn what is relatively enduring from our experience with the transient and vice versa: a dialectic process. The clearly articulated concept of death that one may be able to express at age 12 had its preparation in a great many earlier experiences with losses, meltings, and disappearances.

3. *"Dying" is often a potent metaphor during transitional situations and the extremes of stimulus overload and deprivation.* "I just *died!*" may express the rush of overwhelming feeling experienced by an adolescent in certain situations, while at the other end of the spectrum, the same youth may at times be "dying of boredom." Similarly, "dying" often appears as a metaphor of passage. The newly divorced, widowed, relocated, and retired sometimes express their feelings in this language. Note that adolescence does not have a monopoly on dying-as-metaphor. It seems more likely that it is the transitional situation that gives rise to this metaphor—and perhaps less inhibition about expressing one's feelings in a dramatic way.

By converging these points, it is possible to approach an understanding of "I die, therefore I am." More than the child whose abstract thinking abilities are still limited and more than the adult who has already become habituated to certain ways of seeing/not seeing the world (Kastenbaum, 1980), the adolescent has a vivid awareness of the dialectic between being and not-being. The actual often seems a mockery of the possible. This heightened sense of futurity allows a glimpse of what one might be—but also the recognition that one might *not* be. Daily experience provides occasions for assertions of a new self or "dyings" of the old self and apparent abortions of the new self.

And so it is precisely when the adolescent is most endangered by the polarities of being and not-being that the concept of self emerges with singular force. "I am the one who is torn. . . . I am the one who struggles. . . . I am the one whose future is so in doubt. . . ." The perception of a self-under-reconstruction is vouchsafed most keenly as one experiences the possibility of failure, loss, catastrophe, and death. Dying-as-metaphor becomes associated with the newly found ability to understand the universality, inevitability, and finality of death. Blurring is possible between the metaphoric and objective meanings. The death that is produced by suicide, for example, may be fused and confused with its metaphoric counterparts. Suicidal ideation in general may have a philosophical quality and an experimental function: "Who would I be, if I weren't? Could I accomplish more by ending it all? Will I be my own self most securely in the act of killing this self?" The tragedy of actual suicide is so compelling that sometimes we ignore the potentially valuable role of suicidal *ideation* in the development of a reconstructed view of self and world.

"Living for What? Dying for What?"

The period of life we call adolescence has not always been as extensive and salient as it is today. Through much of history, people moved into adult responsibilities rather quickly, unencumbered by such institutions as compulsory education and such personal agendas as "finding myself." Often the society one entered as an adult was characterized by fixed belief systems, explicit moral/behavioral codes, and (by our standards) limited choices of personal life style. Born into Aztec society, prior to the conquistadors, one would move from childhood through an apprentice period and into full adulthood without having to trouble one's self over fundamental decisions of choice and action (Todorov, 1984). The elderly women who told us about her adolescence "We didn't make that much of a do about it in those days" faced many more choices than did the youths of ancient Mexico and most other previous societies, but fewer than those confronting her grandchildren today. The meanings of both life and death tend to shift somewhat with the distinctive configurations of stress and opportunity experienced by each generation as well as by the sheer numbers of youth in the general population.

The two young men quoted in an earlier section face two variations of the perplexities that our present society visits upon itself. The "greying of America" makes it easier than ever to associate death with the elderly. Encased in a sort of symbolic ghetto, the elderly—especially those vulnerable enough to be institutionalized—are expected to end their now-insignificant lives with equally insignificant deaths (Kastenbaum, 1978; Miller, 1976). The inequity of such a stereotype has frequently been addressed in the gerontological literature. Here, however, it is more relevant to consider the implications for youth.

The young aide who found one of the nursing home residents dead received no emotional or moral support from the institution. There were certain physical procedures to be carried out, and these he performed with a little help. But what did this death "mean"? How was he supposed to feel about it? What should he take of this death back into his own life? Like almost all the young men and women who work with the institutionalized elderly, this person could not help but feel that this death *should* mean something—to somebody! No guidance was forthcoming from the institutional bureaucracy. This failure was itself a kind of message that one is simply to do and not to think or feel. The joking and window-opening represent attempts both to relieve personal discomfort and tension and to avoid an abrupt and complete severance of the relationship with the deceased: "Maybe his ghost is listening and will have a few laughs in the next life." For this young man, entry into the adult work force also provided evidence that it is not appropriate to care very much for his elders, in life or in death. Experiences of this kind are repeated daily throughout the nation. Adolescents are thrown back upon their personal resources and limited life experiences as "The Establishment" processes death in a cost-efficient manner.

"Nineteen-year-old bodies with thirty-five-year old minds" in Vietnam were in jeopardy for their own lives at the same time that they encountered death on many sides. Asking "Why? Wherefore?" cannot be dismissed as a characteristic adolescent mind-set: these questions have not yet been answered satisfactorily. One of the many impacts of the Vietnam War on American life can be seen in the reemergence of so-called adolescent concerns. The "why" of war is a concern now shared by many people of all ages. Some of the excellent philosophical questions that become so urgent to thoughtful adolescents have also reawakened in the minds of their elders—those who had opted not to cope with these issues by growling that we should "nuke 'em all!"

A FINAL WORD

Society's conceptions of life and death cannot hide from the penetrating inspection of each adolescent generation which, for its own part, cannot reconstruct personal world views unless not-being and its meanings are somehow encompassed. Serious questions may be raised about the guidance and models our society provides, but there should be nothing astounding in the fact that adolescents often turn to each other for lack of alternatives.

In this brief introductory chapter, it has been my purpose to suggest that adolescents are more like people than anything else. Yes, there are distinctive biological, psychological, and socio-cultural factors operating in the life of the adolescent, but, no, not every thought, response, and feeling is to be interpreted as a manifestation of "adolescenceness." Theories that are special to adolescence or special to death may not contribute as much to understanding as we would like to believe.

Having offered some cautions along the way, I will take the liberty of disregarding my own advice with the following generalizations: It is in adolescence that we glimpse for the first time what we and the world *might* be. Intellect and feeling are united in the same quest, albeit one subject to confusion and misdirection. The life and death questions we raise in adolescence create a sense of vulnerability that we spend most of our adult years trying to conceal and forget. In later life, one may be caught up again in the challenge of a new transitional situation. And there it is again—the gleam is back in the eyes. The "old adolescent" is fresh again with philosophical questions and experiments in life style. Although we do outgrow some of the predicaments and concerns that marked our adolescent years, I wonder if we are too quick to put aside in our adult lives the impelling questions that we generated in youth.

REFERENCES

Abramowitz, R. H., Petersen, A. C., & Schulenberg, J. E. Changes in self-image during early adolescence. In D. Offer, E. Ostrov, & K. I. Howard (Eds.), *Patterns of adolescent self-image* (pp. 19–28). San Francisco: Jossey-Bass, 1984.

Adelson, J. (Ed.). *Handbook of adolescent psychology.* New York: Wiley, 1980.

Ariès, P. *The hour of our death* (H. Weaver, Trans.). New York: Knopf, 1981.

Baker, M. *Nam.* New York: Quill, 1982.

Caplow, T., & Bahr, H. M. Half a century of change in adolescent attitudes: Replication of a Middletown survey by the Lynds. *Public Opinion Quarterly,* 1979, *43*, 1–17.

Choron, J. *Death and western thought.* New York: Collier, 1963.

Field, T. M., Huston, A., Quay, H. C., Troll, L., & Finley, G. E. *Review of human development.* New York: Wiley, 1982.

Gatch, M. *Death: Meaning and mortality in Christian thought and contemporary culture.* New York: Seabury, 1969.

Goethe, J. W. von. *The sorrows of young Werther* (R. D. Boylan, Trans.; revised by V. Lange). New York: Holt, Rinehart & Winston, 1949. (Original work published 1774)

Hartlage, S., Howard, K. I., & Ostrov, E. The mental health professional and the normal adolescent. In D. Offer, E. Ostrov, & K. I. Howard (Eds.), *Patterns of adolescent self-image* (pp. 29–44). San Francisco: Jossey-Bass, 1984.

Kastenbaum, R. The kingdom where nobody dies. *Saturday Review,* 1973, *56* (January), 33–38.

Kastenbaum, R. Dying, death, and bereavement in old age: New developments and their possible implications for psychosocial care. *Aged Care and Services Review,* 1978, *1*, 1–10.

Kastenbaum, R. Habituation as a partial model of aging. *International Journal of Aging and Human Development,* 1980, *12*, 159–170.

Kastenbaum, R., *Death, society and human experience* (2nd ed.). St. Louis: Mosby, 1981.

Kastenbaum, R. Dying and death: A lifespan approach. In J. E. Birren & K. W. Schaie (Eds.), *Handbook of the psychology of aging* (2nd ed.). New York: Van Nostrand Reinhold, 1985.

Maeterlinck, M. *Before the great silence.* New York: F. A. Stokes, 1936.

Miller, M. B. *The interdisciplinary role of the nursing home medical director.* Wakefield, MA: Contemporary Publishing, 1976.

Piaget, J. *The growth of logical thinking from childhood to adolescence.* New York: Basic Books, 1958.

Todorov, T. *The conquest of America.* New York: Harper & Row, 1984.

2

The Tattered Cloak
of Immortality

Audrey K. Gordon

CHILDREN AND ADOLESCENTS

When we are born, we enter into a life of finitude and mortality. Through nature's wisdom, we are shielded from the full realization of this characteristic of our lives while we are children. Wrapped in the cloak of childhood's perceived immortality, the child ventures forth on unsteady legs—to explore while parents tremble, to play with fire and be burned, to chase balls rolling into the street—while unaware of mortal danger. Could we undertake the tasks of childhood while fully aware of the implications of death? I think not. The child's certainty of permanence allows him or her to challenge the environment without fear and to grow in experience and knowledge. Most theories of childhood concepts of death stress that the finality of death eludes the very young child, who only gradually reaches complete awareness somewhere around ages 11 or 12 (Lonetto, 1980; Wass, 1984a). However, if the child has a personally significant experience with death before this, awareness may come earlier (Bluebond-Langner, 1978). Moreover, fears and anxieties may be present—and perhaps fostered—in the absence of full conceptual clarity (Bertman, 1984; Wass & Cason, 1984).

The first signs of wear in the cloak of immortality appear in the latency-age child. From about six to nine, the world is peopled with villains and monsters. There are things that "go bump" in the night and strange creatures that inhabit the bedroom. This first consciousness that something "out there" can get you is often associated with the child's personification of death. A frequent response to these feelings of vulnerability is the development of a macabre sense of humor (for example, dead baby jokes) to relieve anxiety. For many people, the use of this kind of humor to ventilate fears continues throughout life.

The death of an adult the school-age child knows tears a hole in the cloak. "Mommy, will you die?" the child inquires anxiously, not able to fully accept the premonition that death comes to all. The shorter life span of pets and other "small deaths" occurring naturally throughout life can instruct children about the permanence of death (Carson, 1984), but only if the event is sensitively and realistically handled by the parents. Too often, it is not. The goldfish is replaced with its twin and the aged dog appears to be quickly forgotten by the child absorbed in the antics of the new puppy. Unless the death is ritualized and given meaning, the child has no constructive way to store the memory.

Frequently, children are "protected" by adults from the sights and sounds of death and dying because it is assumed that young people are unable to comprehend their total meaning without adult help. It has been suggested that well-intentioned, but misguided, protectionism of this sort came into favor less for the sake of children than because it allowed the avoidance sought by adults (Corr, 1979; Wass, 1984b). In any event, it would appear that this situation is slowly changing. There is a definite trend toward the education of children in the complete life cycle from birth to death (Gordon & Klass, 1979; McNeil, 1984; Wass & Corr, 1984). This is to be commended. Children need to be prepared to cope in responsible ways with the realities of life and death.

More to the point, adolescents also need to be liberated from the umbrella of adult protectionism. Adolescents have concerns and capacities in relation to death that are distinct from those of younger children. Recognition of adolescent developmental needs concerning the topics of dying, death, and bereavement requires a separate focus from the recognition of a child's developmental needs in this area, since adolescence has its own biological, cognitive, and emotional landmarks.

INTERPRETATIONS OF ADOLESCENCE

Adolescence is a new time in the life experience of humans, new in the sense that centuries ago childhood ended quickly and adulthood began at 11 or 12 due to a shorter life expectancy and the labor demands of marginally productive societies. In a heavily technologized society such as ours with its greatly increased longevity, a longer training process is both feasible and deemed necessary to meet the needs of both the society and the individual. This training process, resulting in delayed social maturation, has become a significant period between childhood and adulthood called adolescence.

Adolescence, the time from 12 to 19, is really composed of two significant periods preceded by liminal stages in which important transitions
occur. The period from 12 to 15 (with 11 as the threshold) encompasses
the acquisition of formal logical thought, the onset of biological sexuality, the growth of the physical structure, and a myriad of psychosocial
tasks. These latter include entrance into a mixed gender peer group, experimenting with adult behavior and rules, and expanding geographi-
cally the territory available for experience. The second period, from 16 to
19 with transition around 15, is characterized by the completion of physical maturation, increasing intimacy with the opposite sex, continued acquisition of adult social skills, clarification of ethics and values, further
expansion of territory (including separation from family of origin), and
the ability to make long-term commitments to persons and goals. These
two periods in adolescence are both biologically and socially determined.

Theories differ as to the meaning and description of adolescence. Adolescence seems to straddle two worlds, that of child and adult, and to
be secure in neither. It is, however, its own time rather than an unsteady bridge between other spheres. Much of the literature on adolescence characterizes it as a time of disruption and turmoil. However,
Offer, Ostrov, and Howard (1981) studied thousands of adolescents in
three countries in the 1960s and again in the 1970s, and concluded that
in general adolescents face life situations with little fear and with a reasonable amount of confidence. They determined that the American
teenager is confident, happy, and self-satisfied.

This is in sharp contrast to the traditional psychoanalytic view that depicts adolescence as a time of fragmentation, mourning, and normal depression. Feinstein (1981) writes that "Anna Freud believed that all adolescents could be thought of as being in a state of mourning and, in fact,
longing for the period of childhood when solutions were relatively simple" (p. 323). Feinstein also states that "partial regressions, in the service
of mastering ego stresses related to the necessary loosening of ego structures, subject the adolescent to frequent loss experiences" (p. 322). Depression is thus seen as a "normal" state for adolescents, unless it mani-
fests itself in maladaptive functioning not associated with the usual
course of adolescence.

My own experience with adolescents agrees with that of Offer et al.
(1981). Most adults remember their adolescence as a time fraught with
anxiety, rebellion, and indecision. Offer and his colleagues think that
adolescence is "the world's most perfect projective device for adults" (p.
121). From an adult perspective, if it is painful dealing with questions of
identity, self-esteem, sexuality, and body image now, how much more
painful must it have been when these questions first arose. To the extent

that adults create self-fulfilling prophecies about adolescence, there may be more rebellion and anxiety at this stage than at other times of life. But the experience of midlife surely equals adolescence in rebellion and anxiety. Indeed, midlife is frequently called a "second adolescence," and some are beginning to speak of "middlescence" as a distinct period with its own problems and opportunities. My point is to agree with Bandura (1980) who has said: "If a society labels its adolescents as 'teenagers' and expects them to be rebellious, unpredictable, sloppy, and wild in their behavior, and if this picture is repeatedly reinforced by the mass media, such cultural expectations may very well force adolescents into the role of rebel" (p.30).

The years from 12 to 18 or 19 are stages in the life cycle like any other and have their idiosyncratic as well as repetitive tasks (Erikson, 1950; Levinson, Darrow, Klein, Levinson, & McKee, 1978). Failure to complete these tasks has the same consequences as failure to complete a task in any other stage. Yet writings on adolescence stress that it is a pivotal time, as if there is a more delicate balance at this point between pathology and health. It is a presumption that a turned-up biological thermostat presupposes an unstable emotional base. In fact, the unstable emotional quality of adolescents has much to do with how they are treated by adults not yet able to accept the adolescent's transition from childhood into a new stage of development. Healthy, confident teenagers are the products of parenting that respects and fosters the growth of the emerging adult, largely by making available experiences that teach adolescents how to cope with adult tasks and how to achieve personally significant goals.

Healthy adulthood does not depend entirely upon the successful resolution of what are presently seen as issues unique to adolescence. Young adults in their twenties are still working out issues of sexuality, intimacy, and self-esteem. Maybe we never finish dealing with such issues. So much attention is focused on the "embryonic" years (infancy, childhood, and adolescence) that we tend to forget the effects of a lengthy educational process resulting in delayed marriage and childrearing, and in a delayed social maturation. Adolescence, as defined earlier, may extend into the middle twenties.

Too often, the young adult is cut adrift without the kind of support and concern that was exhibited in earlier periods of life. We seem to say, "Okay, now you're a grown-up. If you can't do what adults are supposed to do, something must be wrong with you." Unfortunately, being an adult when it comes to coping with death and dying is something often not taught to adolescents and must instead be learned from painful experience as so many adults have discovered.

ADOLESCENT DEVELOPMENT AND DEATH

When the child is able to conceptualize the meaning of life, that is, distinguish between what is animate and what has never lived, then the idea of death emerges. Acording to Piaget (1958), when formal logical thought is achieved (around 11 or 12), it is possible to contemplate the finality of personal death. Physically, the onset of puberty and of the rapidity with which the familiar body changes brings with it the anxiety that nothing is certain—even life itself. Cottle (1972) describes his own perception of life during adolescence in the following way:

> To a great extent, the knowledge of the existence or actual setting and place of parents and food contributed to the feeling I am certain I shared with my twelve-year-old friends, namely, that underlying the whole affair—life, that is—was a sense of permanence. (p. 312)

And then there was the awakening knowledge of death which he experienced as four steps:

> First, the image that someday I just wouldn't be anymore always stung me in bed at night. Then a fright would envelope me, a physiological jolt that like an H-bomb hit every outpost in my entire body at once. Second, with knees folded up into my chest, I invariably sought to ward off the fright, employing the solution that when you're dead you cannot think about anything so it's not so bad, at least not as bad as what you're presently experiencing. Third, my warding off strategy never varied, and never worked. Fourth, I spoke about this death thing with my friends and laughed as again and again I realized that millions of kids went through the same four steps. (p. 313)

When the idea of death overwhelms, sometimes the future does not seem worth the experience of terror. De Varon (1972) recalls her first awareness of mortality in this way:

> When I was about twelve, I was very afraid of death. I didn't see the point in living if I was going to die. I used to cry and cry for my parents' attention, but they couldn't take away this fear from me; they were helpless. (p. 342)

Like masturbation, adolescent death fears are universally experienced and furtively discussed with equally uninformed peers.

It is one of the tasks of adolescence to begin to grapple with the meaning of life and death (a process that continues throughout life) and to emerge with a philosophical and/or religious stance that promotes optimism for the future. There has to be a reason to go on living. How many of us who are older can honestly say, that if we knew what life had in store for us when we were adolescents, we would have eagerly faced those years that lay before us? Without prescient knowledge, adolescents develop a way of handling life's events that is continuously being modified by experience. If the experiences are positive and successful in continuing the development of self-esteem, intimate relationships, sexual and social identity, and autonomy, then the course to adulthood is relatively smooth. If the experiences are not successful or contributory to growth, the result is pessimism about the future and a belief that the present coping strategies are inadequate (and therefore the adolescent is inadequate) to handle present and future stress.

I am suggesting that the prevalence of such behaviors as family violence, teenage pregnancy, chemical dependency, and suicide during adolescence results from the failure to develop a *modus operandi* for handling present and projected future stresses. The social reasons for that failure are many, including the notion, now recognized as mythical, that the family is a protective environment from stress. Adolescent stresses result probably more from conflicts within the family than from any other single cause. Take suicide during the adolescent years as a paradigm case. In a world faced with the possibility of nuclear holocaust, a focus on economic achievement, constant disruption and realignment of the family structure, the necessity for mobility with its consequent lack of support networks, and the demands of technology and acquisition of knowledge, the adolescent may be overwhelmed. Families overloaded by the same stresses cannot comfort and reassure their teenagers: too many decisions to make; too many critical things to go wrong. One decision by the adolescent—that of death by suicide—appears to take care of all the others.

In addition to pessimism about the future, contemporary American society presents adolescents with another problem. We live in a society that is basically uncomfortable with aging, illness, and death. Like the poor housekeeper, we attempt to sweep under the rug those aspects of life that are not pretty or pleasurable. We put forward youthful looks and behavior as the standard for every part of the life cycle. Nine-year-olds try to look like teenagers, while 35 emulates 19. Cosmetic surgeries, obsession with body fitness, idealized standards of beauty—all these and more conspire to stave off external signs of aging with its inevitable consequence, death. The adolescent absorbs the adult envy of youthful energies and enthusiasms, and intuits correctly the adult fear of aging and death. The teenager understands that adult society molds itself in the image of youth and learns to fear growing old. Young people may thus have difficulty developing significant relationships with the aged:

The dramatization of violent death in a hostile world . . . without the ac-
knowledgment or depiction of humane responses or expressions of grief
portends serious problems for our youth in the area of loss and separation,
as it possesses the potential to aggravate intergenerational relationships.
(Fulton, 1983, p. 486)

Teenagers frequently see death and dying depicted in the media
as excessively violent, macabre, distant, or unnaturally beautiful. Brutal death results from chain saws [*The Texas Chain Saw Massacre* (Tobe
Hooper, 1974)], power tools [*The Toolbox Murders* (Dennis Donnelly,
1978)], or blenders and microwave ovens [*Gremlins* (Steven Spielberg,
1984)]. *The Big Chill* (Lawrence Kasdan, 1983) opens with the dressing of
a body for a funeral as the titles flash past. Death is both distant and impersonal. It is hard to imagine those clothes covering a real person.
Much of the music aimed at a teenage market focuses on death by violence, drug overdose, or suicide (see Chapter 3). Rarely is death treated
with compassion or sensitivity in any of these depictions.

Our society as a whole inures itself to the face of death, but that engenders a callousness in our youth towards physical deterioration and
death. At the point where the teen has a personal experience with the
death of a significant person, all the cultural messages about death as
distant, violent, or beautiful are challenged. Nothing in previous experience has prepared the youth for the feelings of rage, loneliness, guilt,
and disbelief that accompany a personal loss. Other peers, unless they
have had a similar personal experience, cannot be supportive. In fact,
there may be a withdrawal of peer support because of anxiety and ignorance of what to do at a time of grief. One high school boy reported that
his friends were afraid to tell jokes in his presence or invite him to par-
ties after his father died.

When the early adolescent, profoundly shaken, confronts personal
mortality or profound loss for the first time and looks for solace and answers, he or she often finds adults lacking. There is too little in our culture that is systematically responsive to these important events in human life. The classic texts on adolescence, such as Conger and Petersen
(1984), Josselyn (1971), or Anna Freud (1958), mention death fears only
in passing, if at all. Much is written about teenage suicide, but the emotional development and/or the environment of the suicidal adolescent is
stigmatized as pathological. Experts, with a few exceptions, seem to ignore the fact of death as it affects the teenage years in a generalized way.
Society's attempts to deny death shortchange the normal adolescent by
forcing him or her to deal with the shocking comprehension of personal
extinction or loss alone or with uninitiated and uninformed peers.

Upon becoming an adult, the assumption is made that a personally meaningful philosophy of life and death has been worked out. When did this happen? In childhood? In adolescence? Who helped to do it? Parents? Teachers? Clergy? Death and dying are not topics that have been openly and systematically discussed with children and teenagers until very recently, and still in too few places. Parents and teachers generally do not handle the subject well, but teens do not know that until they participate in a death-related experience and see (or only much later realize) how inappropriately many of their elders can behave. At last they discover why they have not had satisfactory responses to their questions and fears—so they stop asking for guidance.

Adolescents need not stumble around in a darkness which we and they have helped to create. They need not be burdened by individual projections of turmoil leading to a learned helplessness and even terror in the face of death, or by a social context whose inadequate grounding for optimism too readily fosters pessimism or cynicism. These handicaps need not be experienced by adolescents if adults will educate children and teenagers to face life and life's inevitable end with a sense of mastery, purpose, and dignity. With proper preparation and support, early adolescents can be helped to become aware of death in manageable ways, and late adolescents can be aided in imparting a meaning to death (as well as to life) that transcends everyday events and infuses the future with hope.

SITUATIONS AND RESPONSES

Society is created and held together by ritual. There are the morning wake-up rituals, going to school/work rituals, eating rituals, religious rituals, political rituals, and many others. Ritualization provides sanctioned boundaries within which the self can be safely expressed. Dying, death, and grief are all ritualized by society as a way of containing and giving meaning to feelings of loss and vulnerability. The granting of adult responsibility and privilege to adolescents varies from culture to culture, from one ethnic group to another. Most Western religions, harkening to an earlier time in history, confer adult religious status around 12 or 13, although a few may wait until as late as 16. With this assumption of nominal adult status comes the expectation of adult participation in death as expressed in such activities as the funeral ritual.

Because elders all too frequently do not teach children the adult rituals for handling dying, death, and grief, it becomes one of the tasks of adolescence to find out what they are. Because these rituals are so fraught with anxiety for the adult, they are not easily transmitted to a younger generation. The adolescent particularly wants to know what these rituals are, but also wants to feel free to create his or her own rituals with peers rather than merely obey rules imposed by those outside the group. We will come to an improved understanding of this process in adolescence, along with common thoughts, feelings, and behaviors exhibited by these young people, if we look briefly at several situations in which adolescents in our society typically encounter and interact with death-related experiences.

Funerals

Consider your own first experience at a funeral. Did you know what to do? What you were going to see? What other people expected of you? Were you prepared for the intensity of your feelings of grief or bewildered by your lack of feeling? Were you afraid of losing emotional control? Did you feel a sense of impotence or helplessness such that anything you said or did seemed futile and ineffective? Juxtapose this with the maxims offered by adults to children: "Grandpa went away"; "God took Aunt Jane because she was suffering"; "Always behave in a ladylike way"; "Big boys don't cry"; "Children should be seen and not heard"; "Go to your room until you can control yourself"; "Death is something you'll find out about when you get older."

What prepares the adolescent in our society for an embalmed, cosmeticized body, a subdued, awkward crowd of adults who have difficulty speaking to other mourners, the often somber surroundings of the funeral parlor or church, and the smell of flowers and candlewax that will evoke memories for a lifetime? How does the teenager learn what to do *at the same time* that he or she is gripped by powerful emotions that threaten self-control? What an embarrassment to lose emotional control and perceive yourself as a child again, rather than as an emerging young adult! Typical adolescent responses to the first funeral experience are stoicism or the hysteria of being overwhelmed by feelings and the setting. Is it any wonder that the first funeral experience is often so traumatic and that all subsequent feelings about funerals and death are likely to take their cues from this first encounter?

If we can begin to prepare the adolescent *in childhood* for funeral practices and other social rituals surrounding death—while at the same time reevaluating the efficacy of traditional rituals and perhaps developing new ways of responding to age-old needs—we will do much to lift the taboo attached to dying people, bereaved survivors, cemeteries, dead bodies, and funeral procedures. The young child is neither easily embarrassed nor excessively afraid of death. Adolescence is the very worst of times to *begin* death education, but the very best of times to open up a philosophic dialogue based on a foundation that has been previously laid. Adolescents respond eagerly to discussions of biomedical ethics, living wills, hospice philosophy, or euthanasia. Late adolescents no longer want merely to be told what to do. They want to know why things are done that way and then be permitted to make an independent decision as to whether that is how they want to do it. It does not make any difference what the topic is—for adolescents the process of discussion, reflection, and decision is essentially the same.

Parental Death

The death of a parent threatens the emerging independence characteristic of the adolescent. The parent's death occurring in early adolescence frequently causes a regression to a less mature state. All adults wish for or experience a childlike regression under severe stress. In the adult, this regression in the service of the ego is usually temporary. The younger teenager's attempts to seek the succor of childhood may threaten his or her precarious grasp on selfhood. The trauma of the death may draw him or her back into the protective security of childhood emotions, not allowing him or her to venture forth into the autonomy of adulthood until a time later than peers. In addition, it may interrupt completion of the psychosocial process of seeking maturity by leading the adolescent to search throughout life for the lost parent in marital or business relationships, or by engendering a diminished ability to separate from the family of origin.

The impact of parental death may have different effects on adolescents depending on their individual stage of development. For example, in some cases the younger adolescent has not advanced so far in the separation process that a brief return to childhood becomes threatening, *if* the family network is supportive and understanding and encourages continued appropriate adolescent development. The situation is likely to be somewhat different for the older adolescent. That is, the family system, fragmented by the death, may attempt to turn the older adolescent into a surrogate parent, thus truncating the separation process. Responses to this threat to independence include staying home to care for mom or dad and never marrying or, feeling the tug of war between independence and inappropriate family responsibilities, severing ties to the family more quickly and more permanently than would have occurred if the parent's death had not taken place.

The Death of Friends

The death of friends, whether accidental or suicidal, rips asunder whatever fantasies of immortality that may still exist. The death of a peer forces a confrontation with one's own death at any age. For youth, it calls the logic of the natural order into question, challenges God's existence, and violates the ideals of fairness, justice, and goodness held most dearly. Sigmund Freud (1957) said that the ego cannot conceive of its own extinction. Without denying that claim, Lifton (1979) has observed that, "while I cannot imagine my nonexistence, I can very well imagine a world in which 'I' do not exist." (p. 8). This latter ability is obviously heightened when an adolescent suddenly finds himself or herself inhabiting a world in which a friend or peer no longer exists. The ego is most fragile, most open to doubt, when exposed to the death of someone like the self.

The three leading causes of death in adolescence—accidents, suicide, and homicide—are all particularly difficult for survivors. They usually occur quickly, without advance warning or time for preparation. Is it any wonder that adolescents band together under such circumstances, as if the safety of numbers will protect them from the dread truth of mortality? In the company of peers, they attempt to make sense out of the death and to console each other. Outsiders to the group (adults) may not understand their intense mourning or private rituals. At an age that has little knowledge or experience of normative funeral practices, why is it so surprising that adolescents create highly individualized rituals with which to mourn one of their own, while at the same time rejecting as meaningless or impersonal the traditions that society espouses—traditions to which they have not been sufficiently exposed?

Suicide of a Peer

The suicide of a peer is especially frightening since it taps into adolescent fears about the future and the ability to appropriately manage the tasks of adulthood—for example, tasks of intimacy and self-reliance, either as expressed in traditional patterns of career, marriage, and parenthood, or as they might be worked out in alternative life styles. The fantasy of easing the pressures of life by death exists in all of us to some degree. Since one of the most significant fears for both male and female adolescents is fear about the physical vulnerability of the body (Bamber, 1979), the suicide of a peer heightens this fear.

In order to dispel romantic notions about suicide, it is appropriate for teenagers to know how disfiguring death can be, otherwise the full horror of the act may be denied. Recent reports suggesting a "contagion" of suicides among at least some adolescents in a single community reflect not only societal pressures, but also the tendency of adolescents to deny the physical consequences and finality of actual death.

Risk-Taking

Ariès (1974, 1981) has shown how death and sex were related in the Romantic period. The moment of orgasm was perceived to be a break in reality, a loss of control—a little death or *le petit mal*, as the French call it. Adolescent sexuality is similarly threatening for its loss of control. Nocturnal emissions, unexpected erections, unbidden erotic images, gushing sweat glands, crackling voices, anxiety about the menstrual time and containment of blood, budding breasts—all these developments threaten the familiar body of the child within which the adolescent metamorphosis is taking place. The body becomes an unpredictable unknown just as death is. Death stops change and growth as well as the necessity of dealing with an anxiety-producing sexuality. Death is both frightening and fascinating, just as sexuality is. Thus, Gorer in his classic essay "The Pornography of Death" (1965) has established the link between the taboo of death experience (and the human fascination with that which is forbidden) and the taboo of sexual experience, especially for adolescents.

Risk-taking with body safety is common in the adolescent years, though sky diving, car racing, excessive use of drugs and alcoholic beverages, and other similar activities may not be directly perceived as a kind of flirting with death. In fact, in many ways, this is counterphobic behavior—a challenge to death wherein each survival of risk is a victory over death. Descriptions of the emotions experienced in situations of high risk are similar to descriptions of sexual feelings—exhilaration, sensations of danger, heightened physical awareness, exquisite sensation, suspension of logical thought, lack of anxiety, and testing of physical limits. Sexual feelings and death fears are hidden in ordinary situations. Dangerous situations stimulate both. High risk activities are ways of testing the body, while still remaining cloaked in the remnants of belief in immortality. At the same time, such activities may provide an outlet for sexual tensions and fears.

Black Adolescents

Death in the black community is a much more visible occurrence than it normally is in the mainstream of white society. The homicide rate for black adolescent and young adult males is two to three times that of white males of a similar age. The black community also keeps its dying family members at home far more frequently that does the white community, perhaps reflecting socio-economic variables as well as a tradition of family and religious networking that harkens to an earlier time in white, middle-class society when it also retained stronger ties to its ethnic, religious, and family identities. Consequently, black adolescents are typically more socialized at an earlier age to the rituals surrounding death and dying than are most white adolescents. Young black children are routinely taken to funerals and encouraged to interact with family members who are dying in the home. In addition, the strong religious background of most black families helps to develop a belief about survival after death that makes death less threatening than it is for the more secularized white middle class.

This is not to imply that the black culture does not have its fears and superstitions which it readily imparts to its young. But, on the whole, dying and death are not taboo subjects among black adolescents. Most unfortunately, many teenage blacks are readily familiar with the sights and sounds of violent death and drug overdose. The seeming indifference of many black adolescents to death-related topics and education often comes from repeated personal experiences with the reality and finality of death. It is no wonder that books, movies, and articles about dying and death hold less interest for such young people, especially since most media information is based on and directed to white culture.

Generalities are vulnerable to personal experience, as the following incident shows. A few years ago in a Death and Dying class for health professionals, one of my black students boasted that her eight-year-old son attended funerals with her while she sang in the church choir, and consequently he had no fears or questions about death. At the next class, I had the opportunity to meet the boy and to ask him about all the funerals he had attended and what they had meant to him. With a sly look at his mother, he said: "I always close my eyes and hold her hand real tight, and that way I never see anything!"

CONCLUSION

To summarize: the early adolescent becomes aware of death, and the late adolescent attempts to impart a meaning to death (as well as to life) that transcends everyday events and infuses the future with hope. Failure to endow the future with optimism results in death of the spirit or suicide.

The adolescent is confronted with issues affecting his or her philosophy of life and death that are mainly psychosocial in content. This confrontation has three primary aspects. First, after the cognitive and emotional realization that life as we know it is finite, quite frequently no adequate attempt is made by adults to help adolescents construct the philosophical outlook that they need. All too often, society abdicates its responsibility toward youth in neglecting to educate them about dying, death, bereavement, and funeral customs, leaving them instead to flounder.

Second, in our worship of youth and denial of aging and death, we project onto adolescence a reflection of our own turmoil in coping with the problems inherent in life. In this way, a learned helplessness and even a terror about aging, dying, and death is created. This attitude perpetuates denigration of the values of old age and fosters an unrealistic set of norms for attractiveness, vigor, and sexuality that does not apply to a majority of the population.

Third, the increasing complexity and frustrations of modern life give society little cause for optimism (an attitude too readily absorbed by young people). Increased incidence of adolescent suicide, family violence, teenage pregnancy, and chemical dependency reflects these frustrations. Adolescents are expected to stumble around in a darkness that for the most part they need not have experienced. They are left to find meaning and answers through life's experiences alone. But it need not be that difficult if we educate children and teenagers to face life and life's inevitable end with a sense of mastery, purpose, and dignity.

What has happened to the cloak of immortality mentioned at the outset of this chapter? By the end of adolescence it is patched and tattered, no longer able to contain the child's assumptions of immortality. Putting on the garb of adulthood requires doffing the cloak, perhaps exchanging it for another of stronger weave and heavenly hue. Whatever the new raiment, the cloak deserves the same respect as the favorite blanket, beloved thumb, or well-worn teddy bear. It provided comfort and security when necessary, yet could be set aside when its time had passed. After all, during times of stress, many adults reach for their tattered cloak, believing, even if just for the necessary moment, that we will not ever die.

REFERENCES

Ariès, P. *Western attitudes toward death: From the Middle Ages to the present* (P. Ranum, Trans.). Baltimore: Johns Hopkins University Press, 1974.

Ariès, P. *The hour of our death.* (H. Weaver, Trans.). New York: Knopf, 1981.

Bamber, J. H. *The fears of adolescents.* London: Academic Press, 1979.

Bandura, A. The stormy decade: Fact or fiction? In R. E. Muuss (Ed.), *Adolescent behavior and society: A book of readings* (3rd ed.) (pp. 22–31). New York: Random House 1980.

Bertman, S. L. Children's and others' thoughts and expressions about death. In H. Wass & C. A. Corr (Eds.), *Helping children cope with death: Guidelines and resources* (2nd ed.) (pp. 11–31). Washington, DC: Hemisphere, 1984.

Bluebond-Langner, M. *The private worlds of dying children*. Princeton, NJ: Princeton University Press, 1978.

Carson, U. Teachable moments occasioned by "small deaths". In H. Wass & C. A. Corr (Eds.), *Childhood and death* (pp. 315–343). Washington, DC: Hemisphere, 1984.

Conger, J. J., & Petersen, A. *Adolescence and youth: Psychological development in a changing world* (3rd ed.). New York: Harper & Row, 1984.

Corr, C. A. Reconstructing the changing face of death. In H. Wass (Ed.), *Dying: Facing the facts* (pp. 5–43). Washington, DC: Hemisphere, 1979.

Cottle, T. J. The connections of adolescence. In J. Kagan & R. Coles (Eds.), *Twelve to sixteen: Early adolescence* (pp. 294–336). New York: Norton, 1972.

De Varon, T. Growing up. In J. Kagan & R. Coles (Eds.), *Twelve to sixteen: Early adolescence* (pp. 337–348). New York: Norton, 1972.

Donnelly, D. (Director). (1978). *The Toolbox Murders* [Film]. Los Angeles: Cal Am Productions.

Erikson, E. H. *Childhood and society*. New York: Norton, 1950.

Feinstein, S. Adolescent depression. In L. Steinberg & L. Mandelbaum (Eds.), *The life cycle: Readings in human development* (pp. 317–335). New York: Columbia University Press, 1981.

Freud, A. Adolescence. *Psychoanalytic Study of the Child*, 1958, *13*, 255–268.

Freud, S. Thoughts for the times on war and death. In J. Strachey (Ed.), *The standard edition of the complete works of Sigmund Freud* (Vol. 14, pp. 275–300) London: Hogarth Press, 1957.

Fulton, R. Social issues: Death and dying. In R. C. Federico & J. Schwartz (Eds.), *Sociology* (3rd ed.) (pp. 482–487). Reading, PA: Addison-Wesley, 1983.

Gordon, A. K., & Klass, D. *They need to know: How to teach children about death*. Englewood Cliffs, NJ: Prentice-Hall, 1979.

Gorer, G. The pornography of death. In G. Gorer (Ed.), *Death, grief, and mourning* (pp. 192–199). Garden City, NY: Doubleday, 1965.

Hooper, T. (Director). (1974). *The Texas Chain Saw Massacre* [Film]. Los Angeles: New Line Cinema.

Josselyn, I. M. *Adolescence*. New York: Harper & Row, 1971.

Kasdan, L. (Director). (1983). *The Big Chill* [Film]. Los Angeles: RCA/Columbia Pictures.

Levinson, D. J., Darrow, C. N., Klein, E. B., Levinson, M. H., & McKee, B. *The seasons of a man's life*. New York: Knopf, 1978.

Lifton, R. J. *The broken connection*. New York: Simon & Schuster, 1979.

Lonetto, R. *Children's conceptions of death*. New York: Springer Publishing, 1980.

McNeil, J. N. Death education in the home: Parents talk with their children. In H. Wass & C. A. Corr (Eds.), *Childhood and death* (pp. 293–313). Washington, DC: Hemisphere, 1984.

Offer, D., Ostrov, E., & Howard, K. *The adolescent: A psychological self-portrait*. New York: Basic Books, 1981.

Piaget, J. *The growth of logical thinking from childhood to adolescence*. New York: Basic Books, 1958.

Spielberg, S. (Director/Producer). (1984). *Gremlins* [Film]. Los Angeles: Universal Pictures.

Wass, H. Concepts of death: A developmental perspective. In H. Wass & C. A. Corr (Eds.), *Childhood and death* (pp. 3–24). Washington, DC: Hemisphere, 1984a.

Wass, H. Parents, teachers, and health professionals as helpers. In H. Wass &

C. A. Corr (Eds.), *Helping children cope with death: Guidelines and resources* (2nd ed.) (pp. 75–130). Washington, DC: Hemisphere, 1984b.

Wass, H., & Cason, L. Fears and anxieties about death. In H. Wass & C. A. Corr (Eds.), *Childhood and death* (pp. 25–45). Washington, DC: Hemisphere, 1984.

Wass, H., & Corr, C. A. (Eds.). *Helping children cope with death: Guidelines and resources* (2nd ed.). Washington, DC: Hemisphere, 1984.

3

Death Themes in Adolescent Music: The Classic Years

Thomas Attig

One key to understanding adolescents today is cultivating an understanding of the music that occupies a central place in so much of their lives. The days of folk and rock music as forces for change within a developing "counterculture" are past, in part because much of the best of that past has been absorbed into the dominant culture and in part because the success of the music has contributed to its corruption and co-optation. Nevertheless, music continues to function as a defining element in what remains an "alternative culture." Where traditional culture (family, school, church, political institutions) is perceived as silent, irrelevant, hypocritical, confusing, or corrupt, it is not uncommon for adolescents to turn to their music. That music provides an alternative frame of reference within which their concerns can be and are addressed. It affords opportunity for identification with cultural heroes, values and ideals, hopes and aspirations. It provides communication currency and social connection with peers. In short, their music provides adolescents with mirrors of who they and society are, and intimations of what they and society might become.

As with any range of cultural phenomena, the quality of adolescent

I am indebted to Bill Schurk of The Popular Music Library at Bowling Green State University and to his fine staff for assistance in identifying and locating many of the selections discussed in this chapter. I am also grateful to George Ward of the Texas State Historical Association, Donald Scherer, Jeff Siebert, and Cindy Matyi for their interest, suggestions, and readings of early drafts. Thanks are also due to Peter Prunkle and his student, Stan Dyer, of Quincy College.

music varies considerably. At its worst, this music has: corrupted and trivialized values and ideals; encouraged superficiality and deadened sensibilities; provided mindless distraction and escape; reinforced oppressive stereotypes and narrow-mindedness; pandered to commercial interests and the lowest common denominator of consumer appeal; and displayed little imagination or creativity. However, at its best, this music has: been a positive force in the development of individual and societal values and ideals; penetrated the surface and numbness of everyday existence; cried out for attentiveness to problems that cannot be ignored; challenged hypocrisy and injustice; resisted selling out to materialism and popularity; and done all of these things with great energy, style, and imagination.

Understanding adolescent music provides entree into dialogue with adolescents for counselors, clinicians, teachers, clergy, parents, and any others who care to meet these young people on their own terms (Macken, Fornatale, & Ayres, 1980). It allows for access to a dominant idiom among adolescents and to the range of concerns expressed in that idiom (even when the concerns may be semiarticulately or only unconsciously expressed). In addition, it makes possible comprehension of the variety of ways in which adolescents address these concerns. Cultivating such understanding is akin to learning and using a foreign language in a foreign country. It serves as a means of exchange for ideas and issues. The very attempt to understand says much about the genuineness of the act of reaching out. An attempt to penetrate the music is a sign of caring, for in caring about the music, a person is caring about that which the adolescent cares about. In some cases, this may be a very important message to send.

We are faced, however, with two principal problems in the study of death-related themes in adolescent music. First, the music itself continues to develop at an extremely fast pace. Second, despite extensive interest in this music in general, I know of only one other study that has addressed this particular topic (Thrush & Paulus, 1970). In short, there is little to guide us, and no reflective account can expect to keep up with the rapidity, breadth, or depth of change in this music. In such a state of affairs, it is not possible to remain current with this music nor to provide a definitive analysis of the significance of this music, even with regard to our specific topical focus.

In this chapter, therefore, I have concentrated on what I will call "the classic years" of adolescent folk and rock music, and on the fundamental work of identifying and systematizing the treatment of its death-related themes. The chronological era runs roughly from the mid-1960s—the post-Kennedy, early Vietnam period—to the end of Jimmy Carter's presidency and the return of the American prisoners from Iran at the start of the 1980s. Musically, it is the period from the Beatles through punk rock and the beginnings of new wave. Any account, even of such a relatively limited number of years, must inevitably be selective. Comprehensiveness is simply not possible, but I believe that my approach has the combined virtues of exploring the music itself in its amazing richness and diversity, of focusing upon ways in which this music treats death and death-related themes, of promoting an understanding of adolescents, of treating formally a history that is well known to the great number of adolescents who are natural rock historians, and of respecting the present limits in our appreciation of this subject. By preparing the groundwork and initiating an analysis, a study of this type also will ultimately suggest some directions in the research of more recent adolescent music.

THE MUSIC ITSELF

The treatment of death and death-related themes in the following sections considers: 1. personal encounters with or reflections on death; and 2. the broader cultural context of death and dying. This approach highlights the diversity of themes treated and displays clearly the rich and at times subtle variation in adolescent music as a cultural phenomenon.

Personal Encounters with or Reflections on Death

The songs included here anticipate old age and death, speculate on the meaning of life in death's shadow, deal with immortality and continuity, focus upon loss and its meaning, and address issues of suicide.

Old Age and Death

It is reasonable to expect the music of youth in a youth-oriented society to reflect some distance from old age and the prospect of imminent death. Yet, the stark aversion to old age, bordering on contempt, in some of this music is startling. The clearest explicit example of this is Blondie's "Die Young, Stay Pretty" (*Eat to the Beat*, 1979), which repeats the title as a refrain coupled with contrasts favoring fast living over what is perceived as the slow but inexorable deterioration of aging. In what for many became an anthem for a teen generation, "My Generation" (*The Who Live at Leeds*, 1970) by The Who, the lead singer repeatedly asserts a wish to die before becoming old, seemingly in part because of a repugnance that is attached to old age itself and in part because of the perceived empty values that the older generations represent. Randy Newman's "Old Man" (*Sail Away*, 1972) recounts a visit to an old man during which the visitor points out that virtually no one cares about the old man's life or impending death.

By contrast, several songs express wonder about what it is like to be old and to see life from its end. For example, The Beatles in "When I'm Sixty-Four" (*Sgt. Pepper's Lonely Hearts Club Band*, 1967) wonder principally about connections with others in old age when they ask whether they will still be needed and cared for as elderly people. Paul Simon in "Old Friends" (*Bookends*, 1968) sketches a lonely scene of two old friends sitting on a park bench, "winter companions . . . waiting for the sunset." Life is passing them by as the sounds of the city are heard in the distance, and the singer wonders:

> Can you imagine us
> Years from today
> Sharing a park bench quietly?
> How terribly strange to be seventy.
> Old friends,
> Memory brushes the same years,
> Silently sharing the same fears[1]

Here there is empathy and gentle respect for the experience of the elderly.

John Prine's "Hello in There" (*Prime Prine*, 1971) demonstates empathy as it expresses the viewpoint of an elderly man and his wife facing the years after the kids have grown and gone their separate ways. Conversation between them has quieted; she sits and stares; the news is all old and stale; contact with others has diminished; and dreams are mostly dead. Beyond empathy, and rare indeed, is the sentiment expressed by John Denver in "Poems, Prayers and Promises" (*Poems, Prayers and Promises*, 1971) as he conducts a review of his life and anticipates his future, singing, "It turns me on to think of growing old."[2]

Living in the Shadow of Death

Adolescent music includes several interpretations of life and its potential meaning, given that death is in prospect. Cat Stevens in "But I Might Die Tonight" (*Tea for the Tillerman*, 1970) and Pink Floyd in "Time" (*Dark*

---

[1]*Old Friends.* Copyright © 1968 by Paul Simon. Used by permission.
[2]*Poems, Prayers, and Promises* by John Denver. © Copyright 1971 Cherry Lane Music Publishing Co., Inc. All Rights Reserved. Used by permission.

Side of the Moon, 1973) both express resistance to conforming to cultural norms because these norms are likely to lead to a dismal end. Harry Chapin's "Dreams Go By" (*Portrait Gallery*, 1975) underscores the importance of avoiding preoccupation with day-to-day concerns at the expense of the pursuit of one's most important dreams. The song is sung first from the perspective of youth putting off dreams of a bright and anticipated future, second from the perspective of later life when it is realized that important dreams have been permanently shelved but time still remains to realize others, and finally from the perspective of old age when the time for dreaming is wistfully remembered. Anticipating a time of dying, Richard Harris's "In the Final Hours" (*A Tramp Shining*, 1968) suggests the likelihood of being caught unprepared and quite possibly alone.

Although time is short, all of these songs acknowledge that life is potentially meaningful if lived attentively. In contrast, there are songs with a darker estimation of life's potential. In its most cynical moments, this latter music can express the view that existence is absurd, even that it is a joke played upon us by God, as in Randy Newman's "God's Song" (*Sail Away*, 1972).

"Dust in the Wind" (*Point of No Return*, 1977) by Kansas offers still another point of view, one that is pervaded by an atmosphere of quiet acceptance. Contrary to the values of the older generations, this song urges that materialism and possessiveness do not provide keys to meaningfulness. Similarly, in "And When I Die" (*Blood, Sweat and Tears*, 1969) by Blood, Sweat and Tears, the prominent concern is with a peaceful and natural death. Meaningful living is thought quite compatible with the finitude of life, and there is a distinct sense of the continuity of life.

John Denver's "The Garden Song" (*John Denver*, 1979) is an allegory about cultivating human life in a field where each person has fertile ground in which to grow and where death is ever present (in the form of a crow watching hungrily from a perch above the field). To be sure, our efforts can only take us so far, as we seem to be at the mercy of elements and forces beyond our control. Yet, the song suggests that it is possible to conform to the rhythms of life, to take life as it comes, to live it caringly, and to thrive within its limits. The song reflects a quiet acceptance of death that is compatible with the potential for meaningful living. Continuing the garden metaphor, Seals and Croft's "Forever Like the Rose" (*Takin' It Easy*, 1978) suggests that life can be meaningful and beautiful even if it is fleeting:

> Forever like the rose
> I suppose that's the way to live
> Strong and ever giving

Always living with a purpose and a goal
To blossom day to day
Then someday to fade away
Forever like the rose[3]

Immortality: Literal and Symbolic

As Lifton (1983) argues, much of the discussion about the meaningfulness of life is connected with the concept of continuity, either through literal survival after death or through symbolic immortality. This theme of the need for continuity receives varied treatment in adolescent music.

Taking a cue from Freud (1957) and Becker (1973), Paul Simon in "Flowers Never Bend with the Rainfall" (*Parsley, Sage, Rosemary and Thyme*, 1966) offers a song that gives testimony to the extreme difficulty of thinking of oneself as anything but immortal. The self-deception is transparent. After verses detailing confusion, directionlessness, illusion, fantasy and reality, and the need to somehow face tomorrow, the singer concludes:

. . . I'll continue to continue
To pretend my life will never end
And flowers never bend
With the rainfall[4]

In "Eleanor Rigby" (*Revolver*, 1966), the Beatles paint a stark portrait of alienation and meaningless life. The song's title character is virtually, in Shneidman's words, "oblivionated" (1980, p. 5) when she dies and is buried without notice or human concern.

The traditional Christian concept of survival after death is treated in several songs, including Joan Baez' rendition of the folk hymn, "Will the Circle Be Unbroken?" (*David's Album*, 1969), and John Denver's "Fly Away" (*Windsong*, 1975). In the former, the singer anticipates being reunited with her dead mother in a life to come; in the latter, the singer recounts peacefully and confidently of a dying woman about to be released from suffering to "fly away" to a life beyond. A less-traditional treatment of the same afterlife theme is found in "Stairway to Heaven" (*Led Zepplin IV*, 1971) by Led Zepplin, one of the most requested songs on the radio for nearly a decade. A woman's illusion that heaven can be attained through material means and the purchase of a stairway to

[3]*Forever Like The Rose* by James Seals and Dash Crofts. © 1980 Dawnbreaker Music Co. Used by permission only. All rights reserved.
[4]*Flowers Never Bend With The Rainfall*. Copyright © 1965 by Paul Simon. Used by permission.

heaven is rejected, and the importance of a transformation of being for salvation is affirmed.

It is interesting to note the extent to which the Lifton (1983) theme of "symbolic immortality" is treated in adolescent music. The meaning of investing oneself in works to be appreciated by survivors is poignantly, but ironically, explored in Neil Diamond's "Morningside" (*Moods*, 1972). After an account of how an old man spent his last days lovingly making a table so his children would remember him, the song reports that when he did die, no one wept and no one claimed the legacy that he had left behind. In contrast, in "Dancin' Boy" (*Living Room Suite*, 1978), Harry Chapin gives an autobiographical glimpse of his relationship with his young son as he reflects in a bittersweet way on the time when the boy will be dancing to his own music. Still another possibility is found in "Joe Hill" (*Carry It On*, 1971) in which Joan Baez sings of a union organizer who, though dead for 10 years, has achieved symbolic immortality in serving as an inspiration to those who sustain the cause for which he died. Continuity in the memory of survivors is also treated in Mary McCaslin's "Old Friends" (*Old Friends*, 1974):

> But for the ones whose journey's ended
> Though they started so much the same
> In the hearts of those befriended
> Burns a candle with a silver flame.
> Remember old friends
> We've made along the way
> The gifts they've given
> Stay with us every day.[5]

Loss, Grief, and Bereavement

The theme of loss and grief is so prominent in adolescent music that treatment of it must be subdivided into the following categories: songs which pay tribute to departed, prominent figures; "coffin" songs expressing longing for departed lovers; songs reflecting the depth of grief and personal loss; and songs about the means of coping with loss.

Songs of tribute are among the best known and the most maudlin in the death-related music. The list is endless, including the Righteous Brothers' "Rock and Roll Heaven" about prominent rockers (1975); countless songs about Elvis Presley; and Dion's "Abraham, Martin and John" about Abraham Lincoln, Martin Luther King, Jr., and John F. Kennedy (1975). Typically, the deceased is portrayed through the dis-

---

[5]Words and music by Mary McCaslin. Copyright © Folklore Music (ASCAP). Available on Philo Records.

torted vision of a mourner who can see only the good and who refuses a balanced, fully human portrait of just who and what has been lost. More rare and more honest are songs such as Rubberband's "Hound Dog Man" (1977), which recalls Elvis Presley, flaws and all, and which laments not only the loss of his vibrancy to the world but the dispiriting of the generation he represents. Also noteworthy is Don McLean's "American Pie" (*American Pie*, 1972), which views the death of Buddy Holly and other early rockers as a turning point in rock's loss of innocence.

Teen "coffin" songs, a phenomenon of the late 1950s and early 1960s (Denisoff, 1971), antedate our historical boundaries but nevertheless deserve notice here. The endless list includes The Fleetwoods' "Tragedy" (1962), Mark Dinning's "Teen Angel" (1960), Ray Peterson's "Tell Laura I Love Her" (1960), Dicky Lee's "Patches" (1962), and the Shangri-las' "Leader of the Pack" (1964). Romanticized teen love is disrupted by accidental death, foiled by meddling parents, undermined by social distance, and fueled by rebellious defiance. Suicidal ideation and suicide itself in the attempt to be reunited with the lost love are common themes. (In one grotesque song of this type, Jimmy Cross's "I Want My Baby Back" [1964], the drive to reunite is so strong that the young man returns to his lover's grave to retrieve her remains.) Although some might find the feelings superficially expressed, the phrases of yearning and searching in these songs do reveal grief.

Personal loss is treated more directly, honestly, subtly, and probingly in later songs, typically authored by singer-songwriters in the wake of their own experiences. Among the very best of these songs are James Taylor's "Fire and Rain" (*Sweet Baby James*, 1971), David Gates' "Everything I Own" (*Best of Bread*, 1973), and Jackson Browne's "For a Dancer" (*Late for the Sky*, 1974). Taylor captures well the typical denial preceding an impending death and the shock of realization when it happens. Gates, in mourning the death of his father, thinks of the shelter, warmth, freedom, love, and guidance his father had provided, thereby recalling themes of yearning and searching for the deceased. Again, Taylor expresses feelings of helplessness, self-doubt, and the need for support, even as he communicates confidence that the blow can be absorbed and renewal is possible. In lyrical form we can illustrate much of this by quoting at length from the words of Browne's "For a Dancer":

> Keep a fire burning in your eye
> Pay attention to the open sky
> You never know what will be coming down
> I don't remember losing track of you
> You were always dancing in and out of view

I must have thought you'd always be around
Always keeping things real by playing the clown
Now you're nowhere to be found

I don't know what happens when people die
Can't seem to grasp it as hard as I try
It's like a song I can hear playing right in my ear that I can't sing
I can't help listening
And I can't help feeling stupid standing 'round
Crying as they ease you down
'Cause I know that you'd rather we were dancing
Dancing our sorrow away (right on dancing)
No matter what fate chooses to play
(There's nothing you can do about it anyway)

Just do the steps that you've been shown
By everyone you've ever known
Until the dance becomes your very own
No matter how close to yours another's steps have grown
In the end there is one dance you'll do alone

Keep a fire for the human race
And let your prayers go drifting into space
You never know what will be coming down
Perhaps a better world is drawing near
And just as easily, it could all disappear
Along with whatever meaning you might have found
Don't let the uncertainty turn you around
(The world keeps turnin' around and around)
Go on and make a joyful sound

Into a dancer you have grown
From a seed somebody else has thrown
Go on ahead and throw some seeds of your own
And somewhere between the time you arrive
And the time you go
May lie a reason you were alive
But you'll never know[6]

Coping with loss may take alternative forms and may or may not be supported and sustained by others. Here, too, though perhaps indirectly, adolescent music has something to offer. Though the songs do not deal at all directly with loss through death, the very titles of Melissa Manchester's "Don't Cry Out Loud" (*Don't Cry Out Loud*, 1978) and Gloria Gaynor's "I Will Survive" (*Love Tracks*, 1978) reflect two prominent modes of coming to terms with hurt, that is, holding it in or persisting in spite of it with a resolve to be stronger because of it.

Several songs treat the response of others to persons who are hurting during the time of bereavement. Barbara Mandrell's "Hold Me" (*Lovers, Friends and Strangers,* 1977) is a plea for the comfort and security that may come from human touch, warmth, and tolerance of temporary regression and dependency. Mary McCaslin's "Old Friends" (*Old Friends,* 1974) also reminds us of the comfort that can come from the memories of those now dead, memories which "stay with us every day."[7] Two other songs worth noting call attention to the importance of friendship among survivors. Paul Simon's very well-known "Bridge Over Troubled Waters" (*Bridge Over Troubled Waters,* 1970) expresses the singer's assurance that he can be counted on in troubled times. Abba's "The Way Old Friends Do" (*Super Trouper,* 1981) stresses the importance of sharing sorrows and finding comfort in friendship.

Suicide

Suicide is treated from many perspectives in adolescent music. Elton John's "I Think I'm Gonna Kill Myself" (*Honky Chateau,* 1972) gives expression to the wish to commit suicide in order to provoke major grief in survivors and in order to get newspapers to take notice of teenage troubles. By contrast, Don McLean's "Vincent" (*American Pie,* 1972) explores the soul of the artist Vincent Van Gogh as he must have contemplated his suicide. Though his love for the subjects he painted was evident in his work, they could not love him in return:

> And when no hope was left in sight
> On that starry, starry night
> You took your life as lovers often do
> But, I could have told you, Vincent,
> This world was never meant for one as beautiful as you.[8]

Though the picture here is romanticized somewhat, the motif portrayed is clearly one of heartfelt despair.

Simon and Garfunkel's *Sounds of Silence* (1965) album contains two songs of suicide rooted in alienation and failure of communication. "Richard Cory" echoes the E. A. Robinson poem of the same title and expresses the disbelief of a worker in Cory's factory that a man of considerable wealth, power, grace, and style could be moved to suicide. As with the original poem, the song expresses the surprise of the survivor

[7]Words and music by Mary McCaslin. Copyright © Folklore Music (ASCAP). Available on Philo Records.
[8]By Don McClean, Publishers: Mayday Music (BMI) (A div. of Merit Music Corporation)/ Benny Bird Music Co. Inc.

and distorts the picture of typical suicide by suggesting that Cory gave no prior indication whatever of his intentions. In contrast with the original poem, the singer expresses a suicidal inclination of his own as he notes the disparity between the wealth of the dead Cory and his own cursed poverty. The second song, "A Most Peculiar Man," is about the suicide of a man who lived alone and made very little impression on those around him. The most telling line describes his apparent desire to turn on the gas "so he'd never wake up to his silent world" where he was viewed as a "most peculiar man."[9]

In The Little River Band's "Suicide Boulevard" (*Time Exposure*, 1981), sympathy is expressed for the deep hurt suffered by one who is contemplating suicide. An attempt is made to discourage the act by reminding the would-be suicide victim that a reason for living can still be found. But in the end, the decision is left in the hands of the person walking suicide boulevard. In a similar vein, the option of suicide is left open in the familiar theme song from M*A*S*H, "Suicide is Painless" (*M*A*S*H*, 1970). The singers have experienced pain, and they can see much more is in store. Thus, when asked to choose life or death, the singers refuse to answer, apparently taking comfort in the availability of the option and remaining nonjudgmental should others decide to exercise a choice.

Open encouragement of suicide is found in "Don't Fear the Reaper" (*Agents of Fortune*, 1976) by the Blue Oyster Cult. In fact, this song is apparently one in which a young man is urging his lover to join in a suicide pact:

> Seasons don't fear the Reaper.
> Nor do the wind, the sun, or the rain.
> We can be like they are (come on baby)
> Don't fear the Reaper.[10]

In the end, she succumbs. By contrast, Queen's "Don't Try Suicide" (*The Game*, 1980) rather harshly discourages the suicide of a young girl intent upon drawing attention to herself by threatening to complete this act.

Perhaps the most moving of the suicide-related songs is Jackson Browne's "Song for Adam" (*Jackson Browne*, 1972). It tells of the death of a friend the singer had not been able to get to know well. Yet, when the story came back to him that Adam "jumped," he is moved to conclude that he "fell." The story is stunning news to the singer who had always thought that if either of the two would fall along life's way, the singer

---

[9]*A Most Peculiar Man*. Copyright © 1965 by Paul Simon. Used by permission.
[10]Copyright © 1976. B.O. Cult Songs Inc. Used with permission.

would be the one. Self-doubt, a reluctance to judge the motive of the suicide, and deep grief are expressed in this poignant lyric.

The Broader Cultural Context of Dying

In addition to the largely personal context of the music considered previously, there is much in the music of adolescents that focuses upon and reacts to death and death-related themes in the broader cultural context. Included here are: songs that deal with perceptions of death distorted by the filters of media and materialistically dominated culture; songs about war, peace, and the nuclear shadow; songs about hunger; apocalyptic music; songs of alienated youth, drugs, and death; music about violence, guns, murder, mayhem, outlaws, and death in the ghetto; pornographic rock; and nihilistic rock. We shall consider each of these categories in the following sections.

The Distorted Image of Death

The reality of death is threatening, awe inspiring, profoundly significant, mysterious, painful, chilling, sad, frightening, inevitable, unpredictable, uncontrollable, always possible, and a reminder of human finiteness, limitation, and vulnerability. Prominent elements within contemporary American culture have a decidedly distorting influence upon the perception of death as it really is. When filtered through these elements, death in America is all too often homogenized, sterilized, domesticated, controlled, managed, packaged, plasticized, cosmetized, marketed, and trivialized. The distorting influence of material and commercial values upon the ritual response to death in the funeral is nowhere more clearly or succinctly captured than in John Denver's singing of "Forest Lawn" (*An Evening with John Denver*, 1975), a satirical send-off to the well-known southern California cemetery establishment and all of its excesses. Sadly, many people would gladly invest money than themselves in the period following death.

Less well known, but far more powerful, is Don McLean's "Prime Time" (*Prime Time*, 1977). Much is made today of the distortion of reality as it is depicted through the medium of television. The pace is frenetic; life is fragmented; the significant is presented in distilled and capsulated form, and is juxtaposed with the utterly trivial; viewers are bombarded with bits and fragments they can barely take in; and all is reduced to a formless hash devoid of its true force or meaning. McLean's song captures all of this with a perfect combination of lyrics that mimic the television announcer's articulation of life's events and with a rhythm that replicates the numbingly incessant onslaught of television pacing. The chorus insists that television and living in the United States are one and the same:

> Well this is life, this is prime time,
> This is livin' in the U.S.A.
> This is life, this is prime time.
> This is livin' the American way.

Imagine for a moment that living is analogous to being a game show contestant:

> Well, spin the magic wheel. Try to break the bank,
> Think about your life when you fill in the blank.
> There's a game that's real, if you want to try.
> One spot on the wheel that says you must die.
> American roulette is the game we play.
> But no one wants to have to be the one to pay.
> You get to pass go. You get to pass away.
> But before we start the show, here's our sponsor to say:

At this point the chorus is repeated, and you begin to believe it. In a later verse, the experience of taking in a war over dinner is portrayed as follows:

> My supper's on the stove, and war is on the screen.
> Pass the bread and butter while I watch the marine.
> They shot him in the chest. Pass the chicken breast.
> The general is sayin' that he is still unimpressed.
> We had to burn the city 'cause they couldn't agree
> That things go better with democracy.
> The weather will be fair. Forget the ozone layer.
> The strontium showers will be here and there.[11]

In the middle of the final verse, McLean asserts that "They don't keep the promise in the promised land," and the vividness of the imagery and the power of the presentation in the song make the listener stop and ponder.

War and Related Themes

Adolescent music is so rich in this area that it becomes necessary to subdivide the topic into treatments of war and its victims, on the one hand, and the nuclear possibility, on the other hand.

---

[11]Composed by Don McLean. Published by The Benny Bird Co. Used by permission.

War and its victims figured prominently in the music of the 1960s and early 1970s paralleling the course of the Vietnam War. The songs of protest against war had their beginnings in the folk music of the early 1960s with such songs as Pete Seeger's "Where Have All the Flowers Gone?" (*Rainbow Quest*, 1960) and Bob Dylan's "Blowin in the Wind" (*The Freewheelin' Bob Dylan*, 1963). By the mid-1960s, America was immersed in a largely unwanted war, and newer, harsher, and more sharply focused protest songs emerged. Dylan's "Masters of War" (*The Freewheelin' Bob Dylan*, 1963) attacked those who built the big guns and death planes while safely sitting behind desks. Buffy Sainte-Marie's "The Universal Soldier" (*The Best of Buffy Sainte Marie*, 1970) appealed to the conscience of the fighters themselves, charging them with being the instruments of those who would continue the war. The Bob Seger System's "2 + 2 = ?" (*Ramblin' Gamblin' Man*, 1969) echoed the doubts of many would-be draftees who wondered why they were being asked to die.

Later, and likely out of frustration, protest songs turned to black humor. Powerless individuals faced a situation perceived to be absurd and vented their rage against the apparent insanity of the war effort. Center stage was "I-Feel-Like-I'm-Fixin'-To-Die-Rag" (*I-Feel-Like-I'm-Fixin'-To-Die*, 1967) by Country Joe and the Fish. The chorus mocks the tone of the unquestioning soldier:

> And it's one, two, three, what are we fightin' for?
> Don't ask me—I don't give a damn. Next stop is Viet Nam.
> And it's five, six, seven, open up the pearly gates—
> Well, there ain't no time to wonder why.
> Whoopee!—We're all gonna die.

Following the early verses that ridicule the military establishment and Wall Street, the last verse invites the family to join in the promotion of the war in tones that echo television advertising:

> Come on Mothers throughout the land,
> Pack your boys off to Viet Nam.
> Come on Fathers, don't hesitate,
> Send your sons off before it's too late.
> Be the first ones on your block
> To have your boy come home in a box.[12]

Another example of the same bitter treatment is found in Eric Burdin and the Animals' "Sky Pilot" (*The Twain Shall Meet*, 1968), which focuses on the perceived hypocrisy of chaplains and the religious establishment as they supported the war effort.

[12]"I Feel Like I'm Fixin' To Die Rag." Words and music © 1965 by Joe McDonald, Alkatraz Corner Music Co., 1977. Used by permission.

In the late 1960s, when it became apparent that the protest efforts were largely futile, few new protest songs were written. Instead, the impotence of the protest movement was reflected in such songs as John Lennon's "Give Peace a Chance" (*A Hard Road*, 1970). Similarly, from the point of view of a soldier, John Prine's "Sam Stone" (*Prime Prine*, 1971) provides a compelling portrait of a veteran who returns home with shattered nerves, an injury, and a drug habit. Early verses describe his condition, and the impact of his habit and the resulting poverty on his wife and children. The last verse reports his death from an overdose (quite possibly a suicide) and concludes that heroism has only brought him to a premature grave.

The prospect of nuclear holocaust characterizes the atmosphere in Pink Floyd's *The Wall* (1979). An early song, "The Thin Ice," suggests that we are all skating on the thin ice of an uneasy peace, threatened by the fear of global annihilation. Another early song, "Mother," treats the repression and defensiveness (the wall) that builds up as questions of the trustworthiness of the world are explored with the mother. The song begins as the child asks the mother if she thinks someone will drop the bomb, and goes on to explore other nightmares that may well come true. A later song, "Comfortably Numb," depicts the state of mind Lifton (1983) refers to as "psychic numbing."

Other powerful treatments of this subject echo many protest songs in resorting to black humor (Denisoff, 1983). Tom Lehrer's "We'll All Go Together When We Go" (*An Evening Wasted with Tom Lehrer*, 1966) speaks of the crowning achievement of modern civilization as the "universal bereavement" that would result from nuclear conflagration. Randy Newman's "Political Science" (*Sail Away*, 1972) notes that within the international community even our friends put us down and urges, somewhat puckishly, that we go ahead and drop the bomb. Newman would have us save Australia in order to spare the kangaroo, allow for building an American amusement park, and enjoy the surfing opportunities, but in the end he thinks all will be peaceful since everyone will have been set free through death.

Hunger

Direct expression of social concern and protest extends to treatment of world hunger. John Denver's "I Want to Live" (*I Want to Live*, 1978) pleads for the children of the world who ask only to be allowed a chance to live, to grow, to be, to know. Harry Chapin's "Shortest Story" (*Greatest Stories—Live*, 1976) is sung as if in the voice of a newborn in a famine-torn country. The first day of life is hopeful and filled with promise. By the seventh day, the mother's breast has gone dry, brother and sister are crying, and the newborn begins to feel the hunger and falls asleep. The last stanza reads:

It is twenty days today
Mama does not hold me anymore
I open my mouth
But I am too weak to cry
Above me a bird slowly crawls across the sky
Why is there nothing now to do but die?[13]

Apocalyptic Music

A repeated theme in adolescent music is that of impending disaster or total destruction. These songs express concern about the current state of affairs and warn of what may be in store. Among the earliest songs here is Barry McGuire's "Eve of Destruction" (1965), which expresses a feeling of impending doom and fear that others seem not to sense or share, much to the distress of the singer. The basis of the prediction is an analysis of racial and international hatred, and the ever-present nuclear button. Another song, richer in imagery, far more reminiscent of the biblical *Book of Revelations*, is Bob Dylan's "A Hard Rain's Gonna Fall" (*The Freewheelin' Bob Dylan*, 1963). In response to a mother's inquiry about what her son has seen as he has surveyed the world, the singer speaks of weapons wielded by children, a crying clown, and a man twisted by hatred. The images are many, and they snowball to create a devastating effect.

"Before the Deluge" (*Late for the Sky*, 1974) by Jackson Browne expresses the perspective of a person who has survived a destructive deluge that has swept away most of the world as we know it. In looking back, the singer characterizes the people populating the world before the deluge: some were dreamers; some were fools; some were seeking to return to nature; some turned to each other for refuge; some knew pleasure; some knew pain; and some lived only for the moment, losing themselves in the quest for eternal youth, and finally trading "their tired wings for the resignation that living brings." Some were angry at the abuse of the earth and at the powerful who abused her, expending their energies in protest. A few survived and, without time to understand, believed nevertheless that they were meant to live after the deluge. The need for understanding a better way is left unanswered in a chorus that ends:

13© 1975 Sandy Songs Ltd.

Let creation reveal its secrets by and by, by and by.
When the light that's lost within us reaches the sky.[14]

A particularly bitter song is Chicago's "When All the Laughter Dies in Sorrow" (*Chicago III*, 1971), which expresses wonder at the prospect of the passing of the entire human population:

When all the great galactic systems
Sigh to a frozen halt in space
Do you think there will be some remnant
Of the beauty of the human race . . .
Do you think a greater thinking thing
Will give a damn that man was here[15]

Alienated Generations, Drugs, and Death

The limited space allotted here does not allow an extended treatment of alienation as it is reflected in adolescent music. It is against the background of such alienation—resulting from the view that "they don't keep the promise in the promised land," the perceived threat to meaning of life posed by the institutions casting the nuclear shadow, the sense of impending doom reflected in the apocalyptic music treated in the preceding section, and other factors—that much of the more violent and even nihilistic music to be treated in this and the following sections must be understood.

As is only too well known, many alienated and otherwise disaffected or lost adolescents turn to potentially lethal drugs to get a high that life does not afford or to find an escape. The San Francisco sound of the late 1960s encouraged and promoted the drug culture, which is still very much with us. Yet, tragically, many prominent performers, including Janis Joplin, Jimi Hendrix, and Jim Morrison, died from drug overdoses. Many songs express alarm over the potentially, sometimes all too real, lethal results of drug use. Lynyrd Skynyrd's "That Smell" (*Street Survivors*, 1977) describes the smell of death in the air in the aftermath of the deaths of the above-mentioned performers. Paul Simon's "Save the Life of My Child" (*Bookends*, 1968) depicts a scene in which a crowd is gathered beneath a young man perched on a ledge and under the influence of drugs. Some spectators ask, "What's becoming of the children?" while others celebrate a freaky holiday; the police go on about how they are powerless and, anyway, "the kids got no respect for the law today."

A desperate mother repeatedly cries, "save the life of my child." But then darkness falls and:

> When the spotlight hit the boy.
> The crowd began to cheer,
> He flew away[16]

Things are not quite so bleak in Neil Young's " The Needle and the Damage Done" (*Harvest*, 1972), although the song laments the damage done by drugs and the tragedy that results even when junkies die. More positively, in The Little River Band's "Don't Let the Needle Win" (*Time Exposure*, 1981), the singer urges a drug-using friend who comes to ask for money to reflect upon what he is doing to himself, offers to help in any other way, and refuses to give the money. The song concludes with a plea to fight for life, and not to give in to "the needle."

Violence, Guns, Murder, Mayhem, Outlaws, and Death in the Ghetto

There is considerable preoccupation, if not a profound fascination, with themes of violence in adolescent music. The figures depicted in these songs include outlaw "heroes" who in real life were quite unsavory characters but who in song are often rendered as a Robin Hood. Perhaps the fascination is in part:

1. rooted in the American frontier experience in which each made his own law;
2. a function of the distorting influences of cowboy, detective, and spy novels; and
3. a reflection of the exposure to violence in the movies and on television.

Whatever its source, this fascination is real. In this category belong songs dedicated to Mack the Knife, Frankie and Johnny, Bonnie and Clyde, Pretty Boy Floyd, Billy the Kid, Frank and Jesse James, Machine Gun Kelly, and even the gang responsible for the St. Valentine's Day Massacre! Although the romance here is clearly misplaced, these examples are not nearly as offensive as those discussed below.

More schockingly realistic and disturbing treatments of murder include: R. Dean Taylor's "Indiana Wants Me" (*I Think, Therefore I am*, 1970), Jimi Hendrix's "Hey Joe" (*Foxy Lady*, 1967), Warren Zevon's "Roland the Headless Thompson Gunner" (*Excitable Boy*, 1968), The Doors' "The End" (*The Doors*, 1967), and Harry Chapin's "The Sniper" (*The*

---

[16]*Save The Life of My Child.* Copyright © 1968 by Paul Simon. Used by permission.

Sniper and Other Love Songs, 1972). In the first two songs, there is an inti-
mation that the motive for the murder justifies the act: the fugitive from
the law in the first song "had to" kill his victim because of something
that had been said, and Joe from the second song was caught with the
singer's woman. Roland, the subject of the third song, was a mercenary
warrior who was especially proficient with a Thompson automatic
weapon. Following his death, he returns as a headless ghost and blasts
his killer away in an act of revenge. His spirit is said to be alive wherever
arbitrary violence prevails. In the apocalyptic "The End," the end of time
is pictured as desolate and pervaded by images of death, decay, and destruction. It culminates in the singer's systematic, brutal, and remorse-
less slaughter of his siblings and parents. There is almost a psychotic
love of death captured in the mood and events of this song; no wonder
that it was selected to hold a prominent place in the film *Apocalypse Now*
(Coppola, 1979). Chapin's "The Sniper" explores the frame of mind of
another contemporary monster: the campus sniper of the mid-1960s.
The portrait is not heroic, yet the description of the sniper's paranoia,
lack of self-esteem, and pathetic attempts to assert his existence is oddly
compelling and chilling.

   As a counterbalence to the uncritical portrayal of violence, there are
songs that directly express concern about the terrible price exacted by
such violence. Lynyrd Skynyrd's "Saturday Night Special" (*One More
From the Road,* 1976) tells of violent results, both intended and unintended, of the pervasive availability of hand guns in our society and
urges that they all be gathered up and thrown into the sea. The well-
known "Stagger Lee" (*The Exciting Lloyd Price,* 1959) is a song representative of the outlaw hero genre and unchecked ghetto violence. There
are many songs, including a cluster released about the time of the popularity of the movie *Superfly* (Parks, 1972), that take strong exception to
such violence and urge the rejection of such figures as Stagger Lee.
Among the most important songs here are Curtis Mayfield's "Freddie's
Dead" (*Superfly,* 1972), War's "The World is a Ghetto" (*The World is a
Ghetto,* 1972), and the Temptations' "Papa was a Rolling Stone" (*All Directions,* 1972). The last of these ends by observing that the only legacy
from the death of a violent man is that he leaves behind others who are
all alone. Sly and the Family Stone's album, *There's a Riot Goin' On*
(1971), has been plausibly construed as a powerful indictment of indifference to ghetto violence (Marcus, 1982).

Pornographic Rock

Among the most disturbing music from this period is that which Gorer
(1965) would instantly recognize as reflecting the pornography of death.
Fantasy has completely taken over; death is dehumanized and distorted;

and entertainment value is found in the grotesque menacing and slaughtering of innocent women. This music is the equivalent of the "slasher" movies, and it sustains and reinforces sexist oppression. Caputi (1982) analyzes such behavior by tracing the legend of Jack the Ripper into the twentieth century—connecting it with the careers of real-life serial murderers of women, including the Yorkshire Ripper (Peter Sutcliffe), the Boston Strangler (Albert DeSalvo), the Hillside Strangler (Kenneth Bianchi), the Son of Sam (David Berkowitz), and Ted Bundy—and linking the pattern of sex crimes with patterns in popular media. An overview of the lyrics of a few songs suffices to capture their temper.

Warren Zevon's "Excitable Boy" (*Excitable Boy*, 1968) sets the tone as he describes the rape and killing of "Susie" after a junior prom date, explaining cynically that the boy was just "excitable." The Rolling Stones' "The Midnight Rambler" (*Let It Bleed*, 1969) salutes the Boston Strangler, depicts a rape/murder scene right out of DeSalvo's confession, and ends with a threat by the killer to stick his knife down the throat of the listening victim. Thin Lizzy pays tribute to Jack the Ripper with "Killer on the Loose" (*Chinatown*, 1980). This song and Trevor Rabin's "The Ripper" (*Face to Face*, 1980) were, astonishingly, released at the time of the reign of terror of the Yorkshire Ripper. What is especially disturbing about the latter three songs is that the singer adopts the voice of the killer himself.

Nihilistic Rock

The pornographic rock described in the previous section is at least akin to, if not itself a strain of, what I can only term nihilistic rock. Although the Rolling Stones' well-known "Sympathy for the Devil" (*Beggar's Banquet*, 1968) may be a precursor here, it is The Door's "The End" (*The Doors*, 1967) (described on p. 50) which captures the utterly barren negativity of this genre more closely. The roots of this music may well be in the soil of frustrated protest movements, failure to define or sustain a viable counterculture, numbness in the nuclear shadow, profound alienation, and fear of annihilation. Representative is the rage of Johnny Rotten and the Sex Pistol's punk anthems, "God Save the Queen" (*Never Mind the Bollocks, Here's the Sex Pistols*, 1977), which reiterates a denial of any future, and "Anarchy in the U.K." (same album), which forcefully and blatantly dwells on rejection of society with no hint of concern beyond venting that rage destructively. Consider this list of punk bands, their singers, and songs as indicative of the temperament:

Dead Boys. Hot Knives. Werewolves. Rat Scabies. Bitch. Crime. Stone Man. Blitzkrieg Bop. Aliens. Clash. Richard Hell. Stranglehold. Vultures. Storm Troopin'. The Dictators. Killer. Search and Destroy. The Stilettos. Heart Full of Napalm. Kill Me. Mondo Bondage. Quay Lewd. Master Race Rock. The Grenades. Death Race. Alan Suicide. (Selzer, 1979, p. 113)

An album by a group called The Dead Kennedys (*Fresh Fruit for Rotting Vegetables*, 1981) features such tunes as "Drug Me," "Chemical Warfare," "Kill the Poor," and "I Kill Children." Another album by Jerry's Kids (*This is Boston, Not L.A.*, 1981) features such songs as "Uncontrollable," "Letter Bomb," "Murder the Disturbed," and "Decadence." A comparable array of titles can be found in albums produced by such "heavy metal" groups as Steppenwolf, Black Sabbath, Kiss, Judas Priest, and Quiet Riot.

It may be that few take the lyrics, titles, or names of the artists involved with nihilistic rock (as distinct from the beat) seriously and that many find these songs to be a "joke." If so, we might ask, "What is thought to be funny here, and why?" Fuller (1981) offers a plausible beginning to an analysis of the phenomenon of nihilistic rock. In trying to account for the deaths at the 1979 Cincinnati concert by The Who, he explores the treatment of the theme of violence in the music of the 1970s. Fuller appropriately chronicles not only the demonstrative violence so commonly a part of the stage acts of rock groups but also the frenzy frequently stirred up in audiences, frenzy that occasionally breaks out in violence. Especially noteworthy is the Rolling Stones' 1969 concert at Altamont for which Hell's Angels had been hired as a security force and at which murder took place in the audience. Fuller also draws attention to an adolescent tendency to identify with rock performers and the not uncommon abuse of such identification by the artists themselves as they hold almost hypnotic sway over their concert audiences. This much of the book is highly suggestive, even if the author fails to explain The Who concert deaths, which in fact took place prior to the performance largely as a result of the use of "festival seating" and failure to open enough doors to accommodate the crush of the crowd. Nevertheless, I share Fuller's concern about the presence and appeal of nihilism in adolescent music, however limited its audience.

A PROVISIONAL CONCLUSION

I have tried throughout this chapter to let adolescent music from the classic years speak for itself through its titles and lyrics. This music is both personally and socially significant. Whether touching or outrageous, poignant or rebellious, absorbing or challenging, distorted or subtly insightful, the treatments of death and death-related themes in this music provide unexpected clues to understanding both death and adolescents. It is apparent that adolescent music can be an important locus for discussion and communication between adults and adolescents. What is required in the future is additional research conducted in two steps. The first would record the evolution of adolescent music, with particular emphasis on the presence of death and death-related themes, as it moves from its classic period into and through the 1980s. Special attention should be paid to the new phenomenon of music video and the frequently violent images that often have little, if any, relation to the music itself. The second step would be to conduct a psychological, sociological, and historical analysis of the underlying causes that motivate the production of this music and that make it attractive to so many. While the music is clearly an outgrowth and reflection of the adolescent experience of death within a culture that has not come to terms with death, there still is much to be done in order to articulate the complex relationships among that experience, that culture, and their treatment in the music. I hope to have laid useful groundwork upon which to build future analyses.

REFERENCES

"Abraham, Martin and John." Dion. Mousey, NY: Laurie, 1975.

Agents of Fortune. The Blue Oyster Cult. New York & Los Angeles: Columbia Records, 1976.

All Directions. The Temptations. Los Angeles: Gordy/Motown, 1972.

American Pie. Don McLean. Los Angeles, New York & Nashville: United Artists/EMI, 1972.

Becker, E. *The denial of death.* New York: The Free Press, 1973.

Beggar's Banquet. The Rolling Stones. London: London Records, 1968.

Best of Bread. David Gates. Los Angeles, New York, & Nashville: Elektra/Asylum/Nonesuch Records, 1973.

The Best of Buffy Sainte-Marie. Buffy Sainte-Marie. New York: Vanguard, 1970.

Blood, Sweat and Tears. Blood, Sweat and Tears. New York & Los Angeles: Columbia Records, 1969.

Bookends. Simon and Garfunkel. New York & Los Angeles: Columbia Records, 1968.

Bridge Over Troubled Waters. Simon and Garfunkel. New York & Los Angeles: Columbia Records, 1970.

Caputi, J. *The age of sex crime.* Unpublished doctoral dissertation, Bowling Green State University, Bowling Green, OH, 1982.

Carry It On. Joan Baez. New York: Vanguard, 1971.

Chicago III. Chicago. New York & Los Angeles: Columbia Records, 1971.

Chinatown. Thin Lizzy. Burbank, New York, & Nashville: Warner Bros., 1980.

Coppola, F. F. (Director/Producer). (1979). *Apocalypse Now* [Film]. Los Angeles: United Artists.

Dark Side of the Moon. Pink Floyd. Hollywood, New York, & Nashville: Capitol, 1973.

David's Album. Joan Baez. New York: Vanguard, 1969.

Denisoff, R. S. Since I Lost My Baby: The Pop Way of Death. *Creem*, 1971, *3*, 28–31.

Denisoff, R. S. *Sing a song of social significance* (2nd ed.). Bowling Green, OH: Bowling Green State University Popular Press, 1983.

Don't Cry Out Loud. Melissa Manchester. New York & Los Angeles: Arista, 1978.

The Doors. The Doors. Los Angeles, New York & Nashville: Elektra, 1967.

Eat to the Beat. Blondie. Los Angeles: Chrysalis Records, 1979.

"Eve of Destruction." Barry McGuire. Hollywood: Dunhill/ABC Paramount, 1965.

An Evening With John Denver. John Denver. New York, Los Angeles, & Nashville: RCA, 1975.

An Evening Wasted With Tom Lehrer. Tom Lehrer. Burbank, New York & Nashville: Reprise/Warner Bros., 1966.

Excitable Boy. Warren Zevon. Los Angeles, New York, & Nashville: Asylum Records, 1968.

The Exciting Lloyd Price. Lloyd Price. Hollywood: ABC-Paramount, 1959.

Face to Face. Trevor Rabin. Los Angeles: Chrysalis Records, 1980.

Foxy Lady. Jimi Hendrix. Burbank, New York, & Nashville: Reprise/Warner Bros., 1967.

The Freewheelin' Bob Dylan. Bob Dylan. New York & Los Angeles: Columbia Records, 1963.

Fresh Fruit for Rotting Vegetables. The Dead Kennedys. Houston, TX: Cherry Red, 1981.

Freud, S. Thoughts for the times on war and death. In J. Strachey (Ed.), *The standard edition of the complete works of Sigmund Freud.* (Vol. 14, pp. 275–300). London: Hogarth Press, 1957.

Fuller, J. *Are the kids all right?: The rock generation and its hidden death wish.* New York: New York Times Books, 1981.

The Game. Queen. Los Angeles, New York & Nashville, Elektra, 1980.

Gorer, G. *Death, grief, and mourning.* New York: Doubleday, 1965.

Greatest Stories—Live. Harry Chapin. Los Angeles, New York & Nashville: Elektra, 1976.

A Hard Road. John Lennon. New York: Moriphon, 1970.

Harvest. Neil Young. Burbank, New York, & Nashville: Reprise/Warner Bros., 1972.

Honky Chateau. Elton John. Los Angeles & New York: UNI, 1972.

"Hound Dog Man." Rubberband. New York: October, 1977.

I-Feel-Like-I'm-Fixin'-To-Die. Country Joe and the Fish. New York: Vanguard, 1967.

I Think, Therefore I Am. R. Dean Taylor. Los Angeles: Rare Earth/Motown, 1970.

I Want to Live. John Denver. New York, Los Angeles, & Nashville: RCA, 1978.

"I Want My Baby Back." Jimmy Cross. New York: Tollie, 1964.

Jackson Browne. Jackson Browne. Los Angeles, New York & Nashville: Asylum, 1972.

John Denver. John Denver. New York, Los Angeles, & Nashville: RCA, 1979.

Late for the Sky. Jackson Browne. Los Angeles, New York & Nashville: Asylum, 1974.

"Leader of the Pack." The Shangri-las. New York: Lana, 1964.

Led Zepplin IV. Led Zepplin. New York & Los Angeles: Atlantic, 1971.

Let It Bleed. The Rolling Stones. London: London Records, 1969.

Lifton, R. J. *The broken connection.* New York: Basic Books, 1983.
Living Room Suite. Harry Chapin. Los Angeles, New York, & Nashville: Elektra, 1978.
Love Tracks. Gloria Gaynor. New York & Los Angeles: Polydor, 1978.
Lovers, Friends and Strangers. Barbara Mandrell. Universal City, CA: Dot/MCA, 1977.
Macken, B., Fornatale, P., & Ayers, B. *The rock music source book.* New York: Doubleday, 1980.
Marcus, G. *Mystery train.* (Rev. ed.). New York: Dutton, 1982.
*M*A*S*H.* M*A*S*H. New York & Los Angeles: Columbia Records, 1970.
Moods. Neil Diamond. Los Angeles & New York: UNI, 1972.
Never Mind the Bollocks, Here's the Sex Pistols. The Sex Pistols. Burbank, New York, & Nashville: Warner Bros., 1977.
Old Friends. Mary McCaslin. North Ferisburg, VT: Philo, 1974.
One More From the Road. Lynyrd Skynyrd. Universal City, CA: MCA, 1976.
Parks, G. (Director/Producer). (1972). *Superfly* [Film]. Los Angeles: Warner Bros.
Parsley, Sage, Rosemary and Thyme. Simon and Garfunkel. New York & Los Angeles: Columbia Records, 1966.
"Patches." Dicky Lee. Nashville: Smash, 1962.
Poems, Prayers and Promises. John Denver. New York, Los Angeles, & Nashville: RCA, 1971.
Point of No Return. Kansas. New York: Kirshner Records, 1977.
Portrait Gallery. Harry Chapin. Los Angeles, New York & Nashville: Elektra, 1975.
Prime Prine. John Prine. New York & Los Angeles: Atlantic, 1971.
Prime Time. Don McLean. New York & Los Angeles: Arista, 1977.
Rainbow Quest. Pete Seeger. New York: Folkways, 1960.
Ramblin' Gamblin' Man. The Bob Seger System. Hollywood, New York & Nashville: Capitol, 1969.
Revolver. The Beatles. Hollywood, New York & Nashville: Capitol, 1966.
"Rock and Roll Heaven." The Righteous Brothers. Los Angeles: Haven, 1975.
Sail Away. Randy Newman. Burbank, New York & Nashville: Reprise/Warner Bros., 1972.
Selzer, M. *Terrorist chic.* New York: Hawthorn Books, 1979.
Sgt. Pepper's Lonely Hearts Club Band. The Beatles. Hollywood, New York & Nashville: Capitol, 1967.
Shneidman, E. S. *Voices of death.* New York: Harper & Row, 1980.
The Sniper and Other Love Songs. Harry Chapin. Los Angeles, New York & Nashville: Elektra, 1972.
Sounds of Silence. Simon and Garfunkel. New York & Los Angeles: Columbia Records, 1965.
Street Survivors. Lynyrd Skynyrd. Universal City, CA: MCA, 1977.
Super Trouper. Abba. New York & Los Angeles: Atlantic, 1981.
Superfly. Curtis Mayfield. Chicago: Curtom Records, 1972.
Sweet Baby James. James Taylor. Burbank, New York & Nashville: Warner Bros., 1971.
Takin' It Easy. Seals and Croft. Burbank, New York & Nashville: Warner Bros., 1978.
Tea for the Tillerman. Cat Stevens. Los Angeles: A & M, 1970.
"Teen Angel." Mark Dinning. Los Angeles: MGM, 1960.
"Tell Laura I Love Her." Ray Peterson. New York: RCA, 1960.

There's a Riot Goin' On. Sly and the Family Stone. New York: Epic/CBS, 1971.
This Is Boston, Not L.A. Jerry's Kids. New York & Los Angeles: Modern Method/ Atlantic, 1981.
Thrush, J. C., & Paulus, G. S. The concept of death in popular music: A social psychological perspective. *Popular Music and Society,* 1970, 6, 219–228.
Time Exposure. The Little River Band. Hollywood, New York & Nashville: Capitol, 1981.
"Tragedy." The Fleetwoods. Hollywood: Liberty, 1962.
A Tramp Shining. Richard Harris. New York: Dunhill/MCA, 1968.
The Twain Shall Meet. Eric Burden and the Animals. Hollywood: MGM, 1968.
The Wall. Pink Floyd. New York & Los Angeles: Columbia Records, 1979.
The Who Live at Leeds. The Who. New York & Los Angeles: Decca, 1970.
Windsong. John Denver. New York, Los Angeles & Nashville: RCA, 1975.
The World Is a Ghetto. War. Los Angeles, New York & Nashville: United Artists/ EMI, 1972.

4

The Adolescent Philosopher in a Nuclear World

Dorothy A. Austin and John E. Mack

There is an increasing concern among some mental health professionals, educators, and parents in the United States that the escalating arms competition and the threat of nuclear war are having a detrimental impact upon children and adolescents. Some contemporary studies suggest that young people are keenly aware of the danger they face in a nuclear world. Some of the young people interviewed have reported feeling enraged, despairing, resigned, or fearful about the present-day nuclear arms race (Beardslee & Mack, 1982; Goodman, Mack, Beardslee, & Snow, 1983; Snow, 1984).

For these adolescents, the contemplation of nuclear "war" as a conceivable possibility in their own lifetimes may well result in new ways of thinking about death: the imagined death of oneself in a nuclear holocaust; the deaths of family members and friends; and the death—or, more accurately, the extinction—of the entire world. If this is the case—that some adolescents have been significantly affected psychologically by the threat of nuclear death (and that some adolescents have *not* been affected psychologically)—then that experience is undoubtedly related to the broader question of how particular adolescents think and feel about "ordinary" death.

Further study and understanding of general conceptions of death held by certain adolescents in relation to the *particular* fear of death by nuclear war is called for. This is all the more true if we discover that some adolescents in contemporary society experience the nuclear threat as having an impact on their basic thoughts and feelings about "life and death" issues—the philosophical meaning and purpose of life. One might ask, for example, if the fear of dying in a nuclear "war" influences some adolescents' thoughts and planning for the future. If so, for which adolescents, and in what way? How are we to understand those adolescents who seem not to be affected by nuclear weapons? Does the fact of existing in a man-made nuclear world affect the developmental course of some adolescents' ethical and religious values? Are some adolescents all the more prepared to "fight to the death" to protect their country from being overtaken by the Russians? Does the possibility of planetary mass murder, as a result of unsuccessfully negotiated conflict between nations, give rise to an unprecedented despair, an unprecedented indifference, and an unprecedented interest in human relations and cooperation? Does the increasing build-up of U.S. nuclear weapons persuade some adolescents that the U.S. government is struggling to protect itself against the increasingly deadly intentions of the Soviet government? Does the presence of nuclear instruments of extinction as instruments of government policy give rise to an unprecedented conflict between the older and younger generations? If so, how and for whom? Does the national willingness to use nuclear weapons lessen or heighten the investment of young people in the democratic process? How does the possibility of nuclear death affect (or *not* affect) certain adolescents' ideas about patriotism, strength, national security, military service, and so on, depending upon certain variables such as gender, class, race, ethnicity, geographical location, education, and parents' political or apolitical persuasions?

In this chapter we shall consider the attitudes and responses of certain adolescents to nuclear issues within a general discussion of adolescent development, paying particular attention to moral development and to the building of psychosocial identity. For some young people (and for some adults), the overwhelming presence of nuclear weapons and the possibility of nuclear death poses a special threat to the generational connection between adolescents and adults. "Nuclear death," as one young person reminded us recently, "is a special case of death inflicted on a planetary level, by human beings, not by the hand of God or Nature" (Austin, 1984).

For adolescents generally, a generational connection to significant adults is crucial for the healthy development of an adequate psychosocial identity—a sense of having a purposeful role in the world and in the scheme of things. Optimally, an adolescent should feel that he or she will one day receive an inheritable world from those adults who have gone before him. Adolescent identity depends upon a young person having some sense of psychosocial "place"—of "belonging" both emotionally and socially—within one's family and within the larger world. A sense of historical continuity as well as an inherited purpose as a citizen of the world is instrumental to an adolescent's construction of a viable world-view and a positive faith in the meaning of life. Within such a sufficiently defined psychosocial framework, the adolescent is prepared to conceptualize meaningfully about life and death, whether it be making sense of accidental death, premature death, or other unbidden malignancies of fate.

THE ADOLESCENT IN AMERICAN PSYCHOLOGY

As a stage in human development, adolescence is perhaps the most tumultuous, arising as it does as a marginal period between childhood and adulthood. Broadly speaking, adolescence is a time when physical and sexual development is accompanied by frequent mood swings, new cognitive challenges, and shifting dynamics in relationships with peers, family, and society.

Moreover, adolescence is traditionally a time of questioning, at least in North American society. In their essay, "The Adolescent as a Philosopher," developmental psychologists Kohlberg and Gilligan (1971) point out that "all accounts of adolescence stress both the sense of questioning and the parallel discovery or search for a new self" (p. 1055). This adolescent questioning, however, even when it is quite radical, is nonetheless to be seen in the context of certain "givens." Whatever turmoil takes place developmentally, the adolescent nonetheless wants to become a grownup.

"American psychology," Kohlberg and Gilligan (1971) suggest has always "placed the adolescent discovery of the self against a stable but progressive social order. It saw the discovery of self within a desire to be 'grown up,' however confused or vague this image of the grownup was" (p. 1055). In other words, mainstream American psychology has presumed that the psychosocial order of American society is sufficiently intact to support the coming of age of each and every subsequent generation of young people. What we may now be questioning is whether this foundation, which adolescent development has always depended upon, has been significantly overburdened and shaken by the stockpiling of nuclear weapons. As one teenager said in a recent interview (Austin, 1984): "Nuclear weapons are part of the American landscape, like rivers and mountains. Whatever became of the American dream?"

STAGES OF ADOLESCENT DEVELOPMENT

Nuclear weapons may pose a unique threat to the psychosocial development and self-understanding of certain adolescents and to the developmental path of cognitive and moral development they undergo on the
way to ethical maturity and adulthood. By ethical maturity, we mean
the capacity for a certain mutuality between people—a capacity to
depend on each other for the development of respective strengths and
for a common caretaking and preservation of life in the face of human
mortality.

In cognitive terms, adolescence is the time when young people experience a shift from concrete operational thinking to formal operational
thinking. In the Piagetian scheme (Piaget, 1955), this means that adolescents now have the capacity to "abstract" and to think reflectively. This
includes the capacity to think about the nature of "thinking" itself, and
to consider and evaluate hypothetical situations and arguments while
recognizing that what one observes and conceives symbolically is only a
subset of what may be logically possible. For the adolescent philosopher, this means that it is now possible to consider many different perspectives on life, including the imagined nonexistence of oneself and the
world, the imagined feelings of another's point of view, and certain ultimate questions about the nature of life and death, good and evil, and
the meaning of life.

Similarly, the adolescent's moral awareness is also growing. Most adolescents experience maturational shifts from so-called "preconven-
tional" to "conventional" to "postconventional" morality. This transition
in moral development means that the adolescent boy or girl no longer
follows rules merely out of fear of punishment or because of the physical
power of those who make and enforce the rules, as is the case in "pre-
conventional" morality. Rather, at the "conventional" stage of moral development, the preadolescent perceives the rules of family, community,
school, and nation as being valuable in their own right, worthy of being
followed because of their intrinsic value. "Conventional" morality is
characterized by an adherence to what is expected by society and by a
commitment to the maintenance, support, and justification of the social
order.

At the "postconventional" stage of moral development, which first becomes evident during adolescence, there is a major shift toward independent thinking and principled reasoning that have their own value
and legitimation apart from the sanction of society. The adolescent finds
it possible to value life over property. In addition, life itself is held to be
sacred and representative of a universal human value. The adolescent

philosopher chooses life over death both as a matter of principle and as a shared value held in common with other generations, past, present, and future. The adolescent is now capable of contemplating the characteristics of a just or unjust life and death. Death and dying must now be wrestled into a world-view that contains senselessness, absurdity, injustice, and evil. As one well-educated and thoughtful young man said to us: "Nuclear weapons are the most serious philosophical problem of our day" (Austin, 1984; cf. Camus, 1955).

In Kohlberg and Gilligan's (1971) findings, the adolescent is seen as experiencing himself or herself with a newly found subjectivity and selfhood that defines and solves moral dilemmas and social problems along certain predictable lines. A well-known example from the work of these authors is the response of adolescent boys and girls to a hypothetical moral dilemma posed by the psychological investigator: the so called "Heinz dilemma" in which an insufficiently moneyed Heinz feels compelled to steal a necessary medical drug from the druggist in order to save the life of his critically ill wife. Adolescent boys and girls are asked if Heinz should steal the drug.

Not surprisingly, adolescent answers vary according to stages of moral development. Some adolescents answer that Heinz should steal the necessary drug he cannot afford, but that he should be punished according to the law. His sentence, however, they maintain, should be minimal because of the merciful nature of his crime. Still other adolescents suggest that the druggist should be legally liable for not cooperating with Heinz in a matter of life and death. Still others begin to reconstruct the moral dilemma by suggesting that all drugs necessary for the maintenance of life or the prevention of death should be held in common, to be made available to everyone regardless of monetary assets. In addition, generally speaking, adolescent boys tend to answer in accordance with what Kohlberg and Gilligan (1971) call "principled reasoning," while adolescent girls are more likely to respond to moral dilemmas through "contextual reasoning." That is, girls are more likely to make moral decisions about the maintenance of life according to the contextual connections among persons, whereas boys are more likely to make decisions in accordance with the principle of valuing life over property, regardless of circumstances (Gilligan, 1982).

According to Erikson's (1958, 1964) way of conceptualizing adolescent development, the young person moves from "moral" to "ethical" thinking: from the fear of punishment to the recognition and striving for ideals—notably, the ideals of fairness, inclusion, and the preservation of life over death. In adolescence, the young person strives to make sense of his or her own identity in relation to self, others, and society. In doing so, he or she has to integrate emerging sexuality, competing desires for self determination and dependency, developing cognitive abilities, and ethical awareness into a unique self.

As adolescents struggle with these issues of identity, their resolution to improve the world is often accompanied by great frustration. Equipped with new cognitive and ethical tools and a strong sense of how the world should be, the adolescent oscillates between the two worlds of childhood and adulthood. The following paragraph, written by a 15- year-old girl, portrays one adolescent's ironic determination to inherit the adult world and to re-make it into a more idealistic society:

Childhood dies slowly, but even at dawn I fear the dark. Safe in my house of antiseptic ice cubes, I can view the future with the smug idealism that fifteen years has taught me. War? My generation will have no war. Men must live in peace. (Mary, don't hit Suzy.) Poverty? My generation will eliminate poverty. We must share the riches of the earth with one another. (Sally, do you have any old clothes to go to Goodwill?) "Anticipation," they sing on the radio, and I can hardly wait to make the world as it should be. (Larrick & Merriam, 1973, p. 139)

Adolescents question not only their own values, but those of their family and their society. According to Kohlberg and Gilligan (1971), "the core phenomenon of adolescence as a stage is the discovery of the subjective self and subjective experience and a parallel questioning of adult cultural reality" (p. 1059). Embedded in the adolescent's criticism of the values and practices of the adult generation is the adolescent's determination to change the world according to his or her own ideals. This conception of the "adolescent as philosopher," capable of moral and intellectual questioning, is central to an understanding of some adolescents' experience of death anxiety and the threat of nuclear annihilation.

THE ADOLESCENT AND DEATH

Encompassed within the adolescent's growing awareness lies a new understanding of death. Misperceptions regarding death (that is, that death is a reversible process) have long ago been abandoned by adolescents. They now are able to assimilate biological explanations of death while simultaneously pondering more abstract and philosophical notions of death.

Koocher (1981) has demonstrated that children's emotional comprehension of death depends on, although is not solely determined by, their level of cognitive ability. He writes: "Increased levels of cognitive development are linked with increased levels of abstraction in reasoning about death among children" (p. 92). While asserting the importance of cognitive development in the child's conception of death, Koocher acknowledges that each child's emotional capacity to deal with death will vary according to his or her personal history of loss and family experiences. Beginning only in adolescence can a young girl or boy speak of death metaphorically, or begin to recognize and analyze its abstract consequences.

When one considers the rapidly changing awareness of some adolescents as well as the difficulty of the adolescent stage, it is perhaps not surprising to learn that senior high school students experience a higher level of death anxiety than either junior high school students or adults. Koocher (1973, 1974a, 1974b, 1975) also noted that senior high school students he surveyed experienced a significantly higher level of anxiety and depression than either the younger or older populations. The most salient aspects of the adolescents' death anxiety (as well as those of the other two groups, but to a lesser degree) were fear of dying prematurely and disturbance over leaving loved ones behind. Koocher attributed the higher death anxiety of the senior high school students to a greater level of stress accompanying the physical, emotional, and cognitive changes of adolescence. In addition, he noted possible ramifications of the novelty of the adolescent's philosophical capacity. Adolescents are more aware of their feelings and more willing to report them than are young children. Also, the adolescent's understanding of death's finality and inevitability is new and may lead to a certain fear, fascination, and preoccupation with death. A vivid account of one adolescent's preoccupation and fascination with death is *Vivienne: The Life and Suicide of an Adolescent Girl* by Mack and Hickler (1981). In this book, the authors use extensive material from Vivienne's diary and her collection of poems, letters, and school papers, to present a first-person narrative of one young woman's struggle to live and die.

The fact that adolescents are conscious of death and their own mortality is undeniable. As one can conclude from the title of their study, "Death Anxiety in Normal Children and Adolescents," Koocher, O'Malley, Foster, and Gogan (1976) assume that death anxiety is a normal aspect of adolescent development. Integrating the inevitability of death into a productive, stable life is but one of several cognitive, moral, and emotional tasks challenging the adolescent. The focus of this chapter, however, is on the "abnormal" challenge posed by nuclear weapons —the threat of "absurd" death and the extinction of the entire human race.

DEATH ANXIETY AND
THE FEAR OF NUCLEAR DEATH

In order to understand the psychological consequences of the threat of nuclear war on adolescent development, we need to think more about the relationship of normal death anxiety to the fear of nuclear death.

Psychological development has to be understood in the context of the wider psychohistorical moment. Psychiatrist Lifton (1979) maintains that because of the overwhelming presence of nuclear weapons "we are haunted by the image of exterminating ourselves as a species by means of our own technology" (p. 5; cf. Lifton & Falk, 1982). Lifton argues that the ever-present danger of nuclear annihilation has caused a "broken connection" in the vital link between life, death, and "symbolic immortality"—the sense that one will live on symbolically, through one's children, through one's work, through the eternity of nature, or through the religious belief in immortality and transcendent reality. The point, of course, is that nuclear weapons disturb not only our thoughts about mortality, but our thoughts about immortality as well. For Lifton, the life of the self—and one should include here the adolescent self—is maintained through the self's capacity to create and sustain a sense of vitality and historical continuity in the face of inevitable death. The desire for symbolic immortality is a normal human response to the fact of our mortality; it does not represent escape from death, but fulfillment of life.

But—we should remind ourselves—immortality is dependent for its livelihood upon biological continuity, whether it be through the begetting of generations or through the sense that one participates in the ever-recurring cycle of nature. Biological existence is the genesis of the immortal nature of the self, a self that dies and yet lives on (Lifton, 1976). History and immortality are dependent upon the eternal life of the biological: the preservation of the planet and the human species. Death, as well as death anxiety, is part of history, but is transcended or at least transformed by the human capacity for symbolic immortality. But the anticipation of extinction means the imagined end of everything, an end to the repetitive cycle of life, death, and life. As Schell (1982) puts it: "Death cuts off life; extinction cuts off birth" (p. 119).

Our original question was this: Does the possibility of human extinction through nuclear "war" pose an unprecedented challenge to the developing adolescent and to normal death anxiety? In restating this question now, we need to ask ourselves the accompanying question: Does the possibility of human extinction through nuclear "war" pose an unprecedented challenge to the *developing adult*? We suspect that it does and that the crisis we experience as adults is a profound breakdown in our own *generativity*: the fear that we cannot preserve, care for, maintain, and pass on an inheritable world to the next generation, to the world's children. In turn, the developing adolescent experiences a loss of stability and generational confidence that are crucial if a young person is to have the philosophical ability to give meaning to life knowing that one will surely die.

STUDIES OF ADOLESCENTS AND THE NUCLEAR THREAT

In the past few years, several researchers have studied the psychological consequences of the threat of nuclear war on certain adolescents in the United States. The consistent finding is that adolescents studied are indeed painfully aware of the possibility of nuclear holocaust. A 1982 survey of high school students from four states revealed that 87% of those students feared a nuclear war in the next 20 years (Beardslee & Mack, 1982). One researcher has recorded an increase in teenagers' nuclear anxiety during the 8 years from 1975 to 1982. In 1982, over one third of the high school seniors surveyed assented to the statement: "Nuclear or biological annihilation will probably be the fate of all mankind within my lifetime" (Goodman et al., 1983, p. 501). Adolescents in the USSR and in some Western European countries also report feelings of gloom and fears of nuclear war (Chivian & Goodman, 1984; Mack, 1984). It should be noted, however, that adolescents report concern over nuclear war in varying ways depending upon economic class as well as educational and family experience.

In his unpublished paper, "Children and the Nuclear Bomb," psychiatrist Coles argues that "class separates children with respect to their thoughts (if any) about the nuclear bomb." Coles reports that in his interviews with working-class white children, black children in parts of the American South, and Pueblo children, it is "context" that is determinative. He says of studies that explore the psychosocial aspects of nuclear developments:

> If we are to go further, and try to understand the overall significance of a given element of consciousness, then we need to do what Miss Freud suggests: put in our fair share of time with some children, at least enough boys and girls (who come from different enough backgrounds) to give us a sense of whether an issue such as the nuclear bomb much affects them, and if so, how often, and under what set of circumstances. Again, it is context that matters—the comparative significance of *this* matter as against *that* one in the child's life; and it is the overall context that needs to be understood,

namely, what in the child's life may indeed prompt long and hard worry about a nuclear war, and what may make for indifference in another child. To obtain this kind of information requires a rather long involvement with children—the "direct observation," sustained over the years, Miss Freud has again and again suggested as important. (p. 10)

The first studies of the threat of nuclear war on certain children were undertaken in 1961 and 1962 in response to the Berlin crisis and Cuban Missile crisis. At a conference on "International Programs of Behavioral Research in Human Survival," Schwebel and Escalona reported the findings of their studies. Schwebel (1965) had surveyed 3000 junior and senior high school students in order to elicit their views on war and civil defense. He concluded that children were worried about nuclear war and that they adopted one of two strategies to cope with this fear. Some children openly confronted their anxiety and lived with the consequential unpleasant thoughts, while others denied their anxiety in order to protect themselves against the stress of their threatening fears. Schwebel asserted that mental health professionals have an obligation to respond to children's nuclear anxieties. Indeed, in this area of study, all researchers have stressed the importance of adults acknowledging adolescent worries about nuclear war. Adult intervention appears, in fact, to be one of the most effective coping strategies for containing the death anxiety of adolescents.

Escalona (1965) surveyed 311 children between 10 and 17 to explore their attitudes and beliefs regarding the world's near future. Seventy percent were concerned with issues of war and peace; 35% of those 70% expressed worry regarding a destructive war. Escalona described how children's attitudes reflected those of adults in the society, including adults' fatalism. She then went on to formulate a beginning developmental theory of the effect of the nuclear threat on children. She postulated that:

> The profound uncertainty about whether or not mankind has a foreseeable future exerts a corrosive and malignant influence upon important developmental processes in normal and well-functioning children. (p. 201)

In the early 1980s, concern over adolescent development and the threat of nuclear war has been rekindled (Goodman et al., 1983). Five major areas have been considered and deserve attention:

1. The impact of the threat of nuclear war on adolescents' thoughts about the future;
2. Adolescents' cynicism and distrust regarding political leaders and the adult generation;

3. Adolescents' political views pertaining to the arms race;
4. The influence of the nuclear threat on adolescent personality development;
5. Strategies for adult intervention in helping the adolescent to respond to these crises.

In the remainder of this chapter, we will consider each of these areas in turn.

THE THREAT OF NUCLEAR WAR AND THE FUTURE

All of the 31 adolescents interviewed by Goodman and colleagues (1983) reported that the threat of nuclear war is part of their daily awareness, whether it comes to them through newscasts, discussions with their peers, parents, and teachers, or occasional nightmares. In 1965, Schwebel postulated that children choose either to acknowledge and live with their nuclear fears or to repress and deny them. More recently, Goodman and colleagues have reformulated Schwebel's conclusion to suggest that both kinds of coping strategies are used by each individual. Many adolescents simultaneously fear that they will have no future, yet continue to develop future plans. As one 16-year-old girl said:

> Everyday is living in fear that there's going to be war. I make my plans now for my future and I'm just always wondering: will these plans ever come true? (Goodman et al., 1983, p. 511)

Some adolescents live with the daily threat and worry of nuclear war, while developing adaptive capacities that permit them periodically to contain their fears at a level enabling them to continue to function in their daily lives. In looking at the psychology of adults, Lifton (1979) has described a similar process of adaptation that enables adults to lead double lives: being fearful of nuclear extinction, yet carrying on as though no serious threat exists.

In spite of nuclear death anxiety, most adolescents and presumably most adults continue to plan for the future. Some young people report that the possibility of nuclear war does shake their confidence in having children. And some researchers claim that in the face of an uncertain and unpredictable future certain adolescents resort to "living for the moment." One young girl put it this way:

> I'm probably more carefree. I do the things I want to do. I mean I don't hold back. . . . I feel that's my chance to grab it. Get it if you want it because it will never come again. (Goodman et al., 1983, p. 511)

Another young person, faced with the prospect of a premature death, says:

If this (war) is going to happen, I'll have to accomplish everything I want to, all my dreams, before this happens. (Goodman et al., 1983, p. 511)

These youths embrace the present while they anticipate that a future cannot be relied upon for the fulfillment of their hopes. Psychologist Smith (1982) has linked what he perceives to be young people's inability to make commitments to an anxiety about nuclear war, the consequent result being a determination to live for the present:

We know that commitments come with more difficulty to young people of the present day than to predecessor generations; we know that the impulsivity that underlies many forms of problematic behavior is fostered by a reckless orientation to the "here and now." We know that a good many young people are seriously troubled by the prospects of nuclear war. We therefore have good reason to suppose that the threat of nuclear war must be a substantial contributor to orientations on the part of the young that are the focus of appropriate social concern; that, indeed, as the threat becomes more salient, the psychological costs along these lines may be expected to increase.

ADOLESCENTS' DISTRUST OF LEADERS

Today's adolescents not only distrust the promise of a personal future, but are suspicious of the "peaceful" intentions of world leaders and the adult generation as well. They perceive the world to be chaotic, seemingly out of control, and unmanageable in the hands of adults. As one 17-year-old boy remarked:

I think the whole thing has gotten too out of hand, so complicated that there's nothing that anybody can really do about it. . . . I think that nuclear weapons are going to stay. . . . I'm sure sometime in the future there will be [a nuclear war]. (Goodman et al., 1983, p. 513)

In much of the research already completed by others, it was found that adolescents fear the inevitability of nuclear war. There is also the sense on the part of many adolescents that world leaders are working counterproductively toward the attainment of world peace. Many adolescents interviewed accused the U.S. government of being uncaring, secretive, power-hungry, overly concerned with reelection, and obsessed with impersonal calculations of acceptable risks. As one 16-year-old girl said:

I don't think they [U.S. politicians] want to deal with people. I think that they know what it [the arms race] is doing, but they don't want to stop it. . . . It just frustrates me that they care so little about human life and human society . . . (Goodman et al., 1983, p. 518)

Four major areas of distrust were noted by Goodman and colleagues (1983). Today's youngsters are cynical regarding: leaders, media, the powerlessness of the people, and the ineffectiveness of peacemaking strategies employed by world leaders. A feeling of helplessness and powerlessness underlies the adolescents' sense of distrust. Not only do they perceive the adult generation to be ineffective in preventing nuclear war, but they also view themselves to be powerless. They fear that they can neither rely on themselves nor on adults to make the world a safe and certain environment. As Escalona concluded in 1965:

Children know that an overwhelming danger exists. But what they see also is that parents, teachers, in fact, all adults feel inadequate to cope with this danger. . . . They see in their elders evasion or lethargy based on underlying fear and fatalism. . . . (p. 208)

Of course, as Smith (1982) appropriately notes, an understanding of adolescent cynicism regarding nuclear politics cannot be separated from the broader context of adolescent disillusionment with other human horrors such as conventional war, poverty, pollution, political corruption, violence, and disease. One thing that *has* changed since Escalona's conclusion in 1965, now that many more adults have become active in the antinuclear movement, is that young people have become more hopeful as their parents, teachers, and other adult friends become involved actively in trying to stop the spiralling arms competition.

ADOLESCENTS' POLITICAL VIEWS
ON THE ARMS RACE

Recently, attempts have been made to elicit from teenagers what they regard as a desirable nuclear war policy in relation to other nations. Among the 31 high school students interviewed by Goodman and colleagues (1983) in their pilot study, a majority insisted that nuclear war could neither be limited nor won. The majority reported that no nuclear power has a "first strike capability" (the ability to destroy the nuclear retaliatory capacity of the enemy with a single attack) and that any nuclear confrontation will inevitably escalate to a full-scale nuclear war ending in human extinction. A 19-year-old girl expressed her incredulity at those who maintain a belief in limited or winnable nuclear war, with these words:

You do meet other people who are really planning on life going on after a nuclear war. . . . But it won't go on afterwards after such a huge thing. I don't see how people can plan for it . . . . To have mail after a nuclear war is an absurd thought. But there are so many people in such high positions that are thinking like that. (Goodman et al., 1983, p. 515)

These same students asserted that civil defense planning is madness and frightening in that it makes the possibility of nuclear war more likely if there are people who believe that we can survive a nuclear war. A 16-year-old girl interviewed portrayed the folly of both a theory of limited nuclear war and of effective civil defense:

Everyday I hear the Reagan administration denying if there were a nuclear war that it would be total destruction. He's saying only such and such of the population would die. We could all go into these little bomb shelters and be just as comfortable as could be, wait it out for six months, and then crawl off and start anew. . . . I know that's incredibly dangerous. If we believe that then we are sure to destroy ourselves. (Goodman et al., 1983, p. 516)

THE INFLUENCE OF THE NUCLEAR THREAT ON ADOLESCENT DEVELOPMENT

Escalona (1982) identifies adults' passivity in correcting the world's evils to be detrimental to child development. The consensus of mental health professionals, political activists, and parents, at a February 1983 conference held at Yale University was their concern that children's psychological development may be impaired due to an impediment in the socialization process through which children traditionally establish a sense of security. Children have begun to recognize that not even their parents can protect them in the event of a nuclear holocaust. Other worries concerning the consequences of the nuclear threat on adolescent development have centered on the ramifications of the adolescent's sense of futurelessness.

The American Psychiatric Association Task Force on the Psychosocial Implications of Nuclear Advances, chaired by Dr. Rita Rogers, discussed the possibility that the imminent threat of nuclear disaster negatively influences personality development by preventing adolescents from forming stable ideals or a sense of generational continuity. The study argues that:

The formation of the psychic structures upon which such development depends is compromised in a setting in which the possibility of a future appears to have been destroyed by the adults to whom its preservation was ostensibly entrusted. (Beardslee & Mack, 1982, pp. 90–91)

The process of establishing values and ideals in adolescence is inherently dependent on a sense of a future in which they can be carried out. A fear of futurelessness may impede the natural unfolding of these ideals. Moreover, the fear that one's future may never come to pass may give rise to considerable anxiety if an adolescent feels that he or she may not live a sufficiently fulfilled life before that lifetime is ended.

STRATEGIES OF INTERVENTION

Psychologists, psychiatrists, and educators who have postulated and identified the possible developmental arrests to which children and adolescents growing up in the nuclear age are inevitably exposed, have also proposed strategies of intervention to help youngsters better cope with the nuclear threat. One basic aspect of these recommendations has been the value of constructive action as a route to psychological empowerment and the sense of active mastery. The political initiatives of parents and other adults can help to reassure young people that action is being taken to ensure their future. Likewise, some form of political activity on the part of the child or adolescent may help him or her to overcome feelings of powerlessness and helplessness in the face of the nuclear peril. Many educators and parents have endorsed the benefits of nuclear education. Roberta Snow, who is the founder of *Education for Democracy*, a public high school curriculum project for students, teachers, parents, and communities, suggests that adolescents who have taken a course dealing with nuclear issues "were just as fearful, but they were better able to channel their feelings in constructive ways. They were less cynical about governmental processes and believed that they themselves could and would effect change" (Goodman et al., 1983, p. 528).

Mental health professionals have emphasized equally the need to acknowledge and recognize nuclear anxiety in young people. Many professionals work to dissuade parents and adults from encouraging denial of nuclear anxiety in youngsters. Such denial, they believe, merely buries stress in the child or adolescent and precludes the possibility of social or political action which could be helpful on two levels: 1. to benefit the individual child's mental health through psychological empowerment; and 2. to provide the necessary psychosocial foundations in the developing individual that lead to the achievement of social concern and participatory democracy. Finally, mental health professionals have outlined educational interventions which include self-education regarding nuclear issues, receptivity to and acknowledgement of nuclear anxiety in young people, and the education of children, adolescents, and adults toward the active prevention of nuclear war. One such educational center is in Oakland, California: the Citizens Policy Center*, headed by Laurie Olsen, where adolescents can come to discuss their nuclear fears and take action through educational projects that enable adolescents and adults alike to respond constructively to the threat of nuclear death.

The studies discussed in this chapter suggest that several crises may exist in contemporary adolescent development as a result of the threat of nuclear death. Many of today's youngsters are doubtful regarding the possibility of a future and are therefore reluctant to make or rely upon future plans. Adolescent ambivalence regarding the certainty of the future may impair the normal adolescent task of developing values and ideals fit for adulthood. If today's world is viewed as chaotic, deadly, and out of control, and adults in charge are seen as powerless or not adequately caring, many adolescents may become overwhelmed with a sense of inadequacy and even guilt for not being able to put the world on a safer course. Some adolescents report a feeling of generational betrayal: the adults who preceded them have not kept the world sufficiently intact to be handed down to subsequent generations. Adolescents, after all, are the inheritors of the earth and the human legacy. The nuclear specter places into jeopardy not only the continuation of the world but its integrity as a human dwelling place.

A LATE NIGHT THOUGHT

In a splendid collection of essays, *Late Night Thoughts on Listening to Mahler's Ninth Symphony*, the well-known scientist Lewis Thomas (1983) tells us how he used to hear Mahler's *Ninth*, especially the final movement, as "an open acknowledgement of death" and as "a quiet celebration of the tranquillity connected to the process" (p. 164). In his reflection on death, Thomas writes: "I took this music as a metaphor for reassurance, confirming my own strong hunch that the dying of every living creature, the most natural of all experiences, has to be a peaceful experience. I rely on nature" (p. 164).

Because of the nuclear threat, Thomas (1983) now reports that he hears Mahler differently:

> I cannot listen to the last movement of the Mahler *Ninth* without the door-smashing intrusion of a huge new thought: death everywhere, the dying of everything, the end of humanity. The easy sadness expressed with such

*Citizens Policy Center, 512 62nd St., Oakland, CA 94609; (415)654-5271.

gentleness and delicacy by that repeated phrase on faded strings, over and over again, no longer comes to me as old, familiar news of the cycle of living and dying. All through the last notes my mind swarms with images of a world in which the thermonuclear bombs have begun to explode. . . . (p. 165)

Thomas goes on to say that this recent turn of events is something with which his own generation must manage. What he cannot bear to think about is how the threat of extinction is affecting young people. He writes:

What I cannot imagine, what I cannot put up with, the thought that keeps grinding its way into my mind, making the Mahler into a hideous noise close to killing me, is what it would be like to be young. How do the young stand it? How can they keep their sanity? If I were very young, sixteen or seventeen years old, I think I would begin, perhaps very slowly and imperceptibly, to go crazy. (p. 166)

For some adolescents, this absurd, unrelenting fear of nuclear death is the most serious philosophical problem of the day and of their existence. Can they live out a life "in time?" As one youngster said (Austin, 1984): "Can I live a decent, ordinary life from start to finish before the world ends in a nuclear war?" Is it possible for a thoughtful young person, especially one keen on understanding current world events, to contain what may well be an unprecedented death anxiety on the path to evolving adulthood and social responsibility? The answer of course is that some young people do move ahead into young adulthood, extraordinarily well informed and determined to change the world. As one adolescent said about her plans for the future:

"My generation has been shaped not so much by the Civil Rights Movement or even by Vietnam—that's *your* generation. *We're* the generation that has nuclear weapons all around us. That's what's fencing us in. Now the whole planet's going to live or die, not just one country or one side in a war. Nobody can die in a war anymore. That's all over. Isn't it incredible what my generation has to do? But I think we can do it. I mean, we have to do it. We're going to pass this world on, without war. We have to get along. That's why I'm going into international law. I want to sit at the bargaining table and make sure it happens."
"Do you think your generation can do it in time?" I asked her.
"I have to believe that we can," she answered. "Besides, there's no other way to live. I've already decided that I would rather die trying to save the world, than just die. So that's how I'm going to live." (Austin, 1984)

REFERENCES

Austin, D. Unpublished interviews with adolescents, 1984.

Beardslee, W. R., & Mack, J. E. The impact on children and adolescents of nuclear developments. In R. Rogers (Ed.), *Psychosocial aspects of nuclear developments* (Task Force Report #20) (pp. 64–93). Washington, DC: American Psychiatric Association, 1982.

Camus, A. *The myth of Sisyphus and other essays* (J. O'Brien, Trans.). New York: Knopf, 1955.

Chivian, E., & Goodman, J. What Soviet children are saying about nuclear war. Boston: *International physicians to prevent nuclear war report* (IPPNW Report), Winter, 1984.

Coles, R. Children and the Nuclear Bomb. Unpublished manuscript.

Erikson, E. *Young man Luther*. New York: Norton, 1958.

Erikson, E. The golden rule in the light of new insight. In *Insight and responsibility: Lectures on the ethical implications of psychoanalytic insight* (pp. 217–243). New York: Norton, 1964.

Escalona, S. Children and the threat of nuclear war. In M. Schwebel (Ed.), *Behavioral science and human survival* (pp. 201–209). Palo Alto, CA: Science and Behavioral Books, 1965.

Escalona, S. Growing up with the threat of nuclear war: Some indirect effects on personality development. *American Journal of Orthopsychiatry*, 1982, *52*, 600–607.

Gilligan, C. *In a different voice: Psychological theory and women's development*. Cambridge, MA: Harvard University Press, 1982.

Goodman, L. A., Mack, J. E., Beardslee, W. R., & Snow, R. The threat of nuclear war and the nuclear arms race: Adolescent experience and perceptions. *Political Psychology*, 1983, *4*, 501–530.

Kohlberg, L., & Gilligan, C. The adolescent as a philosopher: The discovery of the self in a postconventional world. *Daedalus*, 1971, *100*, 1051–1086.

Koocher, G. P. Childhood, death, and cognitive development. *Developmental Psychology*, 1973, *9*, 369–375.

Koocher, G. P. Conversations with children about death: Ethical considerations in research. *Journal of Clinical Child Psychology*, 1974a, *3*, 19–21.

Koocher, G. P. Talking with children about death. *American Journal of Orthopsychiatry*, 1974b, *44*, 404–411.

Koocher, G. P. Why isn't the gerbil moving any more? Discussing death in the classroom. *Children Today*, 1975, *4*, 18–21.

Koocher, G. P. Children's conceptions of death. In R. Bibner & H. E. Walsh (Eds.), *New directions for child development: Children's conceptions of health, illness, and bodily functions* (No. 14). San Francisco: Jossey-Bass, December 1981.

Koocher, G. P., O'Malley, J. E., Foster, D., & Gogan, J. L. Death anxiety in normal children and adolescents. *Psychiatria clinica*, 1976, *9*, 220–229.

Larrick, N., & Merriam, E. (Eds.). *Male and female under 18*. New York: Avon, 1973.

Lifton, R. J. *The life of the self: Toward a new psychology*. New York: Basic Books, 1976.

Lifton, R. J. *The broken connection: On death and the continuity of life*. New York: Basic Books, 1979.

Lifton, R. J., & Falk, R. *Indefensible weapons*. New York: Basic Books, 1982.

Mack, J. E. Soviet children are worried too. *USA Today*, April 3, 1984, p. 1.

Mack, J. E., & Hickler, H. *Vivienne: The life and suicide of an adolescent girl*. Boston: Little, Brown, 1981.

Piaget, J. *The child's construction of reality*. London: Routledge and Kegan Paul, 1955.

Schell, J. *The fate of the earth*. New York: Knopf, 1982.

Schwebel, M. Nuclear cold war: Student opinion and professional responsibility. In M. Schwebel (Ed.), *Behavioral science and human survival* (pp. 210–223). Palo Alto, CA: Science and Behavioral Books, 1965.

Smith, B. *The threat of nuclear war: Psychological impact*. Address to the Physicians for Social Responsibility Symposium, Eugene, Oregon, October 9, 1982.

Snow, R. Decision making in a nuclear age. *Boston University Journal of Education*, 1984, *166*, 103–107.

Thomas, L. *Late nights thoughts on listening to Mahler's Ninth Symphony*. New York: Bantam, 1983.

PART II

Coping with Dying, Grief, and Bereavement

The predeath and postdeath experiences of dying and bereavement present human beings with the task of coping with existing or anticipated loss. Such coping is difficult but not beyond the capacities of most normal adolescents. The proximate expectation or the actual impact of loss through death engenders strong reactions in grieving. Whether it is my own dying, the dying of someone I love, or the aftermath of a death, in the end my obligation —and, some would say, my opportunity—is to find some way of coming to terms with these facts of life.

Much as I might like to do so, I cannot completely avoid these experiences. Even as they threaten the values and the security I have previously enjoyed, such experiences demonstrate that death is a part of life, a defining constituent of the only mode of existence known to human beings in this world. By learning to cope in an effective manner with loss and death, adolescents enhance the quality of their own lives and the lives of those with whom they come into contact. In so doing, those who survive a death also prepare themselves to meet additional responsibilities that will come to them as they grow into mature adulthood. Those who care about adolescents have the privilege of seizing occasions provided by loss and grief to help these young people in this process.

Chapters 5 and 6 explore the experiences of dying and bereavement in adolescence. In the former chapter, David Adams and Eleanor Deveau analyze the needs of adolescents who are dying, common responses made to that experience, and guidelines for constructive intervention. In the latter chapter, Stephen Fleming and Rheba Adolph take a similar approach to grieving in adolescence. Chapter 6 is particularly notable for the model that it advances, which enables helpers to distinguish and set alongside each other tasks and conflicts that are part of normal development in adolescence as contrasted with those that are specific to grieving and mourning. For each of these cases, as well as for coping with dying, a full range of cognitive, affective, and behavioral dimensions is outlined and common misconceptions are disspelled.

Chapters 7 and 8 then turn to two prominent loss experiences that are especially trenchant in the world of today's adolescents. The first is teenage pregnancy and elective abortion; the second is the death of infants whose parents are themselves adolescents. Many adults would prefer not to think about either of these phenomena. That may be understandable, but it cannot be permitted to stand as our final position. Abortion and parental bereavement are undeniable components of the actual experience of many contemporary adolescents. In both cases, one can identify loss, grief, and significant consequences for future quality of life. In each case, how the loss is encountered, what it means to an individual adolescent, and what it portends for the future will be different. In every case, adolescents will be better off when adults are prepared to recognize what is happening and to promote a healthy resolution of these difficult circumstances. Gail Joralemon deserves credit for her unique contribution in Chapter 7 to the exploration of loss and grief associated with teenage pregnancy and abortion, as do Carol Ann Barnickol, Helen Fuller, and Beth Shinners for breaking new ground in Chapter 8 with their discussion of bereaved adolescent parents.

5

Helping Dying Adolescents: Needs and Responses

David W. Adams and Eleanor J. Deveau

To die as an adolescent is to die in the spring of one's lifetime.
(Schneiderman, 1981, p. 58)

Adolescence, the struggle for identity and independence, is a time of growing, changing, discovering, and learning. Adolescents experience many moods, and their goals are ever changing as they work toward delineating their future.

Dying adolescents are forced into a quandary. Their impending death is a personal devastation of all of life's goals. They must follow a totally different and painful direction. Loss of their independence, body integrity, sexual prowess, friends, and family is inevitable.

Kalish (1985) points out that today's society is future-oriented, and holds specific values and personality characteristics in esteem. People value their attractiveness to others. Attraction is generated by physical appearance and prowess, sexual appeal, and other less-visible traits. Knowledge, compatibility, the ability to enjoy life and to instill positive feelings in others, moral "goodness," and possession of sufficient power to ensure respect are all desirable. Adolescents adhere to these same values, and their behavior follows suit. When adolescents are dying, their ability to retain many desirable personality characteristics is in jeopardy.

It is against the very nature of adolescents to accept their own death without contention. They naturally believe that they are going to reach adulthood regardless of their illness and live many more years beyond. Personal death is *not* meant to be in the adolescents' repertoire.

Cancer is the most common disease-related cause of adolescent death (Plumb & Holland, 1974). The course of this illness illustrates almost every aspect of the struggle adolescents must face when dying from any lingering disease. For this reason, this chapter deals primarily with adolescents dying from cancer and draws heavily on the writers' experiences in caring for such young people within the hospital setting.

The path of dying has been called a trajectory—a course of decline that may be altered by people (including the patient), circumstances, or events (Glaser & Strauss, 1968). In cancer and other similar illnesses, adolescents have often experienced intense treatment at diagnosis and at least one relapse involving even stronger treatment complete with experimental chemotherapy, medical procedures, and perhaps surgery. Relapse may be seen as the beginning of the end and a downhill course that adolescents desperately want and need to avoid (Adams, 1979; Adams & Deveau, 1984). This chapter focuses on the time beyond the initial relapse—a time when treatment is ineffective, disease is beyond control, and palliation is in order.

THREE DYING ADOLESCENTS

Here are three examples of dying adolescents to illustrate their needs and coping responses. These needs and responses parallel those of healthy adolescents; however, they are intensified and altered by the symptoms and demands of illness:

> At age 14, Paul had a malignant abdominal tumor excised. He had anticipated a rapid release from the hospital and a return to his home community. Paul was well liked, had many friends, and was the second eldest of four siblings. He missed his family and friends, and was upset that he did not improve. Paul lost weight, was nauseated by chemotherapy, and was too weak to walk. At times he was despondent and became irritable toward the nursing staff. He wanted to go home and kept reminding the doctors that he was only supposed to be hospitalized for a few days. Sometimes he would examine himself in the mirror and be upset by how thin he was. He talked about the future, his friends, his ability to play hockey, and his interest in school. Paul looked forward to his mother's visits but was concerned by the added stress on her. After further tests revealed new tumor growth, care was organized for Christmas at home to be followed by further surgery.
>
> After Christmas, nausea, anorexia, and the need for increased medical care led to rehospitalization. Paul seemed relieved by the return to the hospital. As his tumor grew, he talked about how he was gaining weight, described his belief that God was close to him, and at one point worried that he would not grow up. He became anxious if his mother was late and desperately wanted his friend to stay overnight in his room. He was happiest when his friends came and longed to be with them. His father, who lived at a distance, upset Paul with his visits, especially when he poured out his religious beliefs. Paul gradually spoke less about going home, seemed comforted by his family's presence, and died quietly.

John, age 16, was a lively, outgoing teen whose leukemia relapsed. He willingly accepted chemotherapy and was initially optimistic about his future. He worked hard to remain in school and to be independent. He looked after his own medications and learned to drive so that he could come on his own for treatment. A second relapse and the growth of a visible tumor caused John to panic. He sought help from many people, became overly anxious, and was prone to outbursts. He denied what was happening most of the time, and if confronted he became hostile. At times, he spoke about his relationship with God and how God comforted him. He became upset when he lost his hair, but he refused to wear a wig and talked openly about his baldness. When John was advised that chemotherapy was ineffective and that there was nothing more that his physician could do, he jumped up and ran out of the clinic. John gradually tempered his goals and concentrated on getting through his remaining days.

Mary, age 17, was a popular, caring person. She had recurrence of a sarcoma with metastasis. Mary was determined to remain in school, to carry on her studies, and to maintain her participation in active sports. She fought her disease, struggled against nausea from chemotherapy, and was distressed by her progressive weakness. As she deteriorated physically, Mary chose to return to the hospital for her few remaining weeks. She controlled who visited, set daily goals for herself, and discussed her innermost thoughts with very few people. Mary remained in the hospital until her death.

NEEDS OF DYING ADOLESCENTS

The preceding examples show the immediacy and intensity of the needs of dying adolescents as opposed to those of healthy adolescents. Most teens want to be seen as individuals who are treated fairly and honestly. As they mature, they want and need increasing independence and the opportunity to control more and more of their lives. Most want and need privacy and time to contemplate hopes, dreams, and plans for the future (Adams, 1979; Adams & Deveau, 1984; Blumberg, Ahmed, Flaherty, Lewis, & Shea, 1981; Jacobstein & Magrab, 1981). As death approaches and their personal values and capabilities are threatened, their needs intensify. They must maintain a sense of identity and want to be remembered. More than ever, they need to know what is happening to them (Deasy-Spinetta, 1981; Kikuchi, 1972; Pendleton, 1980; Susman, Pizzo, & Poplack, 1981). Independence continues to be sought but is much harder to attain and must be achieved in less-common ways. Privacy is frequently desired but often violated, and the person vacillates between fleeting hopes of a rescue from death and knowledge that only days or weeks remain. Each need can become an obstacle in a lonely struggle that leads adolescents to require love, comfort, reassurance, and help from family and other caregivers. The following sections discuss these needs in depth.

Sense of Identity

Adolescents have major concerns that affect their behavior, their families, and everyone who associates with them as they struggle to determine who they are. They worry about their bodies, their appearance, and about what others think of them. Much time is spent in thought and some time in admiring bodily changes. Soul searching, a desire to be attractive, and being liked all go together. Most adolescents in advanced stages of cancer have already suffered negative bodily changes and personal losses. Steroids frequently bring unwanted bloating and facial and body hair. Pain, nausea, and hair loss often accompany chemotherapy and radiotherapy. Surgery may leave disfigurement and unsightly scars. Metastasis may distort body parts or cause weakness, emaciation, and cachexia (Adams, 1979; Adams & Deveau, 1984; Susman et al., 1981).

Dying does not remove the desire to be attractive. For instance, Mary would only allow her family and a few staff to see her without her wig. When able, she dressed in her housecoat, put on her wig, and sat up in bed. John and Paul both worried about their appearances. Paul worried about his weight loss and frequently made reference to his scar. Later on, he joked about how fat he was getting or reflected on his anxiety about the rapid growth of his tumor. Although John had previously lost his hair at diagnosis, he was extremely upset when it came out in handfuls during chemotherapy. He struggled with his feelings and purchased a wig, but then decided to be bald and only occasionally wore a hat. His anxiety about the tumor in his arm was related less to his appearance than to the signalling of a return of his disease.

Appearance means most when teens are away from close friends or family. Dying deprives adolescents of the ability to compete sexually and be attractive in public. Sick and dying teens usually look different. They have referred to themselves as "weirdos" and "freaks," and have believed that others stare at them. Bodily changes evoke embarrassment, create anxiety among those who are not close friends, and lead to isolation. Loss of social place is part and parcel of dying. Friends who do remain close are true friends (Pendleton, 1980). Paul was fortunate because his friends worried about him and came to the hospital. One even stayed overnight when Paul was well enough to have him there. John was less fortunate because he had been uprooted from his home community. He had to search for peer support and eventually found it in a church group. Other dying adolescents who have been absent from school for long periods have had few friends left.

In an effort to understand themselves and to be recognized, adolescents often vacillate between fantasy and reality. Their image of themselves may move from grandiosity to degradation. The reality of dying may bring a natural withdrawal and depression. It is easy to push a fragile ego to despair and to erode self-worth. Fortunately, most adolescents struggle to keep on living, and to find meaning and purpose in life and death. Sometimes religious beliefs or the determination to be loved and remembered helps teens to keep going. Stories, poetry, diaries, and special deeds are common ways dying teens implant purpose, bequeath something to others, and leave their mark on eternity.

Honesty

Tell me what I want to know when I want to hear it. When I have heard enough, I will turn you off and we will try again.

Through the years there has been increasing recognition that the honesty of parents and professional caregivers helps children and adolescents cope with cancer (Adams, 1979; Adams & Deveau, 1984; Deasy-Spinetta, 1981; Hofman, Becker, & Gabriel, 1976; Karon, 1973; Moore, Holton, & Martin, 1969; Plumb & Holland, 1974; Vernick, 1973).Spinetta and his colleagues have found that the more open and honest the family system, the more children are able to face both good and bad events (Spinetta, 1981; Spinetta, Rigler, & Karon, 1974). Adolescents are in a difficult position. Shyness, uncertainty, and lack of confidence may inhibit willingness to ask questions, and at times the adolescents themselves may be misread. Caregivers may believe that adolescents know what is happening, assume that others have provided information, or think that teens do not want to know the truth. Sometimes dichotomies between adolescents and parents inhibit honest communication, and specific details are not discussed (Jacobstein & Magrab, 1981). At other times, the extreme reactions of adolescents cause some caregivers to withhold information.

In helping Paul, John, and Mary, the physicians were open and honest. Paul tended to be passive and accepted information stoically. John was more anxious, dramatic, and volatile. He asked for information on his own terms, denied the gravity of his illness, and continued to defy death almost to the end. When Mary learned about the ineffectiveness of the medication, she increased her physical activities as if to fight off the disease and then relied on her religious faith to help her. If families and health professionals are not honest, they will be mistrusted. Although information may occasionally be misconstrued, adolescents are knowledgeable and perceptive. They overhear discussions, read charts, talk with other patients, learn from books and the media, and are usually aware that they have little time left.

Honesty must pervade all communication, not only about the prognosis but about what is happening each day. Information must be shared about tests, procedures, and medication changes. Trust in others and reassurance help to temper the delicate time ahead.

Independence

Adolescents search for independence. One of their favorite behaviors is to "hang out" and to gather with peers away from adult scrutiny (Farrell & Hutter, 1980). Participation in sports, school achievement, resistance to clinic visits, or avoidance of adult functions may be part of the quest for independence. Dying teens have a difficult time maintaining positive feelings about themselves. In the hospital, they lose independence and peer contacts, and are restricted from participating in active sports (Adams, 1979; Adams & Deveau, 1984; Hofman et al., 1976). Efforts to regain independence are sought by maintaining personal care, leaving the ward for short periods, working alone on hobbies, and making decisions on practical matters such as which intravenous sites are selected and when treatments should be received.

Control

Adolescents who are dying from cancer have already learned ways to try to control what is happening. For example, Brian, age 15, kept track of blood counts, left the clinic so that staff had difficulty finding him, and vomited in advance of injections. Such attempts to control are not always positive, and are linked closely to feelings of frustration and the need to be independent. Overt attempts to control such as hiding may be consciously motivated, whereas vomiting is usually linked to unconscious rebellion and is a conditioned response. Control goes beyond a desire for independence and is allied with a need to combat underlying anxiety. Fears of mutilation and separation are not far beneath the surface (Adams, 1979; Adams & Deveau, 1984).

For dying adolescents, death anxiety and fear of suffocation are also real, and may exaggerate the need to control (Adams, 1979; Alexander & Adlerstein, 1958). Anxiety may be somatized as in Paul's case where he focused on bodily changes. It may be directed toward common concerns such as food, lateness of visitors, and worries about school. There is a challenge to find even small measures of control when disease is rampant. Paul determined who could visit him, when to take his pain medication, and when to do his school work. Mary decided to stay in the hospital, controlled who entered her room, and bequeathed her possessions. She tried to accomplish a small task each day and as she became weaker her goals were as simple as putting on her wig or sitting in a chair.

Dying adolescents need to share in decisions about their care (Schowalter, Ferhold, & Mann, 1973). For instance, if nothing remains except an experimental drug with doubtful impact on the disease, the adolescent may not want to take it. This does not mean that the physician's or parents' roles are usurped. It simply means that teens have the opportunity to be a partner in the decision making. As one adolescent put it: "After all, it's my body and my life. . . . "

Privacy

Apart from the food, adolescents in hospitals complain most about the number of staff who poke, prod, and question them. Often staff and students forget adolescents' intense concerns about their bodies. Adolescents also want and need time alone to contemplate who they are and what they will become. Dying adolescents need privacy for the same reasons and for reasons created by their illness (Adams, 1979; Adams & Deveau, 1984). Repeated examinations and tests are exhausting. In their zeal, hospital staff may forget that dying teens have limited physical and emotional resources, and may apply acute care approaches to palliative care situations (Adams, 1984). The interest in the dying adolescent as a teaching case necessitating the display of bodily changes to a variety of learners can be devastating. Fortunately, most physicians are sensitive to this problem.

Any adolescent with cancer will have days known as "bummers" (Farrell & Hutter, 1980). These are usually precipitated by bad news and exhaustion. Adolescents may want to shut the world out and be left alone. This may not indicate a need for psychiatric consultation unless the withdrawal goes on for many days unaccompanied by medical problems such as infections and side effects of chemotherapy (Adams, 1979; Adams & Deveau, 1984). Dying adolescents require respite and sometimes recover with bursts of energy. As their conditions deteriorate and they become thinner, weaker, and cachectic, they have less energy to cope, and a natural distancing takes place (Spinetta, 1981; Spinetta, Rigler & Karon, 1974). Hospital staff and parents need to cooperate to reduce the number of intrusions and bodily insults. As death draws closer, privacy is imperative. Care should be given by a constant nurse and physician, family members should visit in small numbers, and allowances should be made for one or two favorite people.

Orientation to the Future

How do you keep dying adolescents interested in life and free of despondency? Fortunately, most teens have an inherent desire to live and are often resilient. A host of defense mechanisms, especially denial, can be used to provide the strength and energy to carry on (Kagan, 1976; Karon, 1973; Lazarus, 1981). Before his death, John went through a variety of responses. During his first relapse, he was eager to return to school and readily discussed his plans to attend university. With subsequent relapses, he became upset and angry. He needed to fight his leukemia and was determined to overcome it as well as to keep up with his schooling. He vacillated from anger to hope to despair. As his condition deteriorated, he focused on goals directly related to his disease and to the hospital. He was determined to take the new medication, go through with the tests, and learn to drive so that he could transport himself to the hospital. Physical illness reduced his focus on school. He would cope with the hospital first. Making friends was another goal, and he sought out two sources of friendship and support. His other major goal was to remain at home with his family, so he did everything possible to avoid hospitalization. As his illness advanced, his goals diminished. He focused on getting through each day, avoided trips to the hospital, and spent considerable time listening to music. Plans for the future and for the return to school were no longer discussed. He withdrew from medical staff and concentrated his attention on himself and on his family.

Love, Comfort, Reassurance, and Freedom from Pain

Dying adolescents often become frightened by the progression of their disease. Their life is ending, and they feel helpless and defenseless. Nowhere is there a greater need for parent participation and consistency in staffing. Disruptions in established routines such as changes in nursing staff, medical care, and parents' ability to visit may intensify the adolescents' anxiety. Dying adolescents, when severely compromised, will often accept dependency on their parents. One teen realized that her parents had already seen her at her best and her worst (Pendleton, 1980). She recognized that her parents loved her no matter what, that she could not remove the strain on them, and that they wanted to care for her. Whether death occurs in the hospital or at home, the parents' role is similar and often follows the same pattern. Be with me, care for me, reassure me, don't abandon me. . . .

Another part of dying is the need for comfort. Often pain can be controlled either in the hospital or at home by a knowledgeable physician. Addiction to drugs at this time should not be an issue as physicians often need to increase doses of medication in order to control pain (Adams & Deveau, 1984). There should be no need for continued suffering. However, it must be recognized that the response to pain may be increased by anxiety, previous experiences with discomfort, cultural expectations, family responses, and events such as the death of other children (Adams, 1979). Each situation is unique and requires individual attention.

Understanding the needs of dying adolescents is the first step in learning to help them face what lies ahead. Next, we will examine the common responses of these teens.

RESPONSES OF DYING ADOLESCENTS

Dying adolescents are in the ambiguous position of being neither adult nor child (Jacobstein & Magrab, 1981; Lowenburg, 1970; Susman et al., 1981). They vacillate between adulthood and childhood in a world that is alien, hurtful, and frightening. It is a world filled with strong and changing emotions, and decreasing hope for life beyond a few weeks or months. This is a time that works against the natural need for the minds and bodies of adolescents to develop, forcing a regression that must be faced by everyone involved. In effect, there are three basic variations in the coping ability of adolescents that are linked to development and age. In older adolescents, from age 17 on, rationality and increasing maturity frequently allow them to function with less denial and overt emotion than adolescents who are 15 or 16. Middle adolescents are usually at the peak of turmoil and anxiety, and are prone to sudden emotional fluctuations and extreme reactions. Young adolescents tend to be more dependent on parents and more easily influenced so that compliance with medical treatment can often be more easily obtained.

Although it can be a mistake to stereotype, it is important to recognize the impact of culture, environment, and other factors. Gullo (1973) in examining dying children over age 10 discussed several categories of responses:

1. "death acceptors" face whatever comes realistically;
2. "death deniers" deny the gravity of their illness;
3. "death submitters" are overwhelmed, isolated, and helpless;
4. "death facilitators" engage in behaviors that aid their own death;

5. "death transcenders" have internal value systems about the existential or religious meaning of death; and

6. "death defiers" are usually older children who fight to maintain their dignity and freedom even though they do not expect to live.

Dying adolescents may exhibit any of the above with the exception of "death facilitation" which is not frequently seen. Some may fluctuate and change categories at different points in the dying trajectory.

SOME COMMON RESPONSES

Denial

Weisman (1972) suggests that in terminally ill adult patients, there are three orders of denial: 1. denial of the facts; 2. denial of the worst implications; and 3. the refusal to accept one's extinction. Lazarus (1981) points out that denial can be dynamic and subject to change generated by mood or new information. Denial is part of the process of trying to understand what is happening. It can be a positive or negative reaction.

For dying adolescents, denial can provide a chance to rest from reality and to go on living. Denial allows them to absorb small amounts of information over time. John's denial that his cancer might ever materialize again slowly weakened as his physical abilities deteriorated.

Denial was most beneficial early in John's terminal phase when he was bombarded with new information and needed time to prepare to face reality. Denial can be negative if it is rigid and entrenched (Lazarus, 1981). For instance, when Harry, age 15, was dying, he acknowledged that he had leukemia and was becoming sicker, but he denied that his disease could be fatal. When a child with leukemia died, Harry became quite upset because he suddenly realized that he could also die. In most situations, denial is used to advantage by adolescents who have a willingness to allow reality to seep in. The greatest problems usually occur when adults promote denial and will not allow adolescents to face reality on their own terms.

Anger

Adolescents with cancer often endure many provocations. Discomfort, restrictions, isolation from friends, and immobility have usually been part of their lives prior to terminal care. In the terminal period, feelings about these impositions may be intensified by the fact that life is ending. Anger may well up and burst forth. In the hospital, most anger is directed toward the surroundings and the routines by complaining or lashing out verbally. When adolescents are still well enough to resist, anger may be shown in rebellion or refusal to cooperate with hospital staff. Adolescents react in anger to show how fed up they are with their disease, hospitals, treatments, and all of the trappings of the illness.

We seldom have seen adolescents overtly angry with God. Dying adolescents frequently invest in a Supreme Being who will provide help in this life, the next one, or both depending on their beliefs.

Anxiety

From diagnosis on, anxiety plagues both dying adolescents and their families. The disease, the uncertainty of the prognosis, and the strain on the family provide continued stress. As death approaches, adolescents are faced with new anxieties concerning pain and the meaning of death. Egocentric qualities may temporarily vanish as teens worry about how family members will carry on without them. New medical information, bodily changes, the death of other children, and the feeling that nothing will be left as a remembrance can all add to existing anxiety. An interest may be generated in poetry or art in a desire to create something that may be left for posterity. Dying adolescents may also develop a new interest in God as a means of trying to cope with their own impending death. As one teen stated, "it is a type of insurance."

Sadness and Depression

It is understandable that dying adolescents experience considerable sadness and bouts of depression. In extreme cases, sadness may bring symptoms of clinical depression, including a deepening sense of worthlessness and hopelessness, inhibited sleep patterns, flattened affect, and inability to enjoy life. Depression in dying adolescents is a complex problem. Clinical depression may be precipitated by medical sequelae or by entrapment without resolution. As noted earlier in this chapter, some professional caregivers may confuse depression with the adolescent's need for respite from emotional and/or physical exhaustion. Kübler-Ross (1969) contends that depression is to be expected as a part of the dying process. Age makes no difference. Depression may be interpreted as a giving in, yet there is evidence that dying persons move in and out of depression. The concern about depressive symptoms should focus on their duration, intensity, and impact on the quality of the life that remains.

We believe that in many instances temporary resolutions of medical factors, changes in medication, and alteration of circumstances frequently change depressive responses. Sadness tends to be intermittent, and in most situations complete clinical depression is not that common.

Guilt

Denial, anger, and sadness can be positive responses that enable dying adolescents to shut out, lash out, or sort out the implications of what is happening to them. Guilt is a residual feeling that seldom has positive qualities. Although guilt may lead adolescents to treat others with more kindness or to perform some useful tasks, it is usually a burden (Adams & Deveau, 1984; Blumberg et al., 1981). Guilt may prevent dying adolescents from expressing their feelings or seeking the kind of help that they require.

Sometimes when cultural or family influences instill guilt feelings, they cannot be resolved. For example, Peter, age 17, was dying of cancer. Peter and his family displayed no emotion when his illness was diagnosed and when his disease metastasized They were not willing to discuss his illness except on a superficial level. The expectation was that Peter was to be strong and that he was destined to be an army officer. He continued to talk about his career right to the end. When the physician confronted him about his behavior, he replied that "my parents know what I'm going through and I know what I'm feeling and going through." He became silent and would speak no more—a soldier to the end. To break the silence would have broken the family trust. Peter was controlled by guilt. He felt guilty if he spoke because he believed he would let his family down. Outwardly he denied what was happening and repressed the feelings that most adolescents would acknowledge.

Withdrawal

One of the most common responses of dying adolescents is to withdraw (Adams, 1979; Adams & Deveau, 1984; Lowenburg, 1970). For example, fear of what is ahead, the need to recoup resources, uncertainty about how people will accept them, or feelings of rejection are common reasons for withdrawal. Peggy, age 14, withdrew to a quiet room before and after chemotherapy. She needed time to gather the courage to face treatment, as well as time to recover before returning home. Betty, age

13, withdrew from her friends when she could no longer keep up with them and felt isolated. Mary opted for refuge in the hospital because she believed care at home was too difficult for her parents. Withdrawal allows adolescents to temporarily escape from anxiety-provoking situations. It provides time to regain strength needed to confront what lies ahead.

Overcompensation

When people feel inadequate and are incapable of competing in one forum, they may try other areas. Some adolescents have maintained their studies as long as possible and have excelled beyond all reasonable expectations. Donna, age 18, was so determined to keep up her studies that she kept going at considerable personal and emotional cost. She was accepted into college but died before she could attend. Mary played active sports as long as she could, and George continued running until his health gave out totally.

The determination to achieve such goals provides adolescents with an immediate channel for their energy and directs them away from anxiety about their impending death.

Regression

Adolescents who become overwhelmed by their illness may revert back to behavior that is common at an earlier stage of development (Adams, 1979; Adams & Deveau, 1984; Karon, 1973). Dying adolescents who are forced to relinquish their independence may allow their parents to provide love, comfort, and physical care similar to that provided in their younger years. Occasionally, regression may be more severe with reversion to temper tantrums, childlike irritability, and unreasonable demands. These behaviors can be confusing and upsetting to dying adolescents and their families.

In most instances, regression is precipitated by severe physical and emotional stress. Parents need help to understand what is happening. With support and encouragement, they can provide the love and security necessary to help their adolescents temper these behaviors.

The needs and the coping responses of dying adolescents have been examined in detail. Now it is important to consider the role of caregivers. The following section contains guidelines to assist them in providing help to these adolescents and their families.

GUIDELINES FOR CONSTRUCTIVE INTERVENTION

Factors to Consider

The death of an adolescent is taxing for everyone. Young caregivers in particular have difficulties because their closeness in age adds to the tendency to identify with dying adolescents (Adams, 1979). Caregivers working with these teens need to consider the following factors:

1. Dying often goes against the need and desire to heal and cure, especially when involvement is primarily in acute care.
2. Avoidance and abandonment may occur as they often do in the care of dying adults.
3. The transition from acute to palliative care can be difficult if nursing staff are expected to provide care for a variety of patients (Adams, 1984).
4. Limited numbers of staff make it difficult to spend time talking with patients. The team approach utilizing social work and child life staff can be helpful if it is available.
5. Nurses can be key people particularly during evening and night hours because adolescents will often single out one nurse in whom to confide.
6. Staff tend to become attached to adolescents. It is important to monitor personal feelings and behavior. If staff are unable to keep a rational perspective and lose control of their emotions, it is very difficult to be helpful.
7. If dying adolescents direct their anger toward staff, the affront must not be taken personally. Staff must recognize why such behavior occurred (Adams, 1984).
8. Parents should be respected and encouraged in helping to provide care. Staff have the responsibility to perform medical procedures and to supervise care; consequently, parents should not be burdened with tasks that they are not equipped to handle (Adams & Deveau, 1984). Caring is truly a cooperative venture and parents should feel welcome. The needs of dying adolescents should come before personal pride and other priorities.

Specific Guidelines

We have found that the following guidelines are helpful in working with adolescents who require terminal care in the hospital. Many of these measures are also applicable when care is given at home.

When terminal care begins, staff should be:

1. calm and maintain control of their feelings;
2. clear and consistent in their expectations; and
3. honest and realistic yet willing to allow denial, understanding that it is a method dying adolescents use to try to restore order.

In the process of terminal care, staff can help by:

1. providing the time to listen;
2. explaining everything clearly—there should be no surprises;
3. preventing unnecessary examinations;
4. continuing to be honest;
5. respecting adolescents' wishes and allowing them to make decisions when suitable;
6. helping to establish achievable goals without removing all other goals;
7. allowing some hope and some fantasies to remain, for example, going home or eating a large steak may not be feasible, but adolescents may hope that it is possible;
8. reducing doorway discussions;
9. placing dying teens in a quiet area of the ward; and
10. maintaining personal appearance and comfort, for example, hair washing and dressing in their own clothing.

As death nears, staff can continue to meet needs of dying adolescents by:

1. facilitating access to parents and special health team members;
2. keeping the nursing staff as constant as possible;
3. narrowing down the total number of staff involved in providing care;
4. allowing a continuing role in decision making;
5. involving parents and dying teens together in discussion about the right to refuse extraordinary treatment or resuscitation measures;
6. encouraging the participation of siblings;
7. providing time alone to rest, free from interruptions;
8. recognizing that distancing from staff and family is a natural phenomenon;
9. providing opportunities for parents to help their adolescents by hand holding, gentle stroking, rubbing and washing, rearranging pillows, providing mouth care, providing diversion, and monitoring changes in physical status;
10. giving pain medication without hesitation and making sure that it is effective; and

11. providing nursing measures such as warm baths, gentle rubs, warm milk, soft and clean sheets, and quiet music.

Throughout terminal care, it is important to continue to involve parents and to remember that they need encouragement, reassurance, and frequent advice about what is happening. They may require help to overcome the natural communication and relationship dichotomy that separates adolescents from the world of adults.

HOME CARE

This chapter cannot be concluded without explicitly discussing care at home. When death is inevitable, care of dying adolescents at home can be a valuable alternative to remaining in the hospital. The major concern is often related to whether or not families can cope with death at home. It may be too frightening or difficult for them. For example, single parents may lack the emotional support and practical assistance needed to provide 24-hour care (Adams & Deveau, 1984). In families who do cope well, anxieties may arise about the management of pain, the way teens will die (that is, how they would control pain and hemorrhage), and the availability of immediate and continued medical attention.

For the dying adolescent, care at home means: familiar surroundings; access to music, pets, and fresh air; the potential for peer support; and the companionship of family and friends. When the total family is prepared and members are reassured by access to medical and emotional support, adolescents at home are often more relaxed, more alert, and may require less pain medication. At home, there is usually less pressure, fewer negative stimuli, and less confusion so that the tendency to be frustrated and direct anger toward family members occurs less frequently.

Although little has been written about sibling reactions to dying adolescents (Coleman & Coleman, 1984; Spinetta, 1981), we believe that the reality of the teen's presence in the home engages many siblings in the care and diversion of their dying brother or sister. The jealousy, hostility, and anxiety that plague siblings may be more readily resolved at home than when care is given in the hospital. Siblings often bring change from constant adult attention and are people in whom adolescents can confide. The closeness and sharing that take place at home can increase positive communication between all family members, and the teen's progressive decline is shared by everyone in a supportive way.

CONCLUSION

There is no question that the care of dying adolescents is difficult, frustrating, and emotionally painful for everyone. A lifetime has been reduced to a few precious weeks or months. Caregivers are emotionally taxed as the vigor of adolescence is replaced by anxiety, fear, pain, and decline in physical prowess. The needs and responses of dying adolescents will always require every ounce of staff energy, initiative, and ability. If caregivers are able to come to terms with their own personal feelings, then they will be able to provide the support, encouragement, guidance, and understanding that these adolescents and their families so desperately need.

REFERENCES

Adams, D. W. *Childhood malignancy: The psychosocial care of the child and his family.* Springfield, IL: Charles C Thomas, 1979.

Adams, D. W. Helping the dying child: Practical approaches for non-physicians. In H. Wass & C. A. Corr (Eds.), *Childhood and death* (pp. 95–112). Washington, DC: Hemisphere, 1984.

Adams, D. W., & Deveau, E. J. *Coping with childhood cancer: Where do we go from here?* Reston, VA: Reston Publishing Company, 1984.

Alexander, I. E., & Adlerstein, A. M. Affective responses to death in a population of children and early adolescents. *Journal of Genetic Psychology,* 1958, *93,* 167–177.

Blumberg, B. D., Ahmed, P., Flaherty, M., Lewis, J., & Shea, J. Coping with cancer: An overview. In P. Ahmed (Ed.), *Living and dying with cancer* (pp. 26–31). New York: Elsevier, 1981.

Coleman, F. W., & Coleman, W. S. Helping siblings and other peers cope with dying. In H. Wass & C. A. Corr (Eds.), *Childhood and death* (pp. 129–150). Washington, DC: Hemisphere, 1984.

Deasy-Spinetta, P. The adolescent with cancer: A view from the inside. In J. J. Spinetta & P. Deasy-Spinetta (Eds.), *Living with childhood cancer* (pp. 189–197). St. Louis: Mosby, 1981.

Farrell, F., & Hutter, J. J. Living until death: Adolescents with cancer. *Health and Social Work,* 1980, *5,* 35–38.

Glaser, B. G., & Strauss, A. L. *Time for dying.* Chicago: Aldine, 1968.

Gullo, S. V. Games children play when they're dying. *Medical Dimensions,* October 1973, 23–28.

Hofman, A. D., Becker, R. D., & Gabriel, H. P. *The hospitalized adolescent: A Guide to managing ill and injured youth.* New York: The Free Press, 1976.

Jacobstein, D. M., & Magrab, P. R. The adolescent coping with cancer. In P. Ahmed (Ed.), *Living and dying with cancer* (pp. 81–94). New York: Elsevier, 1981.

Kagan, L. B. Use of denial in adolescents with cancer. *Health and Social Work,* 1976, *1,* 7–87.

Kalish, R. _Death, grief, and caring relationships._ (2nd ed.). Belmont, CA: Brooks/ Cole, 1985.

Karon, M. The physician and the adolescent with cancer. _Pediatric Clinics of North America_, 1973, _20_, 965–973.

Kikuchi, J. A leukemic adolescent's verbalization about dying. _Maternal Child Nursing Journal_, 1972, _1_, 259–264.

Kübler-Ross, E. _On death and dying._ New York: Macmillan, 1969.

Lazarus, R. S. The costs and benefits of denial. In J. J. Spinetta & P. Deasy-Spinetta (Eds.), _Living with childhood cancer_ (pp. 50–67). St. Louis: Mosby, 1981.

Lowenburg, J. S. The coping behaviors of fatally ill adolescents and their parents. _Nursing Forum_, 1970, _9_, 269–287.

Moore, D. C., Holton, C. P., & Martin, G. W. Psychologic problems in the management of adolescents with malignancy. _Clinical Pediatrics_, 1969, _8_, 464, 473.

Pendleton, E. _Too old to cry, too young to die_ (pp. 34–45, 70–83). Nashville, TN: Thomas Nelson Publishers, 1980.

Plumb, M. M., & Holland, J. Cancer in adolescents: The symptom is the thing. In B. Schoenberg, A. C. Carr, A. H. Kutscher, D. Peretz, & I. K. Goldberg, (Eds.), _Anticipatory grief_ (pp. 193–209). New York: Columbia University Press, 1974.

Schneiderman, G. _Coping with death in the family._ Toronto: Chimo Publishing Company, 1981.

Schowalter, J., Ferhold, J. B., & Mann, N. M. The adolescent patient's decision to die. _Pediatrics_, 1973, _51_, 97–103.

Spinetta, J. J. The sibling of a child with cancer. In J. J. Spinetta & P. Deasy-Spinetta (Eds.), _Living with childhood cancer_ (pp. 189–197). St. Louis: Mosby, 1981.

Spinetta, J. J., Rigler, D., & Karon, M. Personal space as a measure of a dying child's sense of isolation. _Journal of Consulting and Clinical Psychology_, 1974, _42_, 751–756.

Susman, E. J., Pizzo, P. A., & Poplack, D. G. Adolescent cancer: getting through the aftermath. In P. Ahmed (Ed.), _Living and dying with cancer_ (pp. 101–116). New York: Elsevier, 1981.

Vernick, J. Meaningful communication with the fatally ill child. In E. J. Anthony & C. Koupernik (Eds.), _The child in his family: The impact of disease and death_ (pp. 105–119). New York: Wiley, 1973.

Weisman, A. D. _On dying and denying: A psychiatric study of terminality._ New York: Behavioral Publications, 1972.

6

Helping Bereaved Adolescents: Needs and Responses

Stephen J. Fleming and Rheba Adolph

Two clear impressions emerge upon examining the published literature on adolescent grief: there is a paucity of research investigating bereavement at this stage of development; and, on a larger scale, no comprehensive model exists to facilitate an understanding of the adolescent grief experience. This chapter proposes a model of adolescent grief relating loss to the tasks and conflicts of normal adolescent development, and discusses aspects of intervention with this population.

RESEARCH METHODOLOGY: ISSUES AND PROBLEMS

Examination of the literature on grief and bereavement reveals an obvious trend. There has been a concerted effort to explore the impact of parental and sibling death on children (Fleming, 1985a; Furman, 1974; Kaffman & Elizur, 1979; Miller, 1972). However, the major focus of research efforts has been on increasing our understanding of the adult grief response either at the death of a child (Helmrath & Stein, 1978; Schiff, 1977; Trowhill & Fleming, 1980) or at the death of a spouse, most

The authors gratefully acknowledge the assistance of Mary Guerriero and Leslie Balmer in the preparation of this chapter.

frequently the husband (Clayton, Halika, Maurice, & Robins, 1973; Maddison & Viola, 1968; Parkes, 1972; Vachon, 1976). Not only has the reaction of adolescents to parental or sibling death received scant attention, but adolescence as a distinct developmental stage has been largely ignored in grief research. In addition, there are major methodological problems with the few studies that have been published.

A subject of dispute in research on adolescents in general is defining what one means by an "adolescent." Haslam (1978) noted that this term has referred to those as young as 10 and as old as 19 years of age, while Laufer (1980) addresses the period from "puberty to about the age of 21" (p. 265). As for the grief literature specifically, with few exceptions (Balk, 1981; Guerriero, 1983b), one finds that adolescence is either considered an extension of childhood or part of adulthood. For example, Caplan and Douglas (1969) studied the grief responses of "children" aged two to 16 years and Van Eerdewegh, Bieri, Parrilla, and Clayton (1982) focused on children from two to 17 years, while Hardt's (1978) research involved participants aged 13 to 26 years. In referring to the onset of adolescence, Seligman, Gleser, Rauh, and Harris (1974) use operational definitions of age 12 for girls and age 14 for boys. This lack of consensus creates problems in the interpretation of data and severely curtails the generalizability of results.

Another problem with adolescent grief research is that it tends to be retrospective in nature. Participants, be they adolescents or adults, are requested to provide information on their reactions to the death of a significant other (most frequently a parent) at a later period in life. Thus, there is great variability in the "time-since-death" dimension. For example, all of Guerriero's (1983b) adolescent responders had reported the death of a sibling within 24 months, while Balk's (1981) sample reflected on grief experiences occurring within the previous 7 years, and the research of Van Eerdewegh and colleagues (1982) was prospective in nature.

An additional methodological concern is the use of clinical samples in research (Cain, Fast, & Erickson, 1964; Caplan & Douglas, 1969; Seligman et al., 1974). Where participants either are in psychotherapy at the time the death occurs or are referred for treatment during bereavement, results are generalizable only to atypical samples. Retrospective, correlational studies often imply a causal relationship between grief and personality development and, where data are derived from clinical samples, little insight is provided regarding why some adolescents do not develop complications during bereavement or after.

Briefly, other confounding factors include the failure to distinguish varying types of "loss," that is death, divorce, separation (Seligman et al., 1974); the use of highly subjective reports restricting descriptions of adolescent grief to accounts provided by their mourning parents (Van Eerdewegh et al., 1982); and the failure to collect follow-up data or to include control groups (Balk, 1981).

In addition to the paucity of research into adolescent grief and the serious methodological problems affecting those few published reports, a model to encourage theory building and provide direction for research is sorely needed. The remainder of this chapter will:

1. outline the parallel issues involved in adjustment to loss and normal adolescent development;
2. present a model of the adolescent grief experience that reflects the distinctive tensions and conflicts of this period; and
3. discuss intervention with bereaved adolescents.

ADJUSTMENT TO LOSS

Grieving involves a progression of changes or phases in which one group of psychological and social experiences predominates over others in subsequent periods. Freud (1957) categorized mourning behavior into periods of profound dejection, loss of a capacity to adopt new love objects, inhibition of activity (or turning away from whatever activities are unconnected with the thoughts of the dead person), and loss of interest in those parts of the outside world that are not related to the dead person. Contemporary clinicians also expect the mourner to hold ambivalent feelings toward the deceased and to experience disturbance and erosion of his or her self-esteem. Lindemann (1944), Parkes (1972), Parkes and Weiss (1983), and Worden (1982) observed somatic distress, guilt, hostile reactions (even generalized anger), preoccupation with the image of the deceased, and loss of one's customary habitual patterns of conduct. Changes in social status and disruption of one's previous social roles may also beset the mourner.

Object relations theorists emphasize the universality of attachment and loss behavior (Bowlby, 1973). They describe a progression in the series of responses the infant exhibits when its first love object is lost. Upheavals are experienced as the infant searches for the love object, as it protests the loss, as it despairs of reunion with the love object, and as it finally adapts (or fails to adapt) to the reality of the lost object. Mourning behavior can be seen as a parallel of this first separation process. The theories of object relations and mourning converge to form three discernible categories of "loss" behavior, thoughts, and feelings. These categories are: protest and searching; disorganization; and reorganization.

In the wake of bereavement or separation, the infant attempts to recover the lost love object and to gain restitution of the loss. *Protest* is exhibited in rage, anger, clinging, and in phobic, rebellious, or hostile behaviors. There is also an attempt at *searching* for the deceased and often a refusal to believe that the loved one has really died. The mourner, too, looks for the deceased, clings to the hope of a mistaken identity, is obsessed with the image of the deceased, and is angry at the deceased for perceived abandonment. Such thoughts, feelings, and actions serve the need to recover and to reunite with the dead person.

When it becomes clear that the usual patterns of interacting with the lost object are no longer possible, a period of *disorganization* follows the infant's attempts to gain restitution. The permanence of the loss is now a reality. The infant rages at the parent and seems to be out of control. Gratification (food) or comfort (mother) are denied. The mourner also feels angry and empty. Self-esteem plummets, mood shifts occur, behavior is impulsive, and agitation may be severe. The mourner pursues gratification alternately with denial of needs. In this period of disorganization, inner feelings of loss are now related to the primitive infantile object loss. Feelings of emptiness, anger, agitation, impulsivity, and comfortlessness are now displaced to external factors. Mourners may use the excuses of other people and events as causing them to be out of control. The perception of being influenced by forces outside one's self creates in mourners the strong need to gain mastery over past and present events.

It is the disorganization phase of loss in which one can to some extent rework the past context of hurts and anger associated with the deceased. One clinician suggests that the antisocial behavior of the disorganization period is actually an optimistic statement (Sugar, 1968). Despite feelings of hopelessness and despair, the attempts one makes to gain control of the past and present testify to the renewal of hope for the future.

Reorganization is a period of calm alternating back and forth between denial of separation, disorganization, and reorientation. The infant looks to others for new attachments and begins to exercise his or her potentials to learn and develop new skills. At this time the mourner is also beginning to make new commitments to others and to the self. Despite the periodic upheavals of phase shifts, the bond to the deceased is severed.

Mourning is all that is involved in accommodating to the loss of an internal object or to the loss of a beloved person. It is an individual's attempt to align one's inner world with external reality. The survivor may attempt to push aside from awareness unpleasant and angry feeling toward the deceased, or attempt to deny the impact of the loss upon his or her life. But it is not until the survivor begins to disengage from the deceased that the process of healing begins.

DEVELOPING ADOLESCENTS: PRIMARY ENDEAVORS AND LOSS

In the developmental period of adolescence, young persons engage in endeavors that are crucial to their futures. They attempt to:

1. organize and integrate early experiences of separation from parental objects;
2. achieve emotional and physical separation (autonomy) from parental figures;
3. gain mastery and control over the emerging surges of the sexual body, strong emotions, and new-found skill abilities; and
4. achieve intimacy in sexual and social relations.

The central question that adolescents address is: "Who am I as an emotional, thinking, physical, and sexual being?" The adolescent years are the period in the developmental growth cycle during which the person struggles to form mental pictures of the self as separate from early identifications and as a person with a fixed sexual identity (Laufer, 1980).

Young persons meet the challenges of forging their "identity" by:

1. regressing temporarily to an earlier and more comfortable developmental phase;
2. identifying with people outside their immediate families as models of behavior and morality;
3. developing their own intellectual ideas;
4. experiencing childhood anger and aggression in a new context;
5. exploring their sexuality by trial actions;
6. distancing themselves from new and powerful affects which they now experience as arising from within themselves.

By the close of the adolescent years, the person has established some predictable patterns of dealing with the anxiety inherent in seeking pleasure and gratification. The dialectic between ego-ideal and conscience is more stable than in childhood or puberty.

During adolescence, the loss of a profound relationship—whether an internalized object or a person in the external world—may interfere in what seems to be the natural progression of intellectual-emotional-psychological "growing up." Changes that are normally expected may be averted, avoided, or may not even take place. Such an arrest of developmental unfolding may put the adolescent "on hold" in one phase, and thus inhibit the energy and skills necessary to meet subsequent phase-appropriate demands. A developmental arrest may also have the opposite effect, that is, of increasing the intensity of a prior phase-specific behavior in a following phase.

Studies of adolescent bereavement leave the clinician perplexed, for they do not clarify whether the adolescent is dealing with the "normal" conflicts inherent in each discrete developmental phase or whether he or she is dealing with the conflicts inherent in the grieving process. Activity-passivity, pleasure-pain, love-hate, dependency-autonomy are conflicts bereaved people share, and they are also acutely present in each phase of adolescent ego development. In effect, the work of adolescence and the work of grief are similar, for both involve adapting to the loss of cherished objects (either an inner image or a person), both involve coping with changed inner and external realities, and both must encounter the ambivalence and conflicts inherent in the phases of separation and loss: protest/searching, disorganization, and reorganization (Sugar, 1968).

Another similarity between the work of resolving grief and normal adolescent development is their paradoxical nature. Adolescence is a time of paradoxes. In order to establish an emotional connection with others and to work as a valued member in collective endeavors, young persons first develop a sense of being emotionally separate from their loved ones. They gain a sense of their own individuality and competence. They earn, in the end, a feeling of self-coherence so that they can join with others. Grief is also a time of paradoxes. At some point, the feelings of isolation and attachment to the deceased lessen. Mourners can then reenter previous activities and attach themselves to other people. But in order to feel separate from the deceased and related to others, mourners first immerse themselves in memories of the deceased. To ease their guilt, they need to encounter their own ambivalence and to remember their anger and resentment toward the deceased.

A MODEL OF ADOLESCENT GRIEVING: CONFLICTS AND TASKS IN THREE MATURATIONAL PHASES

What is needed and useful to clinicians, theorists, and adolescent survivors is *a model of grieving for adolescents* that reflects the distinct and differing maturational levels of adolescence, one that offers insight into what happens to adolescent development when the conflicts of grieving collide with those of ego development.

Table 6.1 depicts the tasks and conflicts of normal adolescent development, organized around three maturational phases and with adolescence defined chronologically as the period from age 11 to 21. For each of the maturational phases there are associated specific tasks and conflicts.

As adolescents move beyond the embrace of their families in Phase I, they struggle to replace family comforts with those of peers. Loyalties are now transferred and shared. There is the excitement of participating in new activities, but this also creates fear as one leaves the security and predictability of the family. Herein is the saga of the newly emerging adolescent and his or her attempts to regain the lost object (internal image or actual person). We can never really do without the internal image of a comforting, nurturing figure, but we have to make a life apart from the physical presence of, as well as the emotional attachment to, this figure. Retaining an inner image of comfort, adolescents untie more of the emotional bonds between themselves and their parents. There is the dawning recognition that one is no longer a part of the childhood past, but not yet part of the adult future. In effect, this is the *protest/searching* phase of normal adolescent mourning as proposed by Sugar (1968).

In Phase II, adolescents may perceive their residual dependency on their parents as a threat to their desire for autonomy. A conviction that they are at least somewhat competent to do things by themselves is augmented by their emerging motor, muscular, sexual, and intellectual skills. If they wish to surpass their parents' achievements or at least meet parental expectations of their children, adolescents may be distancing themselves and adding an element of competition to the relationship. It is risky to compete with those you need. Now, feeling guided by their own goals, adolescents often find themselves without the comforts of convention. "I can do this myself," a familiar proclama-

TABLE 6.1. Tasks and Conflicts for Adolescents by Maturational Phase

Phase I	Age:	11–14
	Task:	Emotional separation from parents
	Conflict:	Separation vs. Reunion
		(abandonment) vs. (safety)
Phase II	Age:	14–17
	Task:	Competency/Mastery/Control
	Conflict:	Independence vs. Dependence
Phase III	Age:	17–21
	Task:	Intimacy vs. Commitment
	Conflict:	Closeness vs. Distance

tion, may imply a rejection of past wisdom without the consolation of its tried-and-true prescriptions. The dynamics of this phase are similar to those of Sugar's (1968) period of *disorganization*.

In Phase III, having achieved a degree of emotional and physical separation from their parents and better able to synthesize their personal and social identities from the context of their childhood dependencies and the turmoil of the unknown, older adolescents struggle with interpersonal closeness. How intimate and committed they allow themselves to become reflects their degree of mastery of the preceding conflicts. Too intimate a relationship creates the risk of being personally overwhelmed and, once again, dependent. Too distant a style risks psychological isolation and abandonment. This period parallels Sugar's (1968) *reorganization* phase.

We have identified *five core issues* around which bereaved adolescents attempt to accomplish some resolution of the ambivalence engendered by phase conflicts. These core issues are: predictability of events; self-image; belonging; fairness/justice; and mastery/control. Each phase has identical core issues that provoke cognitive, behavioral, and affective responses. Although these three response categories of thinking, feeling, and behaving remain the same across all phases, the response content is unique to the particular developmental period.

It is beyond the scope of this chapter to elaborate on how bereaved adolescents think, feel, and behave across all of the five core issues as a function of phasic development. Instead, for illustrative purposes, a single core issue—that of "self-image"—will be developed in detail. Readers may consult Tables 6.2, 6.3, and 6.4 for an outline of the model across all three maturational phases, all five core issues, and all three response categories.

A CORE ISSUE IN ADOLESCENT BEREAVEMENT: SELF-IMAGE

Cognitive Responses

In Phase I, the adolescent recognizes: "I am different from everyone else." No matter how bereaved adolescents attempt to be similar to other young people, their perception is one of being different. The positive repercussions of difference are a voluntary pulling away from parents and a welcoming of this difference since the valued uniqueness enhances self-image. However, the separation of bereaved adolescents from a loved person is unwilled. Here the feeling of being different takes on the pejorative quality of being "marked."

In Phase II, the perception of the adolescent is: "I can do anything."

TABLE 6.2. Phase I. Conflict: Separation vs. Reunion

	Reactions		
Core Issues	Cognitive ("I am different")	Behavioral (Seeking and protesting separation)	Affective (separation anxiety)
Predictability of Events	Unsafe world for individual and/or parents; vulnerable to death and/or abandonment	Overly cautious or excessive risk-taking	Fear Anger
Self-image	"I am marked" "I am different. . . . I am bereaved"	Adult and/or altruistic behavior not typical of adolescents "Acting out"—dramatic, flamboyant behavior or prominent resistance to home and school rules (to attract care)	Predominantly flat/shallow Depressed (agitated)
Belonging	Belief that only peers understand, as parent(s) are preoccupied with their grief Peer rejection	Seeking peers Avoiding peers Withdrawal from peers and at times, through projection, provoking rejection from peers	Manic (especially with peers Anger (at parents and peers Isolation/ alienation
Fairness/ Justice	Why *my* brother? and Why *my* family—typifying adolescent attachment to the family for it is also the center of his or her universe	Self-protection or Self-destructive behavior	Fear of dying (self, parents) Envy Guilt Anger (at deceased, parent[s], self, etc.)
Mastery/ Control	Dead sibling is idealized; survivor would rather have died in his or her place Dead sibling is rejected and assigned characteristics dissimilar to survivor	Over-identification with deceased to gain perceived magical/positive characteristics Distancing from deceased by: denial of good memories and importance of deceased	Emptiness Inferiority (to de-deceased) Ambivalence (toward deceased Fear (of not being able to control and cope with the unknown) Anger (at all of the above)

105

TABLE 6.3. Phase II. Conflict: Independence vs. Dependence

		Reactions	
Core Issues	Cognitive ("I can do anything")	Behavioral Independency— dependency	Affective (Fragmented)
Predictability of Events	Unsafe world as the adolescent knows he or she is vulnerable to death (physical)	Fight response of— aggression—risk-taking—independent action	Fears of— personal death —personal dis-integration— parental death
	Perception of not being able to control inter-nal (psychological) as well as external envi-ronment	Flight response of rigid, overcontrolled actions; also dependence on others for stimulation, competency activities, and decision making	Anger (at being afraid)
Self-image	Integrated—the con-viction that "I can handle this"; but, in fact, the awareness that assertions of competency are re-flections of transitory self-competence	Task mastery —for example, Role reversal where adoles-cent assumes responsi-bilities of adulthood	Fear —Loss of compe-tence or loss of the appearance of competence
	Disintegrated—the conviction that "I can't handle this" and the recognition of the fragility of competence	Fight—presenting illu-sions of adult inde-pendence and mastery; often flouting con-ventions of peers and adults	Anger and re-sentment to-ward others as they are not "good enough" and don't un-derstand the bereaved adolescent
		Flight—submission and conforming to rules and regulations	
Belonging	A perception that be-longing to a group enhances confidence; usually transitory	Seeking peers' recogni-tion and approval; may include sexual acting out as a means of ap-pearing adult and in control	Merged/ac-cepted—al-most feeling "at one" with others
	More often the belief is of not belonging	Withdrawal	Feeling misun-derstood/re-jected and dis-liked by peers Anger (when

| | | Reactions | |
Core Issues	Cognitive ("I can do anything")	Behavioral Independency— dependency	Affective (Fragmented)
			feeling one does not belong or is not "good enough") Fear (of belonging, for one can be abandoned—as happened with the deceased)
Fairness/ Justice	Why me?—reflects egocentric orientation; unfairness and arbitrary nature of deceased's death is related personally by survivor	Protest at self as the object of destiny's unconcern Self-punishment as a means of warding off fate; fear of again being victimized	Guilt (for wishing death of others) Anger (at all of the above, as well as at fate and inability of parent[s] to protect deceased and survivor)
Mastery/ Control	"I must and I will do it"—no matter what the activity or endeavor	Academic life—pursued with greater or lesser intensity Social life—frantically enlarged or deliberately shrunk "Don't die!"—the command to self and others as an attempt to be omnipotent Taking more responsibility as a means of proving to self that one is capable of self-protection	Anger and resentment
	"I can't/won't do it"— no matter what the activity or endeavor	Acting out—refusal to "play by the rules" as an attempt at control by defiance	Disintegration (everything is too difficult) Guilt and depression follow

107

TABLE 6.4. Phase III. Conflict: Closeness vs. Distance

		Reactions	
Core Issues	Cognitive ("I can trust. . . .")	Behavioral Investment— Withholding	Affective (Acceptance— (Rejection)
Predictability of Events	Unsafe world because of vulnerability to death and fearing death of another Loss of control (personal) is perceived if someone close cannot be protected from death	Investment in another as an attempt to gain safety through an alliance; also, attempt is to gain affection and attention lost when significant other died	Fears of—personal death —personal disintegration— parental death —death of "significant other" Anger at self and others
Self-image	"I am affirmed by another" is a transitory belief for the adolescent has already experienced profound isolation or	Investment—commitment to another waivers and may alternate with . . .	Feelings of being worthwhile/ accepted/loved
	"I am alone . . . no one has experienced what I have, so no one can really understand me"	Withdrawal	Feelings of being rejected
Belonging	Belonging in another's life is seen as giving life a purpose and meaning missing since the loved one's death	Commitment—faithful and loyal to a partner; almost clinging	Merged with another Accepted and understood by another
	Reduced meaning is seen if another has to be "used" to gain purpose in living	Withdrawal	Alienation/ anomie Fear of risking attachment to another
Fairness/ Justice	"Why must this happen at all?"—altruistic view replaces eogcentrism	Religious pursuits and good deeds reflect altruism	Neutralized affect—evil is part of the world
	"What's the point of anything?"—the world is unfair and goodness is no protection against evil	Abandoning transcendence and altruism— hedonistic behavior	Generalized anger
Mastery/ Control	"I can't risk/trust" because I can lose the "other"	Withholding/withdrawal of help, affection, and praise	Emptiness Despair Failure Alienation

Such thoughts of omnipotence, though they come and go, may push adolescents to risk experimenting with new skills and adventures. With every success, adolescents believe further in their own power, and success breeds more success. But bereaved adolescents know that they cannot do everything. Left without this basic illusion, this awareness may confound their sense of mastery and control. If adolescents do not believe in themselves and in their own efficacy, the central conflict of independence-dependence is heightened.

In Phase III, the cognitive issue is "trust." The adolescent says: "I want to and I can trust others to give me comfort and solace when I am vulnerable," and "I am trustworthy so that I can give comfort and solace to another." Bereaved adolescents are already "marked" by themselves as different; they believe they may not meet the challenges of control and mastery. They hesitate to put their trust in another for they may endure another painful loss if the other dies—an ever-present reality for a bereaved person.

Behavioral Responses

In Phase I, bereaved adolescents have the normal behavioral responses which reflect the conflict of simultaneously seeking separation and protesting it. As well as having to cope with their emerging pictures of themselves without the aid of a parent or sibling, bereaved adolescents may try to resolve this conflict by being the "good" or "parent" child. In this role, they try to achieve the nurturing they are unable to get from their parents by exhibiting adult or altruistic behavior not typical of their age group. Or, bereaved adolescents may adopt the opposite stance and become the "acting out" child, in effect, attracting attention and assuring the sought-after nurturing.

In Phase II, the behavioral trend is toward independence. Bereaved adolescents may engage in "fight" responses (being aggressive, taking risks) or "flight" responses (rigid, overcontrolled reactions). The former can be considered as a behavior directed toward an exaggerated self-image of independence and the latter as an exaggerated self-image of dependence.

In Phase III, the behavioral concomitants of the task of commitment to another may stir up images of oneself as either being overinvested in another or being hopelessly withdrawn from others.

Affective Responses

In Phase I, affects center around the anxiety of separation. Expressions of emotions are depressed and flat or agitated, and young bereaved adolescents seem to see themselves as ineffective as a result. In Phase II, affective responses are fragmented, inconsistent, and reflect the struggle of becoming self-competent. The self-image of bereaved adolescents is pervaded by anger and resentment at their fears of incompetence. Finally, in Phase III, affective reactions of older bereaved adolescents emerge as they feel themselves accepted or rejected by others. Their self-picture seems to be either of one who is "worthwhile at last" or one who is "unloveable." Both are responses to the devastating blow they suffered at death. Feelings of rejection common at this age are augmented by the initial destruction of self-esteem when a loved one dies.

In suggesting age-typical thoughts, feelings, and behaviors, the model we have offered provides order for the varied and complex responses of adolescents to death. It also encourages the matching of age-appropriate conflicts and tasks with grief responses as an indication of how the survivor's developing personality may be shaped and colored by the loss. For example, the isolation felt by survivors may be intensified in a 14-year-old who is immersed in the developmental task of distancing himself or herself from emotional ties with parents. When a parent or sibling dies, the surviving parent(s) are often unable to nurture the adolescent or, as the opposite may happen, tend to hold on too closely so that the adolescent may be unable to reach out for the comfort of peers. If the family encourages extreme autonomy, the youngster must struggle with this separation-reunion dilemma in isolation. The normal tasks of an adolescent of this age are now complicated and may be too taxing for immature abilities. Unable to negotiate appropriate emotional separation and left with protest or despair, the adolescent's future abilities to form intimate relationships are endangered.

HELPING BEREAVED ADOLESCENTS

Interventions with Individual Adolescents and Families

Adolescents frequently exhibit great resistance both to professional intervention, for example individual, group, or family therapy, and to involvement with mutual- or self-help groups. Struggling with the previously discussed tasks and conflicts, the fearful and vulnerable adolescents are now faced with the stigma of "needing help." Concerns centering on their mental health often surface at this time. In response, it is useful to impress upon bereaved adolescents that "one need not be 'sick' to get better." In other words, just as a visit to the family physician to discuss physical concerns may be preventive, seeking psychological assistance may also serve to circumvent complications. In no way does the latter imply that one is "going crazy."

In recent years there has been a growing trend toward self-help or, perhaps more accurately, mutual-help groups to assist the bereaved (Klass, 1985). Groups have been established for those suffering the death of a spouse, others to offer support at the death of a child. As a treatment modality in their own right or as an adjunct to psychotherapy, mutual-help groups for those suffering the death of a sibling need to be developed.

While mutual-help groups for bereaved adolescents are an important option for assistance, though one whose effectiveness has not yet been demonstrated, one cannot consider the adolescent in a psychosocial vacuum. Even as they acknowledged that adolescents often speak to peers about personal matters, Connell, Stroobant, Sinclair, Connell, and Rogers (1975) reported that significantly more adolescent boys used family members as confidants, principally their mothers. Similar results were found for adolescent girls, with an even clearer preference for their mothers. A family is traumatized by the death of one of its members (Fleming, 1985a; Parkes, 1972; Raphael, 1983; Schiff, 1977), and, as a result of their collective and individual pain, survivors are often confronted with a sense of loneliness and isolation as communication with other family members dwindles. It is not surprising, therefore, that Balk (1981) found adjustment to a sibling's death to be a function of family coherence, with adolescents from a family that encouraged closeness and communication experiencing fewer grief complications. The family, then, must be considered in any comprehensive intervention program not only during the period immediately following the death, but for a considerable time thereafter.

With respect to the death of a child, there are recent data suggesting that family maladjustment persists beyond the second year of bereavement. Trowhill and Fleming (1980) and Fleming (in press) administered a social adjustment scale (Weissman, Prusoff, Thompson, Harding, & Myers, 1978) to bereaved parents at one- and two-year postdeath assessments. The social adjustment scale is a self-report measure designed to indicate level of individual role performance and adjustment in five major areas of functioning (work, social and leisure activities, extended family, marriage, and parenting). Up to and including two years after the child's death, bereaved parents reported greater maladjustment in all areas of functioning than a group of nonbereaved controls. Scores on the marital subscale, reflecting a lack of affection, disinterest in sex (and an increase in feelings of dissatisfaction and/or guilt when it occurs), domineering behavior, dependency, and submissiveness, were indicative of the greatest maladjustment.

Education About Bereavement

In addition to direct help for the adolescent and his or her family, educational programs aimed at lessening the risk of postbereavement morbidity need to be developed and implemented. Balk (1981) and Raphael (1983) have stressed the importance of educating professionals (especially those having contact with the bereaved: physicians, nurses, counselors, and funeral directors) and members of the lay community alike. Through popular magazines, professional journals, radio, and television, the nature of grief and adaptive methods to deal with it need to be explored. Topics might include: the necessity for the open expression of grief and frank discussion of the deceased—in effect, granting "permission to grieve"; the need to recognize and accept support during this vulnerable period; the importance of good communication skills; the identification of helpful behaviors; and the recognition of the adolescent at risk.

There is much about the normal grief experience that is frightening, even terrifying. Consider such aspects as: the vulnerability and sense of "no one understanding"; the waves of anger, guilt, and uncontrollable crying that leave the bereaved exhausted with feelings of helplessness and despair; the fear of depression and "going crazy" as one experiences visual and auditory reminders of the deceased; the alarm accompanying strange physical sensations (nausea, chest pain, sweating); and the self-criticism and feelings of inadequacy with the dawning awareness they are not "grieving as they should." The anxiety generated as one confronts this puzzling, unfamiliar, and scary array of physical and psychological experiences can be reduced to manageable proportions through intervention at the cognitive level designed to correct misconceptions regarding grief. In other words, provide the bereaved with grief education.

Two commonly held misconceptions with the potential to create serious complications relate first to the "shoulds" of grief and second to the relationship between grief intensity and time. "Shoulds" refer to widely held prescriptions of socially approved thoughts, feelings, and behaviors: the "do's" and don'ts" of grief. For example, "I *should* not speak ill of the dead" or "I *should* not be angry at God."

"Shoulds" are particularly maladaptive, for they foster a sense of guilt and self-inadequacy as the bereaved seemingly fall short of society's "standards of grieving." Sensing that their experience of loss is somehow atypical or unacceptable, bereaved persons often experience external or internal pressures to abandon genuine feelings of grief in favor of society's expectations of what is acceptable. This failure to plumb the depths of one's own anguish may cause serious problems later when unresolved grief erupts.

The time since death plays a prominent role in this delineation of appropriate thoughts, feelings, and behaviors. Consider, "It's been four months; I *should* be back to my old self again," or "I *should* be able to concentrate on my school work by now." Kastenbaum (1981) has commented that we are impatient with the bereaved and, seemingly perplexed by the irrationality of grief, we coerce them to quickly "return to normal," at least superficially. Society's expectations of the time necessary to accomplish the work of grieving (usually 12 months or less) stand in sharp contrast to the research evidence. As Parkes (1972), Parkes & Weiss (1983), Raphael (1983), and Worden (1982) have indicated, the physiological and psychological repercussions of loss are profound and often extend well beyond the first year of bereavement. Balk (1981) found that one-third to one-half of a sample of sibling-bereaved adolescents reported experiencing such symptoms as guilt, confusion, depression, loneliness, and anger. The mean postdeath interview was conducted at 23.6 months! In this light, one can see why mutual-help groups are invaluable since they offer a supportive forum for not only self-exploration and catharsis, but for validating and "normalizing" one's experiences over time (Klass, 1985).

Unfortunately, one periodically encounters support for the notion of accelerated or telescoped grief. Thus, Rounsaville and Chevron (1982) wrote:

> Grieving normally occurs when a person sustains an important loss of a significant other and, during the bereavement period, experiences symptoms such as sadness, disturbed sleep, agitation, and decreased ability to carry out day-to-day tasks. *These symptoms are considered normal and tend to resolve themselves without treatment in 2 to 4 months.* (p. 112; our emphasis)

Statements such as this one, so obviously at odds with the bulk of the published literature and with the personal experience of the bereaved, cruelly encourage unrealistic expectations of early recovery from the very normal pain of grief.

Intervention, then, needs to be directed toward creating a more realistic, less destructive set of expectations. The bereaved need support and encouragement in their struggle to recognize and curtail the disruptive influence of existing "shoulds." Endeavoring to explore *all* of one's thoughts and feelings about the deceased, no matter how unpalatable, one needs to appreciate a desirable "should"—that of being honest with oneself.

With respect to time, societal pressures to curtail grief expression emanate from the assumption that "time heals." This is simply not true. In working with the bereaved, it is important to stress that "it is not the time you have to use, but how you use the time you have." Simply noting the time since a death has occurred says nothing about *how* this time was used. Factors associated with delayed or chronic grief reactions include: a highly dependent relationship with the deceased; great ambivalence toward the deceased; the survivor's tendency to avoid stress or conflict; current, multiple, and uncontrollable life stressors; and the lack of a supportive friendship network.

Another expectation involving time is reflected in the frequently heard expression, "when will I get over this?" The reality is "you *never* completely 'get over' the death of a loved one, rather, you learn to live with it." Certainly the acute phase of grief begins to subside, and the pain becomes less intense and more intermittent, with increasingly longer periods of peacefulness intervening. However, incidents such as hearing a favorite song or thinking you have seen the deceased in a crowd may precipitate a grief response of surprising intensity. In his analysis of 56 nineteenth-century adult diarists, Rosenblatt (1983) did not find evidence that grief gradually wanes (as in Figure 6.1)—quite the contrary. As Rosenblatt suggests, the typical grief response corresponds to Figure 6.2, with symptoms absent for increasingly longer periods. The peaks of emotional intensity, however, are still elevated even after many years.

SUMMARY AND CONCLUSIONS

There are scarce references in the bereavement literature to adolescents who have suffered the death of a parent or sibling. Indeed, "adolescence" is itself a muddled concept in the clinical literature, and there is little attempt to analyze adolescence as a series of discrete developmental epochs. Methodological problems are evident in studies of adolescent grief, especially the unrepresentative nature of the sample populations as well as reliance on retrospective accounts rather than present experiences of reported grief. What is particularly lacking in the clinical literature on adolescent bereavement is a model that combines a theory of loss with a theory of adolescent development.

The model proposed in this chapter serves several functions:

1. it enhances a clinician's understanding of an adolescent's grief;
2. it highlights the impact of loss upon the adolescent as he or she develops an adult personality;

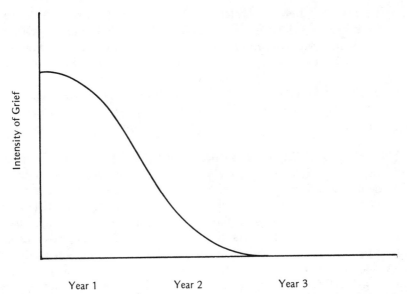

Year 1   Year 2   Year 3

Figure 6.1. Time course of grief: common impression. (After Paul C. Rosenblatt. *Bitter, Bitter Tears: Nineteenth-Century Diarists and Twentieth-Century Grief Theories.* Minneapolis: University of Minnesota Press, 1983. Used by permission.)

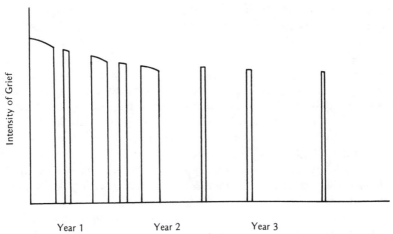

Year 1   Year 2   Year 3

Figure 6.2 Time course of grief: diary data. (After Paul C. Rosenblatt. *Bitter, Bitter Tears: Nineteenth-Century Diarists and Twentieth-Century Grief Theories.* Minneapolis: University of Minnesota Press, 1983. Used by permission.)

3. it guides the helping professional in identifying crucial deficits in the bereaved adolescent's psychological and emotional growth;
4. it aids in understanding the etiology of adult deficits and dysfunctions which may be grief-related if the adult, as an adolescent, suffered the death of a loved person;
5. it offers some appropriate clinical strategies to compensate for these grief-related dysfunctions, and thus aids in the further psychological and emotional growth of the adult.

This model also suggests further research directions, for example, looking more closely at age differences in bereaved adolescents rather than sampling wide age ranges. Second, the model makes clear that grief responses cannot be considered in isolation; attention must be directed to the impact of loss on the conflicts and tasks of normal adolescent development. Third, it is generally recognized that powerful sex role expectations influence the expression of one's feelings. With the possible exception of anger, when distressed or frustrated, males encounter more prohibitions against emotional expression than do females. Where such proscriptions deny the expression of feelings (for example, crying) and aggressive responses clearly do not alleviate a distressing condition (for example bereavement), males may have fewer outlets for their grief. Raphael (1983) has suggested a differential response to death with male adolescents often behaving in a more aggressive manner, testing authority figures, and using drugs and alcohol excessively. All these behaviors serve to punish the bereaved, release tension, and elicit involvement of others. Females, in contrast, often feel a longing for comfort and reassurance reflecting a diffuse need to be held and consoled. Unfortunately, no systematic research has addressed this issue. Fourth, adolescence has commonly been portrayed as a period of great stress, chaos, and instability (Barker, 1976; Haim, 1974; Stone & Church, 1973). Acknowledging that this period is not stress-free, Bandura (1980) and McCandless and Coop (1979) hold that adolescence is characterized by more continuity and stability than originally thought, with the great majority of normal adolescents relatively stable and well adjusted. Furthermore, Offer (1969) reported that many adolescents profited developmentally from situational crises, that is, they used the stressful experience as an opportunity for positive personality changes.

The possibility that the death of a loved one can serve as a catalyst for constructive personality change needs further exploration. With sibling-bereaved adolescents, for example, both Balk (1981) and Guerriero (1983a) found no resulting detrimental impact on self-concept; in fact, there was a tendency for the bereaved respondents to be more self-confident, more satisfied with themselves in general, and more ethically or morally conscious. In accounting for these results, Balk (1981) suggests that death precipitates a reevaluation and examination of ideals, an increased sense of concern and responsibility for others, and a reassessment of life's meaning.

Finally, focus needs to be placed on bereaved adolescents within their grief-stricken families—families that function at different points on the "open/closed" continuums of rules, boundaries, intimacy, communication, and control systems.

REFERENCES

Balk, D. E. *Sibling death during adolescence: Self-concept and bereavement reactions.* Unpublished doctoral dissertation, University of Illinois, Champaign-Urbana, 1981.

Bandura, A. The stormy decade: Fact or fiction?" In R. E. Mauss (Ed.), *Adolescent behavior and society: A book of readings* (3rd ed.) (pp. 22–31). New York: Random House, 1980.

Barker, P. *Basic child psychiatry.* Baltimore: University Park Press, 1976.

Bowlby, J. *Separation: Anxiety and anger.* New York: Basic Books, 1973.

Cain, A., Fast, I., & Erickson, M. Children's disturbed reactions to the death of a sibling. *Journal of Orthopsychiatry*, 1964, 34, 741–752.

Caplan, M. G., & Douglas, V. I. Incidence of parental loss in children with depressed moods. *Journal of Child Psychology and Psychiatry*, 1969, 10, 225–232.

Clayton, P. J., Halika, J. A., Maurice, W., L., & Robins, E. Anticipatory grief and widowhood. *British Journal of Psychiatry*, 1973, 122, 47–51.

Connell, W. F., Stroobant, R. E., Sinclair, E. E., Connell, R. W., & Rogers, K. W. *12 to 20: Studies of city youth.* Sydney: Hicks, Smith & Sons, 1975.

Fleming, S. J. Children's grief: Individual and family dynamics. In C. A. Corr & D. M. Corr (Eds.), *Hospice approaches to pediatric care* (pp. 197–218). New York: Springer Publishing, 1985.

Fleming, S. J., Parental social adjustment after the death of a child. In press.

Freud, S. Mourning and melancholia. In J. Strachey (Ed.), *The standard edition of the complete psychological works of Sigmund Freud* (Vol. 14) (pp. 243–258). London: Hogarth Press, 1957.

Furman, E. *A child's parent dies.* New Haven: Yale University Press, 1974.

Guerriero, A. M. *Adolescent bereavement: Impact on physical health, self-concept, depression, and death anxiety.* Unpublished master's thesis, York University, Toronto, 1983a.

Guerriero, A. M. *Adolescent grief: Existing literature.* Paper presented at the Annual Meeting, Canadian Psychological Association, Winnipeg, Manitoba, 1983b.

Haim, A. *Adolescent suicide.* New York: International Universities Press, 1974.

Hardt, D. V. An investigation of the stages of bereavement. *Omega*, 1978, 9, 279–285.

Haslam, M. T. A study of psychiatric illness in adolescence: Diagnosis and prognosis. *International Journal of Psychiatry*, 1978, 24, 287–294.

Helmrath, T. A., & Stein, E. M. Death of an infant: Parental grieving and the failure of social support. *The Journal of Family Practice*, 1978, *6*, 785–790.

Kaffman, M., & Elizur, E. Children's bereavement reactions following death of the father. *International Journal of Family Therapy*, 1979, *1*, 203–229.

Kastenbaum, R. *Death, society, and human experience* (2nd ed.). St. Louis: Mosby, 1981.

Klass, D. Self-help groups: Grieving parents and community resources. In C. A. Corr & D. M. Corr (Eds.), *Hospice approaches to pediatric care* (pp. 241–260). New York: Springer Publishing, 1985.

Laufer, M. Which adolescents must be helped and by whom? *Journal of Adolescence*, 1980, *3*, 265–272.

Lindemann, E. Symptomatology and management of acute grief. *American Journal of Psychiatry*, 1944, *101*, 141–148.

Maddison, D., & Viola, A. The health of widows in the year following bereavement. *Journal of Psychosomatic Research*, 1968, *12*, 297–306.

McCandless, B. R., & Coop, R. H. *Adolescents: Behavior and development* (2nd ed.). New York: Holt, Rinehart & Winston, 1979.

Miller, J. B. M. Children's reactions to the death of a parent: A review of the psychoanalytic literature. In S. Chess & A. Thomas (Eds.), *Annual Progress in Child Psychiatry and Child Development*, 1972, *5*, 487–506.

Offer, D. *The psychological world of the teen-ager: A study of normal adolescent boys.* New York: Basic Books, 1969.

Parkes, C. M. *Bereavement: Studies of grief in adult life.* New York: International Universities Press, 1972.

Parkes, C. M., & Weiss, R. *Recovery from bereavement.* New York: Basic Books, 1983.

Raphael, B. *The anatomy of bereavement.* New York: Basic Books, 1983.

Rosenblatt, P. C. *Bitter, bitter tears: Nineteenth-century diarists and twentieth-century grief theories.* Minneapolis: University of Minnesota Press, 1983.

Rounsaville, B. J., & Chevron, E. Interpersonal psychotherapy. In A. J. Rush (Ed.), *Short-term psychotherapies for depression: Behavioral, interpersonal, cognitive, and psychodynamic approaches* (pp. 107–142). New York: Guilford, 1982.

Schiff, H. S. *The bereaved parent.* New York: Crown, 1977.

Seligman, R., Gleser, G., Rauh, J., & Harris, L. The effect of earlier parental loss in adolescence. *Archives of General Psychiatry*, 1974, *31*, 475–479.

Stone, L. J., & Church, J. *Childhood and adolescence* (3rd ed.). New York: Random House, 1973.

Sugar, M. Normal adolescent mourning. *American Journal of Psychotherapy*, 1968, *22*, 258–269.

Trowhill, A., & Fleming, S. J. *Parental bereavement: The first ten months.* Paper presented at the Annual Meeting, Canadian Psychological Association, Calgary, Alberta, 1980.

Vachon, M. L. S. Grief and bereavement following the death of a spouse. *Canadian Psychiatric Association Journal*, 1976, *21*, 35–43.

Van Eerdewegh, M., Bieri, M., Parrilla, R., & Clayton, P. The bereaved child. *British Journal of Psychiatry*, 1982, *140*, 23–29.

Weissman, M. M., Prusoff, B. A., Thompson, D., Harding, P. S., & Myers, J. K. Social adjustment by self-report in a community sample and in psychiatric out patients. *Journal of Nervous and Mental Disease*, 1978, *166*, 317–326.

Worden, J. W. *Grief counseling and grief therapy.* New York: Springer Publishing, 1982.

7

Terminating an Adolescent Pregnancy: Choice and Loss

B. Gail Joralemon

Teenage pregnancy and abortion are significant phenomena in the lives of many adolescents in our contemporary society. Whatever one thinks of these phenomena from a legal, moral, or religious point of view, we must realize that they have an important impact upon the lives of adolescents and the people they are close to. Some of the implications may be positive and constructive; others can be negative and dysfunctional. It is the purpose of this chapter to consider the phenomena of adolescent pregnancy and abortion from the perspective of the more or less conscious choices they involve and in terms of the loss and grief they may entail.

Other pregnancy-related experiences of loss and grief occur in the lives of adolescents, but they differ substantially from elective abortion. Most important, of course, is the aspect of choice: an elective abortion involves a *conscious decision* to terminate a pregnancy. Two examples of pregnancy-related losses in which this element of choice is not present are miscarriage and stillbirth, each being a natural phenomenon over which an adolescent has no control. Statistics indicate that adolescents are more likely to suffer these unplanned losses than women in other age groups (Institute of Medicine, 1973; Shapiro, McCormick, Starfield, Krischer, & Bross, 1980). In each of these cases, grief will be the reaction to the nondeliberate termination of an accepted pregnancy and anticipated birth. As such, this grief will be different in character and must be treated in a different manner altogether from the grief associated with elective abortion.

Elective abortions can also be contrasted with cases in which there *is* an element of choice and control. For example, medically necessary therapeutic abortions may also involve a conscious choice. However, such choices are different in kind from the ones that we wish to discuss. That is, the issues surrounding therapeutic abortions are usually more life threatening and immediate for the woman than those faced in choosing an elective abortion. As in cases of miscarriage and stillbirth, it is especially important to remember that therapeutic abortions may terminate very much wanted pregnancies.

Relinquishing a baby for adoption is also a deliberate decision, but one that involves the additional experiences of a full-term pregnancy and childbirth. While the decision-making process and its implications in the case of relinquishment for adoption may be similar to the process leading to elective abortion, the totality of the adoption experience makes it a very different loss. In short, although there may be similarities in the factors that lead to the pregnancy, in the process of making decisions, and in subsequent feelings of isolation and grief, in the end each of these pregnancy-related experiences is different and must be studied and treated accordingly.

Of all the pregnancy-related losses in adolescence, elective abortion is the most common and least often recognized. It is vitally important that this dimension of adolescent life be explored and understood both by adolescents and by those who share their lives. For an adolescent unfamiliar with decision making on a life-affecting scale, the reality of pregnancy and the decision to have an elective abortion can generate a pronounced sense of loss and a grieving for the unknown that may be especially acute. An adolescent's world and world view, how she comes to the decision to have an abortion, and the time frame in which she finds herself will all affect her feelings about her choice to terminate a pregnancy.

The focus of this chapter is on choice and loss in terminating an adolescent pregnancy. The first topics to be considered define the context within which these events take place. They are the factors involved in teenage pregnancy, the role of denial and its consequences, and events leading up to the decision to choose an elective abortion. Abortion and loss, decision making and the loss of childhood innocence, and the need for a broader perspective are examined next. Finally, we will address the question of providing support for postabortion adolescents. One caution should be kept in mind throughout: when dealing with any discussion about abortion, it is important to emphasize that broad generalizations and expectations often do not apply to specific individuals. Each young woman choosing an elective abortion does so from her own, unique situation. There is no single model for the "average" adolescent having an abortion. The following analysis is an introduction to a complex, individualized, and very personal experience of loss and grief in adolescence.

PREGNANCY IN ADOLESCENCE

As the age of puberty declines and sexual activity among adolescents increases, the teen pregnancy rate increases. An estimated 58% of young women in our society have had intercourse by the time they reach the age of 18 (Dryfoos & Bourque-Scholl, 1981). As a result of this there are more than one million teen pregnancies a year in the United States alone (Tietze, 1978), and three-quarters of those are unintended (The Alan Guttmacher Institute, 1981). The majority of pregnant teens (two thirds) carry their pregnancies to term, and more than 96% of those girls keep their babies. Approximately 38% of pregnant adolescents (under age 20) terminate their pregnancies (American Academy of Pediatrics, 1979).

Clearly, adolescent pregnancy is a significant social phenomenon in our society. What are its perceived benefits and realistic consequences?

Perceived Benefits

As Luker (1975) describes in *Taking Chances,* there are many reasons for risking a pregnancy by taking chances on sexual activity without contraception. Adolescents combine those reasons with lack of knowledge, lack of financial resources, and strong peer pressure to be risk takers (Zelnik & Kantner, 1979). Pregnancy, regardless of its outcome, offers a range of perceived benefits (Castleman, 1977). Perhaps the most important is that pregnancy is one of the fastest means of getting attention, negative or positive, from family members. Some change in behavior towards a pregnant adolescent is almost guaranteed: the pregnancy will *focus* attention and *force* a family to deal with her. What clearer way to ask for help, for love, for support? On a relational level, pregnancy will define a sexual or love relationship in terms of commitment. Either a declaration of future intentions will be effected, or an end to the relationship will be forced. The outcome of the attention is less at issue than the attention itself. Other perceived benefits may include: confirmation of the reality of one's fertility, improvement of one's image or sense of self-worth (look what I can do!), resolution of ambiguous sex roles, establishment of a strong focus of energy and ego strength in the midst of personal chaos, and punishment for the family and/or partner.

Our society acknowledges adolescent maternity and copes with it by developing numerous services and programs to handle the problem. The prevalence of these services has removed, to a large extent, the stigma of being an unwed pregnant teenager. We should not be surprised, then, to find that pregnancy and motherhood have become for many young people the new teenage status symbols: proof positive that one can "do it," can be a mother, can father a child. A baby is perceived as being "someone who belongs to me" or "someone who will love me" or "someone whom I can play with." No problems or crises enter into the dream of the perfect baby, the best mother, the little family that will not have the difficulties that, in fact, are known all too well to many adolescents. In addition, the *perceived* financial independence that comes with federal and state aid programs for teenage mothers simply enhances this dream. Why not continue the pregnancy and gain automatic adulthood, independence, love, and affection?

Denial and Its Consequences

For many adolescents whose families' socio-economic status and belief systems reject these unrealistic notions of pregnancy and motherhood, pregnancy is a terrifying experience. When these adolescents are pregnant, the most common reaction is denial: "I *can't* be pregnant" or "But it was only the first time I ever had sex." The probability of a pregnancy may also be rejected as a result of a basic lack of knowledge or understanding of human sexuality and contraception.

The young person's inexperience with crises, real or threatened, may exaggerate the anticipated consequences and contribute to the very real hope that the problem will go away: "I'll just die if I'm pregnant" and "Oh my God, what am I going to do?" Fear of parental reaction to the pregnancy ("My parents will kill me!") is usually masking the real fear: that parents will find out that their daughter has been sexually active.

If an adolescent does not want to be pregnant and cannot face the effects her pregnancy would have on herself and on everyone around her, she may strive to convince herself that she is *not* pregnant ("It's all in my imagination."). In this way, denial may well become the most natural response in these circumstances.

Tragically, denial too often leads to adolescent pregnancies not being confirmed or detected by others until well into the second trimester. Parents who deny their suspicions about a teenage pregnancy can also extend the time between the suspicion and confirmation. We often see adolescents who are four to five months pregnant—but whose parents have "just noticed she was putting on weight" or have only recently be-

come aware that their daughter has been sick or upset. The issues surrounding the next steps to take are then further complicated with additional anxieties, fears, and beliefs concerning abortion at a later stage in
pregnancy.

Pregnancies of very young adolescents as well as those visible pregnancies of older girls which can no longer be denied will most often involve parental support and/or intervention. Younger girls are more
likely to seek the help and financial support of parents or other adults in
order to obtain an abortion. Those whose later pregnancies will require
more complicated arrangements and considerably more money will usually involve an adult. However, more mature teens and those who are
approaching a second abortion are more likely *not* to involve their families in any way. The abortion becomes an example of what they can do
for themselves in terms of decision making, taking responsibility for
their decisions, and acting on their choice without adult help.

ADOLESCENTS AND ABORTION

The hard data that we have on adolescent abortions involve the incidence, age, length of pregnancy, and particular problems adolescents
present for medical care. Approximately 434,000 adolescents have abortions every year in the United States (The Alan Guttmacher Institute,
1981; Cates, 1980). Young women in the 18 to 19 age group have both
the highest pregnancy rate and the largest number of abortions of all
pregnant adolescents. Girls age 17 and under (approximately 13% of the
pregnant adolescent population) obtain about 146,000 abortions a year
(Center for Disease Control, 1980). Of this population, girls younger
than 15 have the highest rate of pregnancy termination: over half of their
pregnancies end in an abortion compared to 40% of the pregnancies in
the 15 to 19 age group (Hatcher, Stewart, Stewart, Guest, Schwartz, &
Jones, 1980).

Adolescents present particular concerns for the provision of quality
medical care during and after their abortions. As the pregnancy prog-
resses, the risks to the pregnant adolescent increase. Unfortunately,
there is a disproportionate number of second trimester abortions among
adolescents; nearly one-half of all abortions after 12 weeks gestation are
obtained by teenagers (Cates & Tietze, 1978). Ignorance of the early
signs of pregnancy, denial, lack of access to abortion services and financial resources, and difficulty in making the decision to have an abortion
all contribute to this phenomenon (Bracken & Kasl, 1975; Bracken, Klerman, & Bracken, 1978). Should any problems arise after the abortion, an

adolescent trying to maintain secrecy is more likely to ignore symptoms and to fail to seek the medical attention she may need. This concern often leads providers of abortion services to require parental involvement.

Decision Making and Abortion

Most of the adolescents seen at the Abortion and Pregnancy Testing Clinic in Albuquerque indicate that their first reaction to the confirmation of their pregnancy included shock, depression, sadness, and worry. Many of them tell us that there were problems with their families when they became pregnant. If their boyfriends know that they are pregnant, either they are not seeing each other any longer or they have grown closer because of the pregnancy. (Note the clarification of relationships and the self-focus that these responses demonstrate.)

Sadness and worry also affect the feelings of these adolescents about abortion. The response they have to the question "How do you feel about abortion in your case?" is most likely to be that they would like to have a family some day, but not now. They will often respond that they feel sad, but that they must have the abortion. These adolescents report that they feel elective abortion is wrong but not as bad as having an unwanted child. Many indicate they believe it is morally wrong but necessary to have an abortion in their circumstances.

In a special consent form for minors having an abortion, these minors frequently state, in their own words, their reasons for needing an abortion: they are not ready to deal with the responsibility of having a child; they are too young to have a baby; and/or they have no money to take care of a baby. However, adolescents worry that other people will think they are "bad" if they should find out about the abortion. They also worry about how they themselves will feel emotionally after the abortion. Many suspect that they will feel depressed, relieved, guilty, and sad afterwards. Most are not sure how they will deal with those feelings. These concerns can often outweigh the certainty of their reasons for choosing an abortion.

After Abortion

Abortion is not the kind of experience that is openly discussed by women of any age. There continues to be a shroud of silence that surrounds the termination of a pregnancy; this implies that, although elective abortion is legal and probably socially permissible, it is not a "nice" thing to do. Or worse, the very fact of having had an abortion *may* be seen as an indictment of the individual, that is, as a morally reprehensible act that will forever brand that person as a sinner. If we were able, somehow, to detect all of those who had ever been involved in an abortion, the number and variety of those people would be astounding! That revelation would put an end to the secrecy, the silence, and the moral condemnation. Unfortunately, for the most part, our society maintains a communal silence in this area.

Feelings that surround the decision to terminate a pregnancy and feelings after the abortion are therefore kept hidden out of necessity. If the abortion has been kept secret from parents, family, partner, peers, and others who might have been helpful, the isolation is nearly complete. Any or all of the following feelings may be experienced after an abortion: sadness, dismay, regret, relief, guilt. Adolescents need to express such feelings and to be reassured that they are not alone in having them. Abortion clinics offer postabortion counseling for exactly this reason.

Whether or not adolescents have the support of family or friends, they are usually expected to leave the experience behind them immediately and to "get on with" their lives. Under the circumstances, this is definitely *not* a realistic or a healthful expectation.

ABORTION AND LOSS

Adolescents who terminate a pregnancy are "giving something up." Typically, they have no realistic understanding of what it would have meant in their lives to have continued the pregnancy. They have no way of knowing whether or not they could have carried the pregnancy to term. All the questions about keeping the baby or relinquishing for adoption will never be answered for *this* pregnancy. And any discoveries about motherhood in their present life situation will remain unknown. At a time when they are developmentally immature, these adolescents have had to make a life-affecting decision under the influence of hormonal changes. It is a vulnerable time for them, and they need support and understanding.

Adolescents may romanticize the perceived benefits of pregnancy and motherhood. But these young women have denied themselves the *experience* that might have de-mythologized the condition and status. The deliberate termination of pregnancy may magnify their sense of loss. The "what-ifs" and "if onlys" can gnaw away at them, and feed the grieving for the unknown. With little or no experience of assessing decision making, adolescents can often become stuck in the regret and sadness of a loss not fully understood. In their experience, no vocabulary exists for verbalizing these feelings.

Adolescent male partners may also experience this regret and loss, especially if they are still emotionally attached to their girlfriends. They may have invested in the dreamy, romantic picture of pregnancy and parenthood, and may feel an exaggerated loss. Or they may have honestly wanted the pregnancy to continue and may have made realistic plans to become part of a new family and to care for their partner and child. The main difference for these boys is that *they* did not decide what would happen. In addition to grieving for the unknown, and perhaps the hoped-for, male adolescents may feel a loss of control and an acute helplessness about the whole situation. They also need support and understanding to help them assimilate the experience and come to terms with the loss.

The adolescent's sense of loss, sadness, regret, and/or remorse after an abortion may have more than one root cause. Lack of decision-making experience may magnify the situation. An exaggerated feeling of loss may be caused by having actively *chosen* that loss rather than being the passive victim of fate. This is a decision of considerable finality: once an abortion is over, that unique pregnancy will never occur again. Without gaining the experience that might deflate unrealistic views of pregnancy and parenthood, dreams and expectations have no closure. If adolescents have little or no ability to consider the "road not taken," the vocabulary for expressing the loss of the unknown is nonexistent. And, of course, for female adolescents, hormonal changes during and after the pregnancy may affect their overall emotional state.

Remorse and regret about the abortion may be directly associated with having been pregnant in the first place. It is not easy to have to deal with a pregnancy or to choose its outcome. In a very real sense, adolescents experience a loss of innocence in this process. They can no longer be "children" for whom decisions are made and difficulties are eased. In this sense, adolescents may be grieving for their own lost childhood.

MAKING DECISIONS AND TAKING RESPONSIBILITY

Most adolescents have little experience making major life-affecting decisions. By their very nature, decisions imply active involvement. When adolescents make a decision for themselves, they have to take responsibility for that decision. Learning how to make major decisions and how to act on them removes adolescents from the world of childhood where everything is taken care of by adults. If this is the adolescent's first major decision-making experience, it could easily magnify the feelings surrounding the abortion. By contrast, this experience can also serve as a positive example of how a major decision is made: how to weigh various factors, deliberate, assess the consequences of each decision, etc. Having made an important decision and having carried it out, the adolescent now has the experience with which to face the next decision.

It is often difficult for adolescents to put an abortion into a wider perspective. That this *particular* pregnancy will occur only once and that the decision to terminate it is *very* final are problematic concepts if one's perspective is totally present-oriented. Many possible pregnancies may occur in the future, and different circumstances may make them welcome. But *this* pregnancy will once and for all be prevented from taking its course. Adolescents need help to gain perspective in their lives, and the experience of facing a decision about abortion requires such perspective if it is to be part of a process of growing and maturing.

Postabortion feelings may also be influenced by not having enough experience in life to see "the road not taken" in any perspective. Each life-affecting decision will involve a decision that was not chosen. Choosing an abortion may be the first of these, but it will certainly not be the last. One may never know what a different decision *might* have brought into one's life. The same regret might be felt if the pregnancy *had* been continued: What would have been different if an abortion had been chosen?

Without the experience of continuing a pregnancy and being a parent, unrealistic ideas are difficult to dispel. It may help to spend time with some teenage parents, to read about how *they* feel concerning the reality of pregnancy in adolescence, and to consider statistics about the effect of adolescent pregnancy upon a whole lifetime. This pregnancy is over, and it will never result in a baby being born. And that *is* a loss. Dreams and romanticized fantasies have emotional investment, too, and are not easy to relinquish. The distinction, however, needs to be made between dreams and reality.

POSTABORTION SUPPORT

Suggestions for Non-Professionals

Parents, siblings, friends, and male partners may have been involved throughout the process of deciding to terminate a pregnancy. Or they may only be informed after the fact. In either case, there are several things to keep in mind that may help them be supportive of adolescent girls after an abortion.

It is important to remember that feelings of loss, regret, grief, relief, and guilt are perfectly normal reactions to an abortion. One or more of these feelings may be related to issues and experiences prior to the abortion. They may also be caused or magnified by the rapidly changing hormonal level during and after pregnancy. It is important to *listen* to an adolescent talk about her feelings and experiences, to allow her to share all of that rather than keep it inside. This is a time in their lives when adolescents are particularly vulnerable to withheld attention, judgmental pronouncements, or any indication that they are not "normal." They need to be assured that they are loved and cared for, even if others do not necessarily agree with their decision.

It may be helpful to put the decision-making process itself into perspective. Others might share decisions they have made as well as questions or regrets they have about the choices they did not make. Reassure the adolescent that it is only possible to make a decision based on the circumstances and resources available at a particular time. Having had the experience of making a major decision, at least the person has now acquired or practiced some of the skills that will be very helpful to her for the rest of her life. Keep in mind, however, that she may be feeling more like reverting to childhood dependency than being pushed further into adult responsibilities. Give her as much love and understanding as you can.

Parents may be dealing with their own feelings about daughters growing up and being sexually active. Those feelings need to be dealt with too, but not in association with their daughter's experience. Once the fact of their child's sexual maturity has been accepted, perhaps sexual values can be discussed. It is unrealistic to assume that having an abortion will turn all adolescent girls away from sex forever; it is not unrealistic to use the experience to promote responsible contraception or to help adolescents avoid facing the same situation again.

Male partners may also be trying to come to terms with their feelings about the abortion. This may be a good time for them to talk with their girlfriends about the relationship, about sexual intimacy, and about the future. In all probability, most adolescent girls will want to refrain from sexual intimacy for a while, but they may still need and want some physical contact. This may be an ideal time to develop other aspects of the relationship and to evaluate the impact that the abortion has had on it.

Guidelines for Professionals

In dealing with adolescents and abortion, it is often helpful for the professional to determine what the grieving is about: loss of a relationship, loss of innocence, loss of the unknown, a hormonal exaggeration of a crisis experience, a change in family relationships, or something else altogether. Therapeutic intervention based on the counselor's mistaken assumptions about the reasons behind the young person's grief often can do more harm than good (Beresford, 1977). Moreover, an adolescent who is not feeling the way a counselor expects her to feel might assume that she *ought* to be feeling that way and thus compound her distress. It is wise never to prejudge an adolescent's reactions to this particular experience—she is likely to surprise you.

If one begins by discussing feelings surrounding pregnancy, it may be possible to identify the specific focus of a particular adolescent's grief (Baker, 1981). As many of us have discovered, pregnancy often has no logical connection to eventual childbirth and parenthood in the minds of pregnant adolescents. Other concerns may dominate their reactions. For example, it may be that an adolescent had believed that she would receive increased love and attention for her pregnancy. When she does not experience these desired benefits and after she has gone through an abortion to escape the unwanted consequences of being pregnant, her feelings of shame and grief can intensify.

The decision-making process is often involved in grief feelings after an abortion. In determining how the decision was reached and who was involved, it is necessary to identify any coercion or pressure exerted by other people. Rather than contributing to the skills of decision making, a coercive force may have caused an adolescent to feel she still was being treated as a child who would never be allowed to grow up. Alternatively, she may be grieving for her loss of childhood innocence if she made the decision on her own, especially if she has carried out her decision by herself. An adolescent who manages the fee, scheduling, transportation, and cover-up involved in obtaining an abortion in secret has truly had to grow up in a hurry.

Not knowing what a continuing pregnancy would have meant in their lives, adolescents often have ambivalent feelings about an abortion. It is difficult for mature adults to assess what might have been, and this can be nearly impossible for adolescents. Exploring their images of a continuing pregnancy, childbirth, and parenthood will help to determine whether or not feelings of loss are directed toward the unknown. Separating the known risks of adolescent pregnancy and parenthood from fantasies about them may be the most useful approach. Distinguishing between this terminated pregnancy and future pregnancies may help to lessen the loss. It may also be useful to acknowledge the physiological effects of hormonal changes on emotions, as well as the impact of the premature end to a natural process.

Adolescents may feel that they must give up love and intimacy for fear that those experiences will again result in an unwanted pregnancy. Vowing never to have sex again or never to be involved with a boyfriend again is not an uncommon response from adolescents. Fears of the potential loss of intimacy may be eased with education about contraception and about assertiveness in personal relationships. The abortion experience can then be a basis for learning about responsibility to oneself in a relationship.

Finally, the experience of the abortion itself may need to be talked out and put into perspective. What was difficult about it? What was helpful? How did you feel about the doctor, the other staff, the other patients, and the office or clinic itself? Did this experience make you feel better or worse than you felt before you went there? Did you find out anything new about yourself? It is unlikely that adolescents will have many opportunities to discuss this experience, but important that they not have to keep it to themselves. When an abortion can be perceived as a unique and very profound experience that is worth discussing, the process of exploration may unleash many other hidden feelings as well. The key is *not* to isolate the experience as something dreadful that must be forgotten as soon as possible.

CONCLUSION

In order to help an adolescent cope with preabortion and postabortion feelings of loss and grief, it is important to understand the many complex aspects of teenage pregnancy. Emotional factors contributing to risk taking in sexual activity without contraception are crucial to an adequate appreciation of the concerns about the decision-making process involved in abortion. Adolescents may need help in putting all of this information together in order to gain the perspective they need to assimilate the experience. It is often the difficult "peripheral" issues, feelings, and experiences that cause the grief symptoms rather than the terminated pregnancy itself. Or it may be a complicated combination of factors.

Whatever the cause or causes of grief following an abortion, the entire experience needs to be examined and assessed thoughtfully. And adolescents deserve to have their feelings acknowledged in understanding and therapeutic ways, so that their emotional development is enhanced and strengthened.

REFERENCES

The Alan Guttmacher Institute. *Teenage pregnancy: The problem that hasn't gone away.* New York: The Alan Guttmacher Institute, 1981.

American Academy of Pediatrics, Committee on Adolescence. Pregnancy and abortion counseling. *Pediatrics*, 1979, *63*, 920–921.

Baker, A. *Training manual for problem pregnancy counseling.* Granite City, IL: The Hope Clinic for Women, 1981.

Beresford, T. *Short term relationship counseling: A self instructional manual for use in family planning clinics.* Baltimore, MD: Planned Parenthood of Maryland, 1977.

Bracken, M. B., & Kasl, S. V. Delay in seeking induced abortion: A review and theoretical analysis. *American Journal of Obstetrics and Gynecology,* 1975, *121,* 1008–1019.

Bracken, M. B., Klerman, L. V., & Bracken, M. Abortion, adoption or motherhood: An empirical study of decision-making during pregnancy. *American Journal of Obstetrics and Gynecology,* 1978, *130,* 251–262.

Castleman, M. HEW and the "sexual revolution": Why teenagers get pregnant. *The Nation,* 1977, *225,* 549–552.

Cates, W., Jr. Adolescent abortions in the U.S.. *Journal of Adolescent Health Care,* 1980, *1,* 18–25.

Cates, W., Jr., & Tietze, C. Standardized mortality rates associated with legal abortion: United States, 1972–1975. *Family Planning Perspectives,* 1978, *10,* 109–112.

Center for Disease Control. *Abortion surveillance report.* Atlanta, GA: Author, November 1980.

Dryfoos, J., & Bourque-Scholl, N. *Factbook on teenage pregnancy.* New York: The Alan Guttmacher Institute, 1981.

Hatcher, R. A., Stewart, G. K., Stewart, F., Guest, F., Schwartz, D. W., & Jones, S. A. *Contraceptive technology 1980–1981* (10th revised ed.) (pp. 174–201). New York: Irvington, 1980.

Institute of Medicine. *Infant death: An analysis by maternal risk and health care.* Washington, DC: National Academy of Sciences, 1973.

Luker, K. *Taking chances: Abortion and the decision not to contracept.* Berkeley, CA: University of California Press, 1975.

Shapiro, S., McCormick, M. C., Starfield, B. H., Krischer, J. P., Bross, D. Relevance of correlates of infant deaths for significant morbidity at one year of age. *American Journal of Obstetrics and Gynecology,* 1980, *136,* 363–373.

Tietze, C. Teenage pregnancies: Looking ahead to 1984. *Family Planning Perspectives,* 1978, *10,* 205–210.

Zelnik, M., & Kantner, J. F. Reasons for nonuse of contraception by sexually active women aged 15–19. *Family Planning Perspectives,* 1979, *11,* 289–296.

8

Helping Bereaved Adolescent Parents

Carol Ann Barnickol, Helen Fuller,
and Beth Shinners

Oh you, core of your father's being,
*Light of joy, extinguished too soon!**

Among the many other death-related experiences that they may encounter, adolescents may themselves become bereaved parents. This subject has received extraordinarily little attention in the professional literature or from society in general. More importantly, even when the fact is acknowledged that adolescents can become bereaved parents, its implications have rarely been explored. We note Ruckert's sensitivity to the depth of loss experienced by a bereaved parent, and we suggest that this loss is as significant in the case of an adolescent as in the case of an adult, if not more so. In this chapter, we identify common misconceptions of parental bereavement in adolescence, describe aspects of grief that are common to both adolescent and older bereaved parents, explore factors unique to the adolescent experience, and offer suggestions for those in a position to help bereaved adolescent parents.

PREVIOUS LITERATURE

While bereavement is a subject of major interest in the professional and scholarly literature, the scarcity of materials that are directly related to bereaved adolescent parents constitutes a stark reminder of the inatten-

*From J. H. Kennell, H. Slyter, & M. H. Klaus, "The mourning response of parents to the death of a newborn infant." In *New England Journal of Medicine*, 1970, *283*, 344. Used by permission.

tion to and perhaps minimization of the experience of adolescents who become bereaved parents. The theoretical models in the literature, from the psychoanalytic (A. Freud, 1958; S. Freud, 1957; E. Furman, 1974; R. Furman, 1973) to attachment (Bowlby, 1977, 1980) and crisis theories (Caplan, 1974), address the adolescent's presumed capacity (or lack of capacity) to mourn, and indeed to form parental attachments or bonds. Perhaps because of this, little effort has been made to relate general assumptions to the actual lives of adolescents. Comparative studies of parental grief exist, but only as a reflection of adult grief patterns (Clayton, Desmarais, & Winokure, 1968; Sanders, 1979). Thus, the literature does address the reactions of adult parents to such experiences as the loss of their infants to neonatal death (Borg & Lasker, 1981; Klaus & Kennell, 1982; Peppers & Knapp, 1980) or to Sudden Infant Death Syndrome (Hagan, 1974; Mandell, McAnulty, & Reece, 1980; *Pediatric Annals*, 1984; Smialek, 1978).

To give but one prominent example, in Yaeger's study (1979), 39% of the mothers interviewed were between the ages of 13 and 19. Adaptive and non-adaptive patterns of mourning were identified based on earlier indicators used by Parkes & Brown (1972). Yaeger's study defined 80% of her sample as demonstrating "adaptive" patterns and 20% as showing "maladaptive" reactions. There was no difference in the patterns by age of the mother. However, the Yaeger study, as well as other parental grief research, does not really pursue the variable of adolescence in order to ascertain patterns unique to mothers in this age group. Teenaged fathers receive even less attention.

A thorough search of existing literature produced only one article (Schodt, 1982) that deals exclusively with the issue of bereavement in adolescent mothers. Schodt presents a review of theories and research on mourning and parental grief as a basis for discussing grief in adolescence. She finds incomplete, conflicting theories and many areas of ignorance. Her conclusion calls for studies on the processes of attachment between adolescent parents and their children. In addition, Schodt recognizes the need for studies to aid in understanding the developmental effect of infants' deaths on their teenaged parents. Additional studies are also called for on the effect of early intervention on patient outcomes and on comparison of grief in younger and older parents.

We concur with Schodt's recommendations and conclusions. We have not attempted here to replicate her thorough discussion of theoretical frameworks and research analyses. Rather, our intention is to analyze the bereavement of adolescent parents on the basis of our clinical experience in dealing with losses due to neonatal deaths and to Sudden Infant Death Syndrome (SIDS). Before going further, it may be helpful to note why we believe these two forms of death are particularly relevant to the

experience of adolescents and to say a bit about the prevalence and nature of each.

NEONATAL DEATH AND
SUDDEN INFANT DEATH SYNDROME

Children may die in many ways. However, the range of possibilities is
perhaps a bit narrower for adolescent parents than it is for parents in
general. In practice, adolescents who conceive new life, carry a pregnancy to term, and then become bereaved parents usually experience
the death of an infant at or shortly after birth. Even here, there can be
many possible forms of death. But the two most prominent and most
likely are neonatal death and Sudden Infant Death Syndrome.

The term "neonatal death" refers to all deaths of infants who are newborn, extending from "perinatal deaths" or those associated with the
birthing process to those occuring during the first 4 weeks of life or before the time at which the newborn has been integrated into his or her
family. In the United States in 1981 (the latest year for which statistics
were available at the writing of this chapter), there were just over 26,800
neonatal deaths out of a total of 3.64 million live births (Wegman, 1983).
Frequently, these occur in the neonatal intensive care unit (NICU) of a
tertiary care institution to which the baby has been transferred for intervention by a multidisciplinary team of specialists in this field (Shinners
& Cape, 1984). As might be expected, even though mortality rates are
decreasing, they remain high in most NICUs, currently amounting to
from 15% to 20% of admissions. In our own case—a newly expanded
52-bed NICU located in a private pediatric hospital that is affiliated with
a major teaching institution—this has meant some 630 neonatal deaths
during the period from August 1977 to November 1981, or roughly one
in every four admissions (Perlman, 1984). More recently, we can expect
some 90 to 120 neonatal deaths per year from among an annual admission rate of approximately 600. Of these deaths, statistics for the period
from 1981 to 1983 show that 12% to 15% occurred to adolescent mothers
(between the ages of 12 and 19) (Perlman, 1984). The death of an infant
under these circumstances is an extremely stressful event for all concerned.

Sudden Infant Death Syndrome is the single leading cause of death in
infancy past the initial 2 weeks of life (*Pediatric Annals*, 1984). Some 7,000
babies die each year in the United States from SIDS. In most of these
cases, infants between 2 weeks and 1 year of life die suddenly and unexpectedly, usually during a period of sleep. Although research efforts

continue, there is to date no known way to predict which babies will die of SIDS or in fact to prevent their deaths even if prediction was possible. Parents, surviving siblings, extended family, and friends need consistent and accurate medical information about SIDS. They also need support from sensitive, experienced professionals in order to deal with the feelings of loss, grief, guilt, and blame that surface with such a death.

While maternal age alone does not appear to be the critical variable in increasing the likelihood of a problematic outcome for teenage childbearing, this factor in combination with socio-economic circumstances and other variables is obviously significant (McAnarney, Lawrence, Aten, & Iker, 1984; Rogel & Petersen, 1984). Consequently, it is not surprising that adolescent parents are well represented in the general population of bereaved parents. Inner-city black families, a population with a high percentage of births to adolescent parents, are also at higher risk for both neonatal death and SIDS. As noted in a recent report (Meriwether, 1984):

> The nation has been alarmed by the fact that white youth, including middle-class youngsters, account for a massive increase in teenage sex, especially among 15- to 17-year-olds, whose sexual activity doubled over a ten-year period. Another surprise is that the birthrate for unwed white teenagers rose more than 45 percent, while for Black teens it fell 3.5 percent. But although Black teenage pregnancy has declined, it is still disproportionately high. More than one out of every four Black babies born is to a teenage mother, compared with one out of every seven born to white teens. Also, 57 percent of all babies born to teenagers under 15 are Black. Every year, from among all unwed Black 15- to 17-year-olds, one out of 14 has a baby. (p. 96)

Most of these adolescent mothers are also single, with teenage marriage rates continuing to drop. Of all babies born to white teenagers some 29% are born outside of marriage, while the corresponding figure is 83% for black teenagers. An important factor in this appears to be chronic discrimination that accounts in part for the high unemployment rate of black men and youth, and their subsequent inability to support a family.

Teenage pregnancy is a concern of major standing since a disproportionate number of these adolescents lack the necessary resources to ensure the delivery of normal, healthy infants. They often do not obtain prenatal care, and black teenagers in particular have the highest rates of toxemia and miscarriage. Adolescents also give birth to more premature and underweight babies, which are major predisposing circumstances for infant mortality and other damaging effects if the infants survive. In any event, the untimeliness of parental bereavement in adolescence, the swiftness that usually characterizes the death, the legitimate involvement or unfounded suspicion of hereditary or other guilt-provoking factors, the relative inexperience of adolescent parents in dealing with grief and life-threatening crises, and complications from extended families and/or ill-defined role relationships all contribute to making a difficult situation all the more problematic.

PARENTAL BEREAVEMENT IN ADOLESCENCE

Many people have difficulty in focusing on adolescents as parents, let alone as parents whose children have died. There are two taboos, sex and death, still widely held in our society, and an adolescent mother whose infant has died has defied both of them. It is no wonder then that society has been unwilling to address this issue and tends to do one of three things when confronted with it:

1. minimizes the meaning of the death of the infant, for example, remarks that the baby was only here a short time and "you can have another one";
2. minimizes what the loss of that baby meant to its parents, for example, "now you can go back to being a teenager again"; or
3. acts on stereotypes that inhibit the provision of necessary support needed by the parents in coping with their baby's death.

For all of us the question becomes: How can we maintain and impart our value system without ostracizing individuals such as bereaved adolescent parents? We need to realize that the significance of a child who has died is as valid and as varied for each adolescent parent as for any adult parent.

In particular, medical and counseling professionals must examine and understand the bereavement experience in adolescent parents in order to set aside stereotypes and minimization. As professionals, we can only provide the necessary help and support if we recognize both the universal and the unique aspects and implications of this sort of loss, whether the death of the child be from a neonatal death, SIDS, or another cause.

The population upon which our experience is based is comprised of parents aged 12 to 19, black and white, and both urban and suburban in residence. It is our hope that the following observations will prompt further research and investigation on this important subject.

FAMILIAR MYTHS:
STEREOTYPES AND MISCONCEPTIONS

When confronted with a death, we all have a tendency to slip into comfortable old clichés, stereotypes, and rationalizations so that we can diminish the reality of the event for ourselves and for others. Rarely does anyone intend to hurt or add to the pain already felt by a bereaved parent (be assured, there are a few exceptions to that rule). Death makes us uncomfortable, and we seem to expect to have the appropriate thing to say, at least to diminish our own discomfort if not that of the bereaved.

Some stereotypic attitudes regarding adolescents as bereaved parents were dealt with in the preceding section. In order to bring out the recurring themes in our professional experience, it may be helpful to report the following statements that we have witnessed being made to or about bereaved adolescent parents by health professionals, "experts" in the field of bereavement, counselors, friends, and relatives:

Now they can go back to being teenagers, finish school, and have some fun again.

The baby would have been a burden when he or she got older.

The baby is better off "with God," because the parents were too young, too poor, etc.

A baby is just another "possession" to an adolescent. They move through the experience of death very quickly because they are too immature to have the same depth of feeling for the baby as an adult parent.

The baby died because the mother was too young to know how to care for it properly.

It was a blessing in disguise.

The relationship between the parents simply wouldn't have lasted anyway.

There is no denying the difficulties faced by adolescents who have become parents when they are not yet ready to cope with an adult world. It is safe to say, however, that most adolescent parents do not share the sentiments that are reflected in these frequently quoted stereotypes. If we are to help young people grow and learn from the momentous experience of parental bereavement, painful as it must be, it is essential that we be aware of our biases and carefully put them into proper perspective. It is one thing to appreciate the realities of life faced by teenaged parents, but quite another to pass judgment on the feelings of those parents on the basis of a superficial understanding of their situation. We have learned in working with young parents who have lost babies to neonatal death or to SIDS that stereotypes do not apply to individual human beings.

COMMONALITIES IN GRIEVING: ADOLESCENT AND OLDER BEREAVED PARENTS

The commonalities of the grief experience for bereaved parents, whether they be adolescents or adults, should be examined as a preface to further discussion of the uniqueness of the adolescent experience. A person's way of coping with the death of someone close to them is governed by the ways they have found to deal with past losses and the meaning that the deceased had for them, as well as by the stability or instability of their life situation. The amount of available support and the extent to which an individual is able to utilize that support affect the eventual resolution and acceptance (or permanent scarring) that may occur.

A parent whose baby dies has to struggle with varying degrees of self-blame as well as with a "search" for something concrete that might have altered the inevitability of their child's death. When the death occurs in a neonatal intensive care nursery, the parents need help from sensitive health professionals to understand and cope with the cause of their baby's death. If the infant has died of SIDS, the family needs good information and support to understand that research thus far has not proven SIDS to be either predictable or preventable.

Bereaved parents of any age most certainly feel anger: at relatives, at God, at medical professionals, at themselves. Permission to examine and express that anger can have a "freeing effect." The alternative to an appropriate outlet for parental anger may be an escalation of self-blame.

The parental grief experience has an effect on family and marital relationships. No one moves through grief in the same way or in the same time frame as anyone else. Family members and/or marital partners particularly need to support each other while at the same time feeling isolated in their grief. This holds true for their day-to-day living as well as for the long-term resolution and acceptance of their child's death.

There is no time limit on how long grief or its effects will last. The literature reports that life does not again resume a reorganized pattern for many bereaved parents for at least a year's time, and it may well take longer (Corr, Martinson, & Dyer, 1985; Miles, 1984; Raphael, 1983). Our experience validates this pattern of integration in a family's life. Even though one does not wholly abandon the past, life as it is after the infant's death never regains exactly the same pattern as before. Too often we mistakenly seek to return to comfortable patterns of daily living. But there is no getting back to secure and familiar routines when a major life event has taken place. Each individual and family will have to find a new "status quo." As Cantor (1978) says:

> The emotional pain caused by loss suffered does not move toward forgetfulness. It moves, rather, in the direction of enriched remembrance; the memory becomes an integral part of the mourner's personality. The work of mourning has been completed when the person (or cherished thing) no longer appears as an absence in a barren world but has come to reside securely within one's heart. Each of us must grieve in his own manner and at his own pace. . . . The mourning process must be given the freedom to find its own depth and rhythm; it cannot be artificially accelerated. . . . When mourning has been completed, the mourner comes to feel the inner presence of the loved one, no longer an idealized hero or a maligned villain, but a presence with human dimensions. Lost irreversibly in objective time, the person is present in a new form within one's mind and heart, tenderly present in inner time without the pain and bitterness of death. And once the loved one has been accepted in this way he can never again be forcefully removed. (pp. 66–67)

Incorporated into the new status quo will be the decision about future children. Medical consultation for those experiencing the death of a child during adolescence can aid in this decision-making process. For the married couple or single parent there will be no clear-cut or easy choice. The majority of parents appreciate that there can be no replacement for the dead infant. There is, however, a terrible void left by the baby's death that often desperately needs to be filled. Depending upon the meaning the baby had for the parents, there is often a repeat pregnancy in both adolescent and older age groups. The meaning seems to be more significant than parental age in determining the occurrence and the timing of the subsequent pregnancy.

Frequently, parents need to be reassured that the many psychosomatic problems they are likely to experience are typical of profound grief. Reinforcement as to the appropriateness of their feelings and behavior is important. Parents need reassurance also about the labile state of their emotions. During the months after the death, some events will trigger a "down time." Some of these can be anticipated, for example, holidays and anniversary dates, but there will be other unexpected triggering events for which there can be no preparation.

Another typical manifestation among bereaved parents is their obsession with death and the fear that they or someone else close to them will die. This feeling of vulnerability and lack of ability to control their own lives can be particularly disturbing as it relates to surviving children.

FACTORS UNIQUE TO ADOLESCENT BEREAVED PARENTS

Our experience is that grieving parents of any age share the preceding factors in differing degrees. In order to put an adolescent parent's bereavement into its own meaningful perspective, it is necessary to consider the factors inherent in adolescence itself that make the adolescent experience unique. Adolescence is a time of idealism and self-centeredness, yet it is this very focus on the self that may enhance the grief when the relationship is broken. As Caine (1974) stated in *Widow*: "Since every death diminishes us a little, we grieve—not so much for the death as for ourselves" (p. 67). Moreover, as Jackson (1984) has observed: "Adolescents are apt to think that they are the discoverers of deep and powerful feelings and that no one has ever loved as they love. As love is the other side of the coin of grief, they are highly vulnerable" (p. 42). Emotional injury at this point in development may last a lifetime unless there is skillful intervention, since self-destructive behavior such as drug usage, alcohol abuse, and acting out is quite common as a mode of resolving grief among teenagers.

In most cases, adolescents have not previously experienced the death of someone close to them. Thus, an adolescent may need special reassurance that a tragic experience *has* happened to them (as it has in most cases) and that the depth of their feelings is not "crazy." To this purpose, there is a strong need for education regarding grief and the mourning process.

Adolescents also may exhibit a stronger aversion than older persons to death and to viewing or touching the dead child. For example, adolescent parents frequently are unable to hold their dead infant in the emergency room or the NICU in order to say their good-byes. We should not assume that this reaction is due to their inability to form an attachment to the baby. It would seem to be due, rather, to limited experience with the death of a loved one. Likewise, their peer support group is unlikely to have previous experience with supporting a grieving friend. For all concerned, this can present the first real, direct provocation to sort out questions of life, death, and fairness (or lack of fairness). An adolescent parent's range and depth of feelings may run anywhere from intense emotionality to rigid stoicism or denial, as may those of adults. However, the time frame often seems to move along at a more rapid, though still intense, pace for adolescents.

Another factor that must be recognized as a part of most adolescent parent situations is that of confused, often fluid, role definitions. Married or unmarried teenage parents may live in the homes of their own parents or those of other family members. Even if they live independently, the infant's grandparents are likely to be involved in major decision making and/or primary caretaking roles. In cases in which there are adolescent parents of a child that has died, grandparents often decide medical questions or make funeral and burial arrangements. The adolescent's parental role may thus be obscured, and caregivers may find themselves trapped into dealing mainly with one or more grandparents, instead of with the parents themselves. There can be no doubt that grandparents also need support, but counselors who initially deal only with a grandparent often find their later access to the adolescent parent limited at best.

Nevertheless, it would be a mistake to conclude in all situations in which the grandparents are "in charge," so to speak, that control was not willingly given over to them by the young parent. There have also been situations in which grandparents and other family members have lovingly supported the adolescent in being "the parent" both during the life and upon the death of the baby. The counselor's recognition of *the adolescent as the parent* is often the necessary first step to any meaningful supportive relationship. Beyond that initial presumption, each family situation must be evaluated according to its own dynamics.

The adolescent mother's way of coping with the baby's death is frequently influenced by her perception of herself as the baby's primary caretaker. A teenage mother may have made the decision to carry this child to term and may have cared for the baby herself (or planned to be the primary caretaker in the case of neonatal loss). Alternatively, a mother may have carried the child to term and delivered it not because of her own desire but because of her parents' wish or that of the baby's father. In either case, she already may have strongly identified with her role as a mother and will be affected by the death in this role. When her child dies, the young mother must readjust suddenly to the role of being the mother of a child who is no longer living. For this reason, it may be very difficult for her then to identify with and rejoin peers who have not yet had the same depth of life experience.

As we have noted above, many adolescent mothers and fathers are single parents. In most cases, the baby's meaning for the father is difficult, if not impossible, to ascertain. All that can be assumed is that meanings will be as varied for single, adolescent fathers as for their adult counterparts. The father's continued involvement or lack of involvement with the baby and its mother will often determine whether any counseling contact with him is feasible. Nevertheless, in any child's death, both mother and father are entitled, at the very least, to medical information regarding the cause of their baby's death. Fathers often experience denial of grief more intensely and for longer periods than mothers, which may give others (and themselves) the impression that they are not experiencing any effects from the loss of the baby. We have found, however, that they are usually just "behind time" in their grieving. Thus, it is important that both mothers and fathers are offered the opportunity for information and support if at all possible.

The adolescent parent, whether single or married, will also have to deal with issues of his or her own sexuality and needs for intimacy during bereavement. Needs for touching, for holding, or for a continuing emotional relationship are not necessarily obliterated by the bereavement experience and may continue even in the absence of plans for marriage. This may be a particularly sensitive point for grandparents to appreciate.

In situations in which the baby survived the neonatal period but died of SIDS or some other cause, the child may have been placed in a foster-care or adoptive home. For the parents, this may or may not add additional guilt feelings to their grief. It certainly means that another entire family will be deeply affected by the baby's death. We mention this because the grief of foster parents, adoptive families, and babysitters is too often minimized.

Other family members will also have to cope with the death, particularly when an infant has been part of or was planned to be part of an extended family living situation. In the case of a neonatal death, the extended family as well as the parents may have to deal with genetic issues. In a SIDS case, if there is another infant in the immediate family, there will be fears about that baby dying, too. Everyone needs to understand medical ramifications of the death so that emotional energy is not drained off inappropriately.

A CASE HISTORY

Grace was a young teenager who helped us learn about what it means to be an adolescent, a mother, and then a bereaved parent. She was 16 when her baby daughter, Tammy, was born. The baby's father, John, was 18 years old and had dropped out of high school. Grace and John were black and unmarried. Grace and the baby lived with several brothers, sisters, and Grace's mother, who had an infant son just 3 weeks older than Tammy. Even though Grace lived with her own mother, she saw herself as Tammy's mother and as her primary caretaker. The baby slept in a crib in Grace's room, and Grace fed and cared for her. John saw himself as Tammy's father, and, even though he was not married to or living with Grace, they spent a great deal of time together and he had some involvement in caring for Tammy.

When Tammy was 3 months old, Grace fed her on one occasion during the night, put her back down to sleep, and awoke in the morning to find Tammy dead in her crib. Grace and John and the entire family were deeply affected by Tammy's death. Grace needed reassurance that she was not "going crazy" because she sometimes thought she still heard the baby crying in the night. She had trouble sleeping, especially in her own room where Tammy had died. The social worker from the family service department stated that "the baby's death was somewhat of a blessing because Grace could now go back to high school and to being a teenager again."

Through counseling, Grace was able to understand that her guilt and anger were feelings shared by all parents whose babies die. Grace's mother was very clear that Grace was the baby's mother and that she should be treated as such. Grace found her church involvement helpful, but even there someone told her that Tammy was probably "better off with God" because Grace was so young. Grace understood that there were problems in her situation, but she also knew that she had been a good mother to Tammy and that she would always have tried to take good care of her child. It was very important to everyone that the autopsy diagnosis was SIDS and that the report stated clearly that Tammy had been a healthy, well-cared-for infant. For many months the whole family had fears about Grace's infant brother dying also. John was very angry about Tammy's death and sometimes took that anger out on Grace. He also had difficulty finding and keeping a job after the baby's death. Grace returned to school through a work-study program. She frequently expressed her desire for another baby, and she and John had a boy 1 1/2 years later. He is now a healthy five-year-old, and Grace is a young adult parent with a history of life experiences not shared by many "older" parents.

SUGGESTIONS FOR HELPING

When dealing with a bereaved adolescent parent, there are a few concrete suggestions that we have found helpful. The adolescent is now a parent who is without his or her baby. The clock cannot be turned back in this situation any more than it can be turned back on any major life event. Life simply does not present the opportunity to "cut our losses" and "get on with it" in some former style.

Helpers cannot make assumptions about what kind of parent the adolescent has been based merely on chronological age. As has been stated, what must be determined is the meaning that the baby had to its parent or parents. Also of importance will be the assessment of the dynamics of the family system, the medical implications of the death, and how best to guide the young parent in using available resources.

We have found the following guidelines helpful in working with adolescents who are bereaved parents:

1. Take as much time as necessary to help the parents understand the medical information to the best of their ability.

2. Realize that adolescents may be nonverbal and less assertive than older persons in asking questions for clarification. This does not, however, necessarily reflect their diminished involvement or attachment.

3. Convey to the family both in attitude and directly that their reaction to the death is "normal" (which in most cases it will be) and that it is this tragic event that is completely "out of synch" with life.

4. Include other family members in counseling sessions when possible and appropriate. Help them realize that all they really need to give is themselves and their love.

5. Take your cues from the adolescents as to which problem is to be addressed at a particular time. Helpers may be concerned about an important issue that looms unresolved, but often no amount of prodding seems to bring it into focus for an adolescent who has other priorities. We can only be effective when circumstances combine to make it "the right time" to deal with "the right issue." Encourage bereaved adolescent parents to write letters to their dead children "telling them everything they want them to know and understand."

6. Issues of "control" or lack of control surrounding the infant's care and death may be viewed differently by adolescents who are sometimes not used to seeing themselves in charge of their own situations. This will have to be assessed on a case-by-case basis. In the intimidating world of the NICU, we run the risk of losing effective contact with many adolescent parents at the very beginning because of their anxieties and ready willingness to "leave things to the experts." We must be very careful not to take away their parenthood by taking away their control at the outset when the infant becomes critical. Otherwise, the parent mourns this initial loss rather than the actual death.

7. Help adolescents understand and put into context the often inappropriate reactions of peers, family members, teachers, or other adults. This sometimes involves helping young persons become advocates for themselves.

8. Support adolescents in bringing some resolution to their pain without experiencing unnecessary guilt about moving on with their lives. At

the same time, make it clear that there is no time limit on your willingness to be available to share a bad time or a good one. Leave them with the confidence that they can handle troublesome emotions when they recur in later years.

9. The school is an important and integral aspect of any adolescent's life. Include the school by keeping teachers and other personnel aware of and sensitive to the needs of adolescent bereaved parents, and encourage adolescents themselves to maintaip this relationship.

10. Take into consideration racial, economic, cultural, and other relevant variables in each particular situation. In our experience, it is often difficult to maintain contact with inner-city, black families. Still, if good communication is established, there can sometimes be long-term, positive contact with adolescent parents.

SUMMARY AND CONCLUSIONS

> *What is death, I ask.*
> *What is life, you ask.**

The question of our understanding and support of adolescent bereaved parents has been given scant attention in the scholarly literature. This reflects society's lack of recognition and minimization of the needs of adolescents when they become parents and then, within a short time, bereaved parents.

There are many commonalities among parents of any age in the grief experience surrounding the death of a child. All struggle with varying degrees of self-blame and anger. Family and marital relationships come under stress. Finding a new equilibrium for daily living is difficult. Often reassurance is needed that psychosomatic symptoms and depth of feeling are typical usually of a profound grief experience as opposed to indications that a bereaved parent is "going crazy." In many instances of parental bereavement, parents will need support in their decision making about possible future pregnancies.

In addition to these commonalities, the experience of adolescents has unique aspects related to age and living situation. Many are single parents, and there may or may not be an on-going relationship between the mother and father. Often, it is difficult or impossible for the counselor to contact the father in order to give necessary information and support. Role definitions between the infant's parents and grandparents may be

*From THE DEATH NOTEBOOKS by Anne Sexton. Copyright © 1974 by Anne Sexton. Reprinted by permission of Houghton Mifflin Company.

fluid and confused, but must be understood if support is to be effective for all. It is also crucial to try to understand the meaning that the baby had for each person involved. Those meanings are as varied in the case of adolescents as they are with older parents.

Because of their age, adolescents are unlikely to have previous experience coping with the death of a loved one. They may need special help in their struggle with questions of life, death, and fairness. Health professionals and counselors who provide support to adolescent bereaved parents can be most effective when they relate to the parents based not on stereotypes but on their value and needs as parents who have experienced the death of their child. Adolescents who become bereaved parents should not be expected to go back to being innocent teenagers, although they can be helped to go forward to living productive and satisfying lives.

REFERENCES

Borg, S., & Lasker, J. *When pregnancy fails: Families coping with miscarriage, stillbirth, and infant death.* Boston: Beacon, 1981.

Bowlby, J. The making and breaking of affectional bonds. *British Journal of Psychiatry*, 1977, *130*, 201–210.

Bowlby, J. *Loss: Sadness and depression.* New York: Basic Books, 1980.

Caine, L. *Widow.* New York: William Morrow & Company, 1974.

Cantor, R. C. *And a time to live: Toward emotional well-being during the crisis of cancer.* New York: Harper & Row, 1978.

Caplan, G. Forward. In I. O. Glick, R. S. Weiss, & C. M. Parkes, *The first year of bereavement* (pp. vii–xi). New York: Wiley, 1974.

Clayton, P. J., Desmarais, L., & Winokure, G. A study of normal bereavement. *American Journal of Psychiatry*, 1968, *125*, 168–178.

Corr, C. A., Martinson, I. M., & Dyer, K. L. Parental bereavement. In C. A. Corr & D. M. Corr (Eds.), *Hospice approaches to pediatric care* (pp. 219–240). New York: Springer Publishing, 1985.

Freud, A. Adolescence. *Psychoanalytic study of the child*, 1958, *13*, 255–268.

Freud, S. Mourning and melancholia. In J. Strachey (Ed.)., *The standard edition of the complete psychological works of Sigmund Freud* (Vol. 14, pp. 243–258). London: Hogarth Press, 1957.

Furman, E. *A child's parent dies: Studies in childhood bereavement.* New Haven: Yale University Press, 1974.

Furman, R. A child's capacity for mourning. In E. J. Anthony & C. Koupernick (Eds.), *The child in his family: The impact of disease and death* (pp. 225–231). New York: Wiley, 1973.

Hagan, J. Infant death: Nursing interaction and intervention with grieving families. *Nursing Forum*, 1974, *13*, 372–385.

Jackson, E. N. The pastoral counselor and the child encountering death. In H. Wass & C. A. Corr (Eds.), *Helping children cope with death: Guidelines and resources* (2nd ed.)(pp. 33–47). Washington, DC: Hemisphere, 1984.

Klaus, M., & Kennell, J. *Parent-infant bonding.* St. Louis: Mosby, 1982.

Mandell, F., McAnulty, E., & Reece, R. M. Observations of paternal responses to sudden unanticipated infant death. *Pediatrics*, 1980, *65*, 221–225.

McAnarney, E. R., Lawrence, R. A., Aten, M. J., & Iker, H. P. Adolescent mothers and their infants. *Pediatrics*, 1984, *73*, 358–362.

Meriwether, L. Essence up front—The black family in crisis: Teenage pregnancy. *Essence*, 1984, *14*, 94–96, 144, 147, 151.

Miles, M. S. Helping adults mourn the death of a child. In H. Wass & C. A. Corr (Eds.), *Childhood and death* (pp. 219–241). Washington, DC: Hemisphere, 1984.

Parkes, C. M., & Brown, R. J. Health after bereavement: A controlled study of young boston widows and widowers. *Psychosomatic Medicine*, 1972, *34*, 449–461.

Pediatric Annals, 1984, *13* (March), 188–261. (This special issue contains seven articles reviewing the whole subject of SIDS.)

Peppers, L. G., & Knapp, R. J. *Motherhood and mourning: Perinatal death*. New York: Praeger, 1980.

Perlman, J. M. Clinical experience: Neonatal intensive care unit 1977–1980. St. Louis, MO: Children's Hospital at Washington University Medical Center, 1984.

Raphael, B. *The anatomy of bereavement*. New York: Basic Books, 1983.

Rogel, M. J., & Petersen, A. C. Some adolescent experiences of motherhood. In R. Cohen, B Cohlar, & S. Weissman (Eds.), *Parenthood: A psychodynamic perspective* (pp. 85–102). New York: Guilford Press, 1984.

Sanders, C. M. A comparison of adult bereavement in the death of a spouse, child and parent. *Omega*, 1979, *10*, 303–322.

Schodt, C. M. Grief in adolescent mothers after an infant death. *Image*, 1982, *14*, 20–25.

Sexton, A. Hurry up please it's time. *The death notebooks* (1974) in *The complete poems*. Boston: Houghton Mifflin, 1981.

Shinners, B., & Cape, L. A multi-disciplinary team approach to death in the NICU. In R. Rubright (Ed.), *Persuading physicians: A guide for hospital executives* (pp. 255–258). Rockville, MD: Aspen Systems Corporation, 1984.

Smialek, Z. Observations on immediate reactions of families to sudden infant death. *Pediatrics*, 1978, *62*, 160–165.

Wegman, M. E. Annual summary of vital statistics—1982. *Pediatrics*, 1983, *72*, 755–765.

Yaeger, R. A. *Bereavement outcomes of SIDS families*. Unpublished doctoral dissertation, University of North Carolina at Chapel Hill, School of Public Health, 1979.

PART III
Suicide and Adolescents

Of all the subjects that have something to do with death and adolescence, surely suicide is the one that has been most thoroughly studied. Frequent reports in the popular media draw attention to tragic examples of suicide among adolescents and to alarming increases in overall rates of suicide in this particular age group. Nearly every adolescent that we encounter knows a peer who has committed suicide, and many have considered this possibility for themselves. What does all this mean? Why has suicide risen to stand among the three leading causes of death in adolescence (the other two being accidents and homicide)? How much do we actually know about this particular subject? And what principles should guide adults who seek to be helpful in this area?

Even though suicidology is an established discipline with its own professional organizations and journals, and the literature on adolescent suicide is extensive, there is still much in this area that we do not know. In Chapter 9, Alan Berman surveys the demographic data, the patterns, and the motives for suicidal behavior in adolescence. In so doing, he reveals the complexity of this subject and delineates the present state of our understanding of its dynamics. Two important lessons from Berman's account are: (1) suicidal behavior among adolescents is most often not the expression of a wish to be dead but the expression of a wish to escape from a crisis or situation perceived as intolerable; and (2) sympathetic parents, teachers, and friends often can do much to mitigate the pain communicated by suicidal thoughts and actions, and to offer constructive options in place of a tragic outcome. Each of these lessons can guide helpers while professionals pursue the research needed for the longer term.

In Chapter 10, Sharon Valente and Joan Sellers investigate the other side of this picture: the situation of adolescents who are survivors of a death by suicide. Surprisingly, we know very little about these young people. If suicide is a particularly difficult death-related experience for survivors in general, must it not be even more significant when those survivors are adolescents? These are bereaved adolescents, but that in itself does not fully describe their situation. Like young parents whose child has died, adolescent survivors of suicide are confronted by a death that is usually sudden, often untimely, and frequently unexpected. Like many of their peers who have elected to terminate a pregnancy through an abortion, adolescent survivors of suicide experience the consequences of an action that someone chose, concerns about their own putative guilt, and social stigma. Of course, these comparisons are only illustrative. The actual experience of adolescents who survive the suicide of a relative, friend, or other significant person has its own issue- and phase-specific typology. Through their pioneering characterization of that typology, Valente and Sellers provide another salient perspective on what death means for adolescents.

9

Helping Suicidal Adolescents: Needs and Responses

Alan L. Berman

Dear Mom, Dad, and everyone else,

I'm sorry for what I've done, but I loved you all and I always will, for eternity. Please, please, please don't blame it on yourselves. It was all my fault and not yours or anyone else's. If I didn't do this now, I would have done it later anyway. We all die some day, I just died sooner.

Love,

John

John was 17 when he decided to end his brief life. His adolescence was dotted with problems, some typical, others perhaps more hurtful than anyone might have guessed. He kept his pain mostly to himself. Only after his body was found did family and friends begin piecing together the mosaic that John's life was. To the now knowing eyes of survivors, figure and ground shifted to reveal what otherwise had been over-looked, denied, and misinterpreted. Left in the wake of John's death were the inevitable "if only's."

In spite of John's protestations, the legacy of youth suicide is guilt and self-blame. The young are not supposed to die; death, including suicidal death, is common to the old. For a young person to find life so hurtful, barren, and hopeless that death would be sought, implicitly points a finger of blame at those who might have made a difference. More than ever before, families and communities are facing the tragedy of youth suicide and asking: Why?

Only now are researchers beginning to seek and provide meaningful answers. The acceleration in empirical research in the area of adolescent suicide in the last several years follows closely and parallels reports of dramatic increases in the incidence of these deaths (Berman & Tanney, 1984). Unfortunately, there is a lag of about 3 years before final mortality figures are published by the government and a lag of several more years before any one empirical study can be organized, carried out, and published. Therefore, to have a body of well-conducted research addressing significantly both the questions of "Why?" and "What can be done?" demands inordinate patience among those eager for answers.

It is not that the problem of adolescent suicide is new. It is that the significance of the problem has only recently emerged. In 1960, the suicide rate for the 15- to 24-year-old age group in the United States was 5.2 per 100,000. This rate was less than a tenth that of accidental deaths for this age group. Homicides, malignant tumors, and cardiovascular diseases claimed more lives than did suicide. By 1980, suicide was the third leading cause of death in this age group. The rate of 12.3 per 100,000 persons aged 15 to 24 reflected an increase of 136% and now was a fifth that of accidental deaths. The 30 year increase from 1950 to 1980 is 173%. In absolute numbers, over 5,200 youths murdered themselves in the United States in 1980; proportionately, about 11% of all deaths among 15- to 24-year-olds in our society are suicides.

As indicated in Figure 9.1, while the rates for youth suicide have increased, the corresponding trend at all ages over 30 is on the decrease. In fact, the Surgeon General has noted that with the exception of the adolescent/young adult (15–24) segment of the population, overall mortality rates have decreased for every age group (*Healthy People*, 1979). The mortality statistics directly implicate the reason: the sharp rise in violent (suicide and homicide) deaths among the young (Holinger, 1979; Seiden & Freitas, 1980). Since modes of death are a reflection of the way we live, they serve as an index of psychosocial stress and lifestyle changes and, therefore, provide tentative hypotheses in our quest for answers (Seiden & Freitas, 1980).

DEMOGRAPHIC FACTORS

The study of any human behavior is best accomplished by observing the behaving human. However, the study of suicidal behavior is hindered by the unavailability of the object of study; that object, the decedent, having gone straight to the morgue. The consequent research problems have been extensively reviewed elsewhere (Berman & Carroll, 1984). Suffice it to say that our understanding of completed suicide is primarily

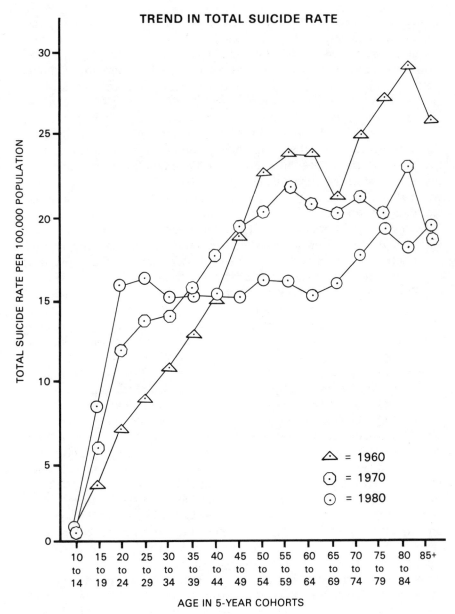

Figure 9.1 Trend in total suicide rate.

limited to what we can garner from statistical analyses of epidemiological, anthropological, and sociological data.

Suicide is most economically viewed as an intensely personal act. However, a great variety of social forces impinge upon any individual's sense of self, needs, resources, and behavior. Berman and Cohen-Sandler (1982) have outlined a sample of indicators of societal change (and relative dysfunction) specific to the adolescent population. Profound increases in rates of divorce —and, consequently, the numbers of children involved—births to unmarried adolescent women, drug use, and juvenile arrests, are but a few of the signs pointing to potential explanatory factors. More will be said of these later. To begin, it is best that we examine the epidemiological trends inherent in the distribution of suicidal death in the adolescent age group.

Holinger and Offer (1982) analyzed the relationship between the adolescent (ages 15–19) suicide rate and population changes among adolescents between the years 1933 and 1978. They found significant positive correlations between these suicide rates and changes both in the adolescent population and in the proportion of adolescents in the population. That is, when there are more adolescents (and more adolescents relative to other age groups), there are more adolescent suicides. Correspondingly, their data predict a downward trend in the number of adolescent suicides as the adolescent population decreases.

As clinical explanations, Holinger and Offer (1982) suggest two models: 1. competition and failure; and 2. progressive isolation. As competition for a relatively fixed number of positions (on teams, for jobs, for admission to selective colleges, etc.) increases with increases in the adolescent population, greater numbers of adolescents fail to achieve their goals, see themselves as failures, and, perhaps, lose sufficient self-esteem and begin a downward slide toward suicide. The second model proposes that the isolated, marginally involved adolescent whose self-esteem already may be fragile will be affected by the larger numbers of adolescents even more. The lonely, depressed adolescent will perceive only that there are many more well-functioning peers, thereby depleting even further those reserves of self-esteem that thus far had defended against hopelessness. The result may be suicide.

Seiden (1983) travelled in the opposite direction and arrived at almost the same explanatory hypothesis. Analyzing the suicide rates by state for the years 1964 to 1978 for 15- to 24-year-olds, Seiden found a strong geographical pattern in the distribution of youth suicides. Of the ten states with the highest rates, nine are located in the western United States. Conversely, all ten states with the lowest suicide rates are located east of the Mississippi River. Furthermore, five of the ten states with the highest suicide rates had rates of increase greater than that of the nation as a whole!

The pertinent characteristic common to these Western states is that their population densities tend to be very low. The rank order correlation between the suicide rates and population densities of these ten highest ranking states was − .78. Thus, Seiden (1983) suggests that low population density may have a significant effect on pathology, increasing isolation from social supports, social controls, and social networks. Withdrawal, increased use of alcohol, and the relative lack of potential interveners in times of crisis all may contribute to an ultimate suicide.

One uncontrolled, yet possibly significant variable in Seiden's analysis is the relative availability in the West of the most prevalent lethal weapon of suicide, firearms. Lester and Murrell (1982) have documented that states with stricter handgun control laws do have lower rates of suicide by firearm. Firearms and explosives accounted for 62% of all suicides among 15- to 24-year-olds in 1980. In descending order of frequency, the following are the principal methods used by the remaining third of completed suicides: hanging (16.8%), poisoning (7.6%), gases (6.3%), and jumping (3.0%).

Table 9.1 tells us that almost two-thirds (64%) of males and slightly more than half the females in the 15 to 24 age range use firearms to accomplish their suicide. The increase in the use of guns accounts for almost all the increase noted in youth suicides (Boyd, 1983). But, as noted in Table 9.1, fully 85% of those using firearms are male. This sex-specific choice of method has long been thought to be one of the main reasons why men are overrepresented in completed suicides and, as we shall see, why women are overrepresented in nonfatal attempts.

As indicated in Table 9.1, one out of every five (21%) suicides in 1980 was that of a 15- to 24-year-old male. Males at these ages are more likely to use hanging as a method of suicide (26% of all male suicides) and less likely than males of other ages to use drowning, poisoning, gases, or cutting. In contrast to women of the same age, males are far less likely to ingest solid or liquid poisons to effect their suicides. Whereas males account for almost five of every six 15- to 24-year-old suicides (83%), they comprise only slightly more than half of the self-poisoners.

Women at these ages represent only 14% of *all* female suicides and 17% of the 15- to 24-year-old suicides. As with males, the majority of young females use firearms to kill themselves. They are overrepresented as drug ingesters: one of five (20%) of all 15- to 24-year-old suicides is by ingestion, and almost half of all poisoning deaths at these ages are those of females.

Racial differences may also be noted in the demography of youth suicide. Blacks aged 15 to 24 account for a greater proportion of all black suicides than do whites in the same age group for all white suicides. Better than one in four black suicides (26%) is aged 15 to 24. Although the suicide rate for minorities is significantly lower than that of the white

TABLE 9.1. Completed Suicides for 1980:
15- to 24-Year-Olds—Sex × Method

	15- to 24-yr-old male suicides		Method of suicide (% of all same sex 15- to 24-year-old suicides)	
Method	A (% *all* male suicides)	B (% all 15- to 24-yr suicides using same method)	Male	Female
TOTAL	21%	83%		
Poisoning	16	54	6	20
Gases	16	79	6	8
Hanging	26	90	18	10
Drowning	16	84	1	1
Firearms	22	85	64	52
Cutting	11	80	1	1
Jumping	20	71	3	5
Other	22	79	2	2
TOTAL			101%	99%

majority (see Table 9.2), suicide among blacks is largely a phenomenon of youth. The greatest increase in rates has been noted in young black males who, in addition, have had traditionally high rates of homicides as well. Relative to all other suicidal methods at these ages, blacks tend to use hanging and jumping proportionately more than their white peers.

THE "AT RISK" ADOLESCENT

As noted in Table 9.2, males, both white and black, complete suicide at rates better than four times those for females. In contrast, females out-number males by about the same ratio when available data on attempted suicide are examined. The modal adolescent attempter is a female (the majority in the home) who ingests pills (with analgesics being the most common) (Berman & Carroll, 1984).

The significance of these data lies in the fact that attempters and completers, as groups, are quite different. Although one may be defined as an attempted suicide in a number of ways (for example, intending to complete suicide but being rescued or intervened with; failing to com-plete; not intending to die but, rather, to communicate an otherwise unaccepted message), the typical completed suicide in adolescence is a

**TABLE 9.2. 1960/80 Suicide Rates per 100,000,
by Race and Sex (Ages 15–24)**

Year	White male	White female	Black male	Black female
1960	8.6	2.3	4.1	1.3
1980	21.4	4.6	12.3	2.3
% Increase	149%	100%	200%	77%

Source: Division of Vital Statistics, National Center for Health Statistics, Hyattsville, MD.

male using a gun and the typical adolescent attempter is a female ingesting pills. Since the attempted suicide remains alive and, consequently, is available for observation and study, what we have learned about the suicidal adolescent has come primarily from our study of young women. Additionally, the study of suicide is always retrospective (after the behavior has occurred). The behavior may lead the survivor to distort information so gathered and may influence any proactive study of the suicidal individual (Berman & Carroll, 1984), making difficult generalizations to that individual's premorbid functioning.

Nevertheless, much can be learned from the suicide attempter. And, it is important to note that there *is* overlap between completers and attempters . Once despairing enough to jeopardize one's life even without intent to die, the likelihood of future and perhaps more lethal suicidal behavior increases. Thus, the assessment of the adolescent at risk for future suicidal behavior must be generalized from findings generated by the study of those who have survived an attempt at suicidal behavior.

The adolescent exists primarily in three venues: in the family, in school, and among peers. Each represents an area of functioning that must be evaluated for possible clues to future suicidal behavior.

Family

The majority of research on suicidal adolescents has focused on family and parental dynamics. Adolescents, by definition, are caught between childhood and adulthood. The often intense and conflictual task of separating from the world of parents and family can be all that more difficult when family dynamics interfere with or make difficult the child's move toward self-sufficiency. Studies of these particular families make it apparent that both past training and present learnings interfere in the adolescents' press for autonomy and growth.

Parents of suicidal adolescents have been found to experience more overt conflict, threats of separation and divorce, and loss of a parent occurring prior to the child's twelfth year (Corder, Shorr, & Corder,

1974; Miller, Chiles, & Barnes, 1982; Stanley & Barter, 1970). Various psychopathologies have been found to characterize parents of suicidal adolescents. These range from general psychiatric problems (Garfinkel, Froese, & Hood, 1982), to current and chronic suicidal behavior (Garfinkel et al., 1982; McKenry, Tishler, & Kelly, 1982), depression, alcohol, and drug abuse (Tishler & McKenry, 1982).

Suicidal adolescents report receiving little affection (Korella, 1972). They hold negative views of their parents and see themselves as different from their parents (McKenry et al., 1982). When families of a suicidal adolescent have been observed interacting on a task, communications to the suicidal adolescent have been found to be punitive and constricted (Abraham, 1978).

It is understandable, then, that suicidal adolescents describe time spent in their family as unenjoyable (McKenry et al., 1982). Perhaps, it is also understandable that suicidal adolescents have been found to have deficient problem-solving skills (Hynes, 1976; Levenson & Neuringer, 1971). Without adequate attention to need fulfillment, skill training, and nurturing—those ingredients essential for psychological growth—the adolescent at risk for suicide is one who lacks the psychosocial supplies needed to deal with the normal *"Sturm und Drang"* of growing. The suicidal adolescent feels expendable, yet lacks the goods to separate and leave. Instead, he or she develops poor reality testing and becomes more hopeless and depressed (Tishler & McKenry, 1982; Topol & Reznikoff, 1982). Suicidal behavior, then, may serve as a form of communication, a cry for help or a way to escape an otherwise poorly solved problem.

Other cues of despair and poor problem solving may be evident in the adolescent's behavior. Drug and alcohol use and aggressive behavior have been found to be more prevalent in histories of suicidal (versus nonsuicidal) adolescents (Garfinkel et al., 1982; Korella, 1972).

School

A close relationship with parents has been found to be inversely related to depressive mood in adolescence (Kandel & Davies, 1982). When depressive mood or a more developed affective syndrome is present, it is often most in evidence in the academic functioning of the adolescent. Unfortunately, no study of suicidal adolescents has, as yet, discriminated them from depressed, nonsuicidal adolescents (Berman & Carroll, 1984). Thus, the research literature suggesting that academic dysfunction and problems are typical of suicidal adolescents may be more descriptive of the much larger body of depressed adolescents as well.

Be that as it may, suicidal adolescents have been found to evidence greater withdrawal from and less involvement with the school milieu (Corder et al., 1974; Gibson, 1982; Korella, 1972). School problems have been found (Sarles, Reynolds, & Heald, 1979), and underachievement and poor school performance have characterized this group's presuicidal behavior (Garfinkel, et al., 1982; Korella, 1972).

The academically capable, but truly depressed and potentially suicidal adolescent is rarely pleased with academic performance, making the error of reasoning that a grade of "B" is the equivalent of an "F." When such perceived failures occur, they have the potential of interactively increasing the sense of despair and hopelessness already felt. Suicidal adolescents have been found to feel more pressure to do well in school (McKenry et al., 1982). Perceived failures, thus, also implicate the loss of even further recognition from those family systems demanding such performance. Interestingly, the long held view that the incidence of suicide for college students is substantially higher than for comparable non-students recently has been challenged (Schwartz, 1980).

Peers

It is common to adolescence that at one time or another suicidal fantasies will be engaged in (Cantor, 1976). It is also normative of adolescence that the present moment has more impact than the future. When an adolescent experiences stress, a constricted view of future possibilities and a momentary fix on present escapes may hold sway. Impulsivity and poor alternative problem solving may make suicidal fantasies turn to suicidal behaviors. A positive and healthy interaction with peers may be a sufficient antidote to this suicidogenic process.

Active peer involvement (dating, shared activities) is negatively correlated with depressive mood in adolescence (Kandel & Davies, 1982). In contrast, suicidal adolescents have been found to have more frequent and serious problems with peers, to be more interpersonally sensitive, and to be less likely to have a close confidant (McKenry et al., 1982; Tishler & McKenry, 1982). Thus, the suicidal adolescent appears, at best, to have a marginal relationship to an interpersonal system that could counteract both the negative effects of a dysfunctional family system and the constriction of a rigid and dysfunctional cognitive style.

Peers have one other, significant effect on the potentially suicidal adolescent: contagion. Adolescents are highly suggestible creatures, eager to imitate others in their quest to establish an identity that fits. Suicidal adolescents are highly vulnerable to influence since they lack reinforcing role models and are low in self-esteem and ego strength. Thus, when a suicidal behavior occurs and receives attention and response in a closed community (for example, school), it is not uncommon to find subsequent suicidal behaviors, often a "rash" or epidemic of followers. It has been proposed that the first suicidal behavior serves as a model or permission giver, precipitating into manifest behavior what had been latent in the follower(s) (Berman & Yufit, 1983). It is most important for us to address the phenomenon of contagion through our interventions and preventative programming efforts at the school and community level.

Case Example

When John's family was interviewed after his suicide, they claimed he gave no signs of being depressed or suicidal. Their response was not unlike that of others who either were ignorant of the family dynamics or had well-prepared defenses against them. John had an intensely ambivalent, perhaps even symbiotic, relationship with his father. John's father had been depressed since he retired from his job due to a medical disability. He spent much of his day and evening in front of the family television set, drinking until he passed out. John's mother constantly spoke of leaving. There was no love, no sexual involvement, no affection. When John's father interacted with John, it was with anger and rigid control. When John sought his father's permission to be more autonomous, his father found reason to restrict and keep him tied to a childlike role in the family.

John was a child seeking permission to leave the home and join the army. He disliked school, lacking passion for study and performing only marginally. At age 17, he had yet to date and was isolated from friends. Small for his age, he had been bullied by some classmates. As a result of the most recent incident, John dropped out of the one extracurricular activity in which he participated. It was then that he asked to join the military. When his father refused him permission, John threw a temper tantrum and was, consequently, restricted to his room. When his mother checked on him early that evening, his suicide note was found on his pillow. His body was not recovered for 3 days.

In spite of the family's protestations, John had given warnings. He was an impulsive, reckless child who did not know when to stop. He did not give evidence of planned behavior and was given to violent outbursts. In anger, he threatened to jump from the roof of his house at the age of eight; and he had told a cousin just last year that he would shoot himself one day. In his last week, he had asked his mother whether she thought that people who killed themselves felt pain.

However, perhaps no one could have known that his pain had reached the level of despair and hopelessness. No one bothered to ask. And no one thought to secure his father's shotgun, just in case. There must have been special meaning in John's choice to use his dad's gun when he decided to shoot himself.

TYPES AND MOTIVES

The decision to end one's life can never be simple. Suicide is a complex, multidetermined behavior that is acted out either on impulse or as a life plan. In adolescence, the motives for suicidal behavior appear largely interpersonal, directed at effecting change in or escape from a conflictual family or peer system. The intended communication may range from hostility to helplessness; each case has its idiosyncratic message. One thing appears clear: No other way to achieve the intended goal is apparent to the suicidal adolescent at the time the behavior takes place.

Some adolescents engage in suicidal behavior as a consequence of severe psychopathology such as psychosis. Others act out of the constricted despair of a clinical depression, interpersonal isolation, or otherwise unexpressable rage. For most adolescents not already defined as severely disturbed, suicide is an extreme method of ending a crisis in their lives.

Case Example

Andrew was a 15-year-old, high school sophomore when his first romance came to an abrupt halt. Surprised that his girlfriend no longer wanted to see him, he wrote a long note to her, in which he entreated her to repair their break or "find [him] dead."

When brought for evaluation, Andrew spoke of this relationship loss as but one of several problems. He had been fighting with his parents and felt they could not understand his problems. He was failing two courses in school and feared further alienating his parents, who were professionals, by disappointing their expectations for him to go to college. He was a failure in athletics as well, since he felt responsible for his team's poor showing in a recent game.

A bright, sensitive, and overtly depressed youngster, Andrew merely "wanted to give up under hopeless odds." Andrew became hopeless in response to an acute loss in a context of no perceived support. What had always appeared to be a close family now felt wrenched by the push and pull of his adolescence. His parents, both only children themselves, had idealized their adolescent years (in spite of much deficit and isolation).

They were simply unable to understand their once loving son; nor were they ready to give him room to grow through his pain. Once involved in therapy, this family was able to place a significant life event in context and support Andrew in easing the burden of his own growth. His suicidal message, while real and honestly felt, was given in a moment of deep pain. Counteracting any suicidal behavior, however, was a parental system that took notice and responded.

Although Andrew's case had a happy ending, it is important to emphasize that the unhappy endings of many other adolescents occurred without possible intervention by family or therapist. Perhaps a brief sampling of these cases will paint a mosaic of implied motives common to completed suicides:

> A 12-year-old son of a military officer shot himself with his father's shotgun. He had been severely punished by his father after being caught playing hooky from school.

> The life of a 15-year-old boy was "wrapped up" in a television space show; his room was cluttered with space models, posters, and related paraphernalia. When not involved with this passion, he spoke of being bored and lacking challenge. When the television show was cancelled, he wrote a suicide note and jumped 200 feet to his death from a bridge.

> A 15-year-old female, on alcohol and PCP (phenylcyclohexylpiperidine), told her friend that she had "messed up [her] life," then put a handgun to her head.

> A 17-year-old male argued with his girlfriend and threatened to kill himself if she walked out on him. She told him, "you're crazy." He pulled a gun out of his pocket and shot himself in the head.

> A 17-year-old hanged himself in a county jail cell. He had been arrested for drunk driving the night after having failed a Marine Corps test.

> A 19-year-old married female drowned herself hours after an abortion. She had been depressed and upset. Her husband was on a training mission with the Merchant Marine.

No vignette can portray adequately the dynamics behind such life stories. No typology can summarize succinctly the multiplicity of motives for deciding on a self-inflicted death. Had the opportunities presented themselves, we can only wonder which and how many of these suicidal decisions might have been redirected toward alternative, life-sustaining choices. That this is possible is without question.

INTERVENTIONS

It is believed by suicidologists that the acute decision to kill oneself is rarely lacking in clues and signs; often these are readily discernible to the trained clinician but unrecognizable to those closest to the victim (for example, as in the case of John). It is apparent, then, that intervention begins with assessment.

Proper assessment of an individual at risk for suicidal behavior requires an awareness of those factors, described earlier, found through research to be associated differentially with that behavior. Furthermore, it demands an interpersonal awareness of messages, verbalized and behaved, that indicate that the individual may be considering a suicidal solution to a life problem. Suicidal communications, however, tend to provoke feelings of anxiety, helplessness, anger, or rage in potential respondents, especially those most intimately involved. In turn, these feelings may unconsciously command the implementation of such defenses as denial or minimization. The result is the surprise and disbelief that often accompanies postsuicidal survivors' descriptions of the suicidal event.

The ability to assess a youth at-risk, therefore, depends on an awareness of such countertransferential reactions and an ability to tolerate the discomforting effect that comes from involving oneself in a life-threatening situation. Teachers must recognize and respond to a student in pain, in spite of the myriad of other responsibilities and needs demanding response. Peers, most often the first turned to and communicated with (Ross, 1980), must understand that what a suicidal adolescent needs is a caring friend and that a caring friend does not hold secret a message that a friend is considering suicide. Both teachers and students fear the responsibility of involving themselves or of "doing the wrong thing." With education regarding commonly held myths and irrational fears (for example, if one talks about suicide, one might suggest it, etc.), knowledge about what can and should be done, and information concerning available resources for professional intervention, teachers and students can be significant gatekeepers in the intervention system (Ross, 1980).

On a more preventive level, student-peers can be taught how to identify signs and symptoms of depression and panic, realities about the mental health system and referrals, etc., in order to promote better self-assessment and problem solving (Ross, 1985). In California, state legislation has been passed (effective July 1984) to provide for the implementation of two pilot youth suicide prevention programs to accomplish these ends.

With awareness and education, basic and effective steps toward intervention in and prevention of a suicidal action can be taken. Suicidal communications can be observed and taken seriously. Warning signs for increased risk of suicidal behavior can be noted and responded to. Channels of communication and empathic support can be opened and provided. Referrals for professional help can be made where both appropriate and necessary.

Intervention at the professional level must take into account the idiosyncratic dynamics of both the suicidal adolescent and crisis. Family therapy, often the treatment with the most impact for the suicidal youngster, may be difficult to effect. Families of suicidal adolescents experience implicit and explicit blame and responsibility for the suicidal behavior and may seek to quickly repair the opened wound (Berman & Carroll, 1984). Less than half the families referred for treatment after initial contact have been found to follow through (Morrison & Collier, 1969).

Individual therapy with the suicidal adolescent must first and foremost ensure the safety of the adolescent. Youths evaluated at high risk for continued self-harm should be considered for hospitalization. In or out of a hospital setting, however, active treatment should be provided. Symptoms must be ameliorated. Ongoing sources of stress must be removed or minimized through distancing maneuvers. Support systems must be stabilized and open communication within them encouraged.

The effectiveness of individual psychotherapy depends, in good measure, on the quality of the therapeutic alliance established between the suicidal adolescent and the therapist. With an empathic, available, and accessible therapist, a nurturing bond can be formed that serves as the foundation of reconstructive, psychoeducational work. Whatever the procedures, the goals of therapy with a suicidal adolescent must accommodate the functional motive of the suicidal behavior. That is, by analyzing the purpose of the suicidal behavior, alternative strategies for accomplishing that purpose can be derived. In the process of seeking nonsuicidal solutions to the problem(s) presented, the more important goal of teaching effective problem-solving skills applicable to a wide range of future problem situations is sought.

As a last word, suicidal behavior—whether ending in death or renewed life—is a communication of pain. For those we have opportunity to help, that communication commands attention. That but one life may be renewed should be sufficient argument for the effort. When suicidal action succeeds in ending an individual's pain, there remain survivors who must bear the burden of that death. Postventive care or bereavement counseling for these survivors, the subject of Chapter 10, is crucial in helping family and peers understand and mourn premature death by suicide.

REFERENCES

Abraham, Y. Patterns of communication in families of suicidal adolescents. *Dissertation Abstracts International*, 1978, *38*, 4669A.
Berman, A., & Carroll, T. Adolescent suicide: A critical review, *Death Education*, 1984, *8* (Suppl.), 53–64.

Berman, A., & Cohen-Sandler, R. Childhood and adolescent suicide research: A critique. *Crisis*, 1982, *3*, 3–15.

Berman, A., & Tanney, B. *Taking the mystery out of research.* Paper presented at the annual meeting of the American Association of Suicidology, Anchorage, AK, May 1984.

Berman, A., & Yufit, R., Suicide: Is it contagious? *Newslink*, 1983, *9*, 3.

Boyd, J. H. The increasing rate of suicide by firearms. *New England Journal of Medicine*, 1983, *308*, 872–874.

Cantor, P. Personality characteristics among youthful female suicide attempters. *Journal of Abnormal Psychology*, 1976, *85*, 324–329.

Corder, B. F., Shorr, W., & Corder, R. F. A study of social and psychological characteristics of adolescent suicide attempters in an urban, disadvantaged area. *Adolescence*, 1974, *9*, 1-16.

Garfinkel, B. D., Froese, A., & Hood, J. Suicide attempts in children and adolescents. *American Journal of Psychiatry*, 1982, *139*, 1257–1261.

Gibson, E. A. H. Adolescent suicide attempts: An examination of critical factors in the school milieu. *Dissertation Abstracts International*, 1982, *42*, 4559B.

Healthy People. (Public Health Service, Publication No. 79–55071). Washington, DC: U. S. Department of Health, Education, and Welfare, 1979.

Holinger, P. Violent deaths among the young: Recent trends in suicide, homicide, and accidents. *American Journal of Psychiatry*, 1979, *136*, 1144–1147.

Holinger, P., & Offer, D. Prediction of adolescent suicide: A population model. *American Journal of Psychiatry*, 1982, *139*, 302-307.

Hynes, J. J. An exploratory study of the affective future time perspective of adolescent attempters: Relationship to clinical identification of lethality and its implications for postvention. *Dissertation Abstracts International*, 1976, *37*, 1404A–1405A.

Kandel, D. B., & Davies, M. Epidemiology of depressive mood in adolescents. *Archives of General Psychiatry*, 1982, *39*, 1205–1212.

Korella, K. Teenage suicide gestures: A study of suicidal behavior among high school students. *Dissertation Abstracts International*, 1972, *32*, 5039A.

Lester, D., & Murrell, M. E. The preventive effect of strict gun control laws on suicide and homicide. *Suicide and Life Threatening Behavior*, 1982, *12*, 131–140.

Levenson, M., & Neuringer, C. Problem solving behavior in suicidal adolescents. *Journal of Consulting and Clinical Psychology*, 1971, *37*, 433–436.

McKenry, P., Tishler, C., & Kelly, C. Adolescent suicide: A comparison of attempters and non-attempters in an emergency room population. *Clinical Pediatrics*, 1982, *21*, 266–270.

Miller, M. L., Chiles, J. A., & Barnes, V. E. Suicide attempters within a delinquent population. *Journal of Consulting and Clinical Psychology*, 1982, *50*, 491-498.

Morrison, G. C., & Collier, J. G. Family treatment approaches to suicidal children and adolescents. *Journal of the American Academy of Child Psychiatry*, 1969, *8*, 140–153.

Ross, C. Mobilizing schools for suicide prevention. *Suicide and Life Threatening Behavior*, 1980, *10*, 239–243.

Ross, C. Teaching children the facts of life and death: Suicide prevention in the schools. In M. L. Peck, N. L. Farberow, & R. E. Litman (Eds.), *Youth Suicide* (pp. 147–169). New York: Springer Publishing, 1985.

Sarles, R. M., Reynolds, B. J., & Heald, R. P., Visual-motor problems of adolescents who attempt suicide. *Perceptual and Motor Skills*, 1979, *48*, 599–602.

Schwartz, A. J. Inaccuracy and uncertainty in estimates of college student suicide rates. *Journal of the American College Health Association*, 1980, *28*,
201–204.

Seiden, R. Death in the west: A spatial analysis of the youthful suicide rate.
Western Journal of Medicine, 1983, *139*, 783–795.

Seiden, R., & Freitas, R. P. Shifting patterns of deadly violence. *Suicide and life
threatening behavior*, 1980, *10*, 195–209.

Stanley, E. J., & Barter, J. J. Adolescent suicidal behavior. *American Journal of Orthopsychiatry*, 1970, *40*, 87–96.

Tishler, C., & McKenry, P. Parental negative self and adolescent suicide attempters. *Journal of the American Academy of Child Psychiatry*, 1982, *21*, 404–
408.

Topol, P., & Reznikoff, M. Perceived peer and family relationships, hopelessness, and locus of control as factors in adolescent suicide attempts. *Suicide
and Life Threatening Behavior*, 1982, *12*, 141–150.

10

Helping Adolescent Survivors of Suicide

Sharon M. Valente and Joan Rifkin Sellers

Suicidologists have focused their attention primarily on the individual who commits suicide and have only recently explored how the surviving family members cope with a death by suicide. How do significant others—and particularly the adolescent—respond to the suicide of a loved one? There is little in the literature that examines the unique experience of adolescent survivors of suicide.

Adolescents are in the process of separation from the family and perhaps from the person who committed suicide. As adolescents strive toward independence, they are struggling to feel worthwhile and attempting to internalize a set of guiding values. For these reasons, the adolescent experiences bereavement differently from other surviving loved ones. Without a firmly established identity or self-image, the adolescent struggles to cope with the stigma, rejection, and disillusionment that accompany a suicidal death. This is doubly hard, since suicide is one of the most difficult types of death for any bereaved person.

The adolescent responds to a suicide by asking heart-rending questions: "Was there something I could have done to prevent this premature death?" "Did I cause this suicide?" Frequently, adolescents wish they had been more loving and had provided a reason for the dead person to continue living. One study (McIntyre & Angle, 1970), which indicated that 50% of preteens who did not believe that the suicider's death was permanent assumed the dead person would magically return to life, suggests that this magical thought pattern may continue into adolescence. This type of egocentric thought process and self-blame is characteristic of childhood defenses that adolescents often use under stress.

The adolescent, like the adult, desperately struggles to understand the course of events of the suicide but is limited by lack of exposure to death, by developmental status, and by immature cognitive skills. Thus, adolescents are particularly vulnerable to feelings of guilt and inadequacy. They often rely on less-mature coping skills than those used by most adults. The literature, in fact, suggests that some youthful offspring of suiciders may feel destined to repeat self-destructive patterns as they near the age of an older individual who committed suicide. The need to study these adolescent survivors is thus quite real, because if they receive therapeutic support and understanding while they are grieving they may develop positive ways to cope with loss rather than imitate self-destructive role models.

LITERATURE REVIEW

The suicide bereavement literature provides no statistical data about adolescent survivors, but it does identify three important themes: suicide survivors experience a variety of physical symptoms, along with strong and long-lasting emotions; support of family and friends may help or hinder the process of grief; and there are important issues in counseling suicide survivors. Case studies and observations of child and adult survivors offer some foundation for an understanding of the adolescent's experience, even though adolescents have been the forgotten grievers — they are absent in the literature and are rarely seen in therapy groups for suicide survivors.

Estimating the Number of Adolescent Suicide Survivors is Difficult

There are no statistics that identify how many adolescents (identified here as the 13 to 19 age group) survive a suicide. Surveys of survivors have not identified how many respondents were adolescents. However, two clinical programs in Los Angeles would estimate that in a group of 20 survivors, from one to three are adolescents. That is, the Los Angeles Suicide Prevention Center Survivors Program (see p. 284) knows of one adolescent for each 20 survivors referred for group therapy, while Hatton and Valente (1984) estimate that their small sample of survivors included three or four adolescents in a group of 20. Neither of these estimates reflects the circumstances of young people and families who cope with their grief without seeking help.

There are many reasons why most adolescents do not go for help or counseling. Some teenagers do not know about available resources; others have not mastered the ability to put feelings into words; and still others fear that needing help may signal weakness. Some adolescents wish to protect their families and themselves from their confusion and inner turmoil by reporting and trying to believe, "I'm fine." They try to act like a grownup and cope alone with the severe physical and emotional responses following a suicide.

Symptoms and Emotions of Bereavement after Suicide

Survivors describe death as a traumatic event causing a confusing and unpredictable array of disruptive physical symptoms and intense emotions that leave the family vulnerable to "physical, emotional, communication, and behavioral disorders" (Lindemann & Green, 1972, p. 64). With all acute bereavement:

> individuals feel physical distress, preoccupation with the image of the deceased, vivid memories of the circumstances of the death, strong emotions such as guilt, hostility, or fear, a tendency to push friends or relatives away, a loss of patterns of conduct, a readiness to copy traits of the deceased or to take over some of the activities or functions of the deceased (Lindemann & Green, 1972, pp. 64–65).

Death by suicide causes additional problems because the death may be premature, self-intended, or violent. After suicide, mourning is very difficult because there usually was no time to anticipate the separation or to say good-bye. Survivors feel added pain because a loved one died before living a full life and because the death was by an unnatural cause; this latter factor carries with it a social stigma. The suicide has made the statement that circumstances were such that it was not worth living on. Suicide survivors face not only the death of a loved one, but also a sense of rejection and disillusionment. Suicide leaves a legacy of shame, reproach, and damaged self-image for the survivor. Survivors seek a scapegoat to blame. They often blame themselves or another family member, and the adolescent may be particularly vulnerable to the effects of this blaming. Not only is the emotional process of mourning exhausting, but it also leaves the survivor "impatient without cause, irritable, withdrawn, isolated, remote, without roots, and incapable of effective action" (Lindemann & Green, 1972, p. 65). The adolescent must cope with the inner turmoil of grief while family members may be in such confusion that they avoid providing any structure such as limit setting, explanations, support, or comfort.

Suicide survivors share many of these responses with survivors of violent death because both modes of death are premature, unanticipated, potentially caused by human agency, and possibly preventable. Survivors of a violent death such as an airplane crash, homicide, or earthquake often experience similar physical and emotional reactions. However, the survivors of violent death are less likely to feel the rejection, stigma, or self-blame that the suicide survivor experiences when he or she thinks: "If I had been more loving, perhaps I could have prevented this death." Further, survivors of violent death are less likely to believe that they are destined to die in the same manner as the deceased.

When grief after suicide fails to resolve normally after about 2 years, the survivor's self-blame may lead to suicide attempts, or hostility may result in destructive acts (Hatton & Valente, 1984). For the survivor, suicide is such a deep wound that it has a great potential of devastating family unity, individual self-worth, and values. While suicidologists agree that suicide creates a period of psychological distress for survivors, they debate the serious consequences of unresolved grief. Several authorities believe that suicide often places the survivors in a high-risk group for committing suicide themselves (Hatton & Valente, 1984). In addition, survivors are at risk for physical problems.

Rudestam's study (1977) of 30 suicide survivors aged 19 to 70 described the range of severe and enduring physical and emotional responses. Initial responses to suicide ranged through feelings of denial, disbelief, fear, calm, control, relief, confusion, guilt, sadness, anger, shock, hysteria, repulsion, or fright. Seven months later, survivors reported new psychosomatic illnesses (for example, peptic ulcer, migraine headaches, hypertension, colitis, physical exhaustion, and other nervous problems). Other behavior problems included crying spells, outbursts of anger, sexual difficulties, withdrawal, anxiety, and use of tranquilizers and barbiturates. Some suggest that gender and culture influence these feelings. For instance, women may be more likely to express intense feelings, while men may be more likely to control most feelings but express anger first (Hatton & Valente, 1984).

While many of these responses follow any death, reactions after suicide or violent death are more prolonged and devastating. Duszynski, Shaffer, & Thomas (1981) hypothesized but could not prove that for the adolescent, the suicide of a parent was one type of trauma that might be a precursor of a developing cancer. Adolescents are likely to seek medical help for physical symptoms of grief while they try to ignore or manage their feelings alone. It is rare that a surviving adolescent does not have some symptoms of grief along with questions or misinformation about suicide. The adolescent may make important decisions about the future based on this inadequate information.

Case studies provide information on disturbed grief reactions and therapeutic interventions that facilitated mourning. Warren (1972) observed disturbed children who stopped developing emotionally when they were traumatized by a parent's suicide. These children continued to use the emotions and defenses prevalent at the time of the trauma, but such childhood patterns were not adequate to the demands of adolescence or adulthood. In part, Warren believed that this developmental arrest was caused by the child's need to preserve a myth that the family was ideal or that the death was natural rather than suicidal. Mourning could not continue until psychotherapy supported the immature and fragile identity and impulses of these individuals, and allowed them to correct the distortions of reality so they could express their hidden feelings safely. This implies that, especially for the younger adolescent, the remnants of childhood thoughts and emotions create a vulnerability to coping with suicidal death. Moreover, families who seek to protect the adolescent by hiding the facts surrounding suicide or their feelings of grief may unintentionally increase this vulnerability.

The Family Can Provide Critical Support for Grief

If the family and significant others can share their grief and understand that each individual may express grief differently, the individual is encouraged to express thoughts and emotions in a safe atmosphere. Richman (1977) suggests that the family network offers this support when members talk openly about the suicidal death with an adolescent and express various feelings. While it may be very difficult to know how to support the adolescent who acts as if everything is fine, families can significantly inhibit grief by isolating or excluding an individual, by displacing unresolved conflicts from the deceased to an individual scapegoat, or by leaving a role hiatus where functions previously conducted by the deceased remain unfulfilled.

In an example of a 14-year-old girl who took on all her dead brother's symptoms (Jensen & Wallace, 1967), the mother inhibited grief because she could not express or recognize her feelings, and the father's need to repress grief suggested that all feelings should be hidden. The adolescent, who had resented how her brother had received all the family's attention, was vulnerable to taking on his symptoms instead of expressing her pent-up rage and her feelings of abandonment and rejection. When therapy provided a safe place for parents and daughter to express grief, it also became clear that the adolescent's prior relationship with her brother contributed to the state of blocked grief or incomplete mourning.

Negative attitudes toward suicide may encourage the adolescent to hide expressions of grief and confine grief to private activities such as writing in a diary, confiding in a trusted pet, or listening to sad music. Private activities of this sort can indeed be helpful, but our point is that other productive expressions of grief may be inhibited by the absence of a safe, supportive atmosphere.

Counseling Provides a Safe Place for Adolescent Survivors of Suicide

The trauma of suicide may make it difficult for survivors to reach out for support as they become overwhelmed by feelings of abandonment, rejection, social isolation, and confusion. Yet some survivors may not be able to cope with the meaning of suicide, feelings of anger or blame, or damage to self-esteem when they are alone. When feelings are blocked, suicide is considered, or life remains empty and joyless, counseling can provide a safe place for sharing grief, confusion, anger, or fear. Schuyler (1973) suggests that counseling must provide a nonrejecting atmosphere to encourage feelings and to support grief and mourning. The counselor also needs to help the adolescent expand social support and build relationships by reaching out for comfort. Because males and females may tend to express grief differently, the counselor helps individual adolescents respect their own styles of grief. Whenever sleep and appetite are disturbed, or alcohol, pills, and drugs are used to blunt grief, then the counselor should help the adolescent both to monitor symptoms and to reconsider the use of dangerous substances. For instance, it is of critical importance to help the adolescent monitor increases in drinking and to avoid drinking and driving (Hatton & Valente, 1984). For some survivors of suicide, individual therapy is most effective because they relate best to one trusted person; for others, a support group of similar survivors facilitated by a therapist knowledgeable in suicide and bereavement is very effective. Still other survivors maintain that they find it most helpful to have fellow survivors lead self-help groups.

In summary, the literature emphasizes how child and adult survivors of suicide have experienced the feelings and symptoms of grief and how families have impeded or facilitated grief.

A DEVELOPMENTAL PERSPECTIVE ON THE ADOLESCENT SURVIVOR'S EXPERIENCE WITH GRIEF

Adolescence is a uniquely human phenomenon characterized by very rapid psychological and physical growth. Adolescents strive to balance conformity and rebelliousness in an effort to secure an identity, to feel worthwhile. They strive to answer the questions: "Who am I?" "What do I deserve in life?"

How then does the adolescent experience the loss of a loved one by suicide? Does this type of trauma significantly alter the already difficult growth process? There is no available data on that point. But it is helpful to consider Bowlby's description of the mourning process. Bowlby's (1969) model defines three developmental stages: protest, disorganization, and reorganization. These will be discussed in more detail below.

Keep in mind, however, that this construct does not accurately reflect the case of every bereaved adolescent. This is due to a number of factors. Adolescents cope differently. Some experience these stages of mourning at different time intervals; others may regress. Circumstances such as age, level of maturity, support network, psychological profile before the suicide, relationship with the deceased, and the features of the suicide itself may influence different reactions.

Protesting the Death: The Beginning of Acute Grief

In the *protest phase* of bereavement following a suicide, strong responses reported include disbelief, denial, anger, fear (especially of loss of control), relief, repulsion, and guilt. Increased substance use, sexual disturbance, and somatic symptoms are also described. Some survivors experience a fear of insanity as well as difficulties concentrating and controlling affect. Some focus on their own behavior, disassociating or separating themselves from their experience in order to assess themselves. Following the suicide, the adolescent often concludes that his or her relationship with the bereaved never had any value from the very beginning.

The adolescent survivor of a suicide, not yet comfortable with a secure self-identity, is likely to feel a sense of personal failure and great guilt. The adolescent may rely upon comfortable juvenile coping skills, especially regression. Alternatively, the adolescent may attempt to react in what is perceived as an adult manner by exhibiting control. The suicide for some may be a first experience with death. As a result, the adolescent may question the value of the struggle to become an adult.

The family frequently responds to a suicide by developing a "family myth"that protects it. Each member assures friends and extended family that all is fine. This distorted communication and the unspoken feelings that it shrouds may confuse the adolescent and contribute to additional difficulties.

Adults appear strong and independent; they exhibit more need behind closed doors. The adolescent may seek to emulate this overt behavior. At the same time, he or she may question whether a traumatized family system that does not offer practical assistance is strong enough to be supportive in future crises. The family, after all, must have failed to support the deceased. Disillusionment and bitterness may then complicate or hasten the separation process normal for adolescents. As a result, constructive growth may remain a difficult private struggle without professional help.

The funeral and other postsuicide occurrences challenge newly formed social skills. For some adolescents, postsuicide rituals such as funerals and family gatherings are helpful especially if their friends can attend and if adults help explain what will happen at the ceremony. For other adolescents, rituals are supportive when the adolescent knows that his or her need for private time away from the ceremony will be respected rather than considered unacceptable. Similarly, the adolescent survivor must continue to attend school and handle other responsibilities after only a brief time period. This is complicated because adolescents are typically expected to behave submissively in our society and are taught that it is unacceptable to express their feelings in public.

Disorganization: Grief Disrupts Thoughts, Feelings, Behavior, and Relationships

In the *disorganization phase*, the mourner begins to deal with the damage to self-image, the death itself, disillusionment, shame, and rejection (Lindemann & Green, 1972). The adolescent may report feelings of unreality or distortions of reality, a need for punishment, symptoms of depression, the idealization of the lost loved one, a sense of powerlessness, intense rage, inability to predict, loss of faith in personal judgment, and a lack of pleasure from accomplishments (survivor's guilt). Objects belonging to the deceased may take on some symbolic significance.

The suicide may cause the adolescent mourner to experience and to attempt to cope with the loss of an adult role model. This also affects the separation process. Prior efforts to disengage may cause guilt. Some adolescents conclude that suicide is an available life option or a destiny. This could result in time distortion, for example, the belief that one must live to the extreme if death occurs early.

Family rules and roles continue to be in disarray. Family members begin to test, restructure, and readjust. Frequently, professionals can identify problems associated with new one-parent families. Living arrangements are often changed, especially if a "breadwinner" is deceased (Cain & Fast, 1972). The adolescent may be called upon to accept an adult role, to be relied upon in new ways. Or, the adolescent may unite the family system by becoming the problem or scapegoat. If a child is perceived as having failed at rescuing the suicide, he or she may be seen as "second best" somehow.

Parents sometimes report that they grow insecure with parenting skills following a suicide (Hatton & Valente, 1984). They may become increasingly lenient and anxious. The adolescent who has relied on consistent parenting may thus feel confused and insecure. Persons who formerly served as "nurturers" are unable to provide the same support offered in prior crises because they are involved themselves with the mourning process.

Survivors of suicide feel ostracized by their communities. They find others do not want to discuss their loss in a meaningful manner and gradually withdraw. Some families move to new communities to enable the "family myth" to survive. This may temporarily ease the experience of the adolescent in the midst of processing social norms and attitudes, even while it causes problems for some adolescents who are forced by relocation to develop new peer-group networks. Although adolescents may be capable of self-expression and rely less than adults on avoidance, society restrains them, preferring to accept the family myth.

Reorganization: Refocusing on Life

In the *reorganization phase*, energy is refocused in healthy directions. Survivors experience hope. They may assert that they "see the light at the end of the tunnel." Although they will never forget, they will survive.

Memories become less intrusive. Strong emotions, however, may unexpectedly emerge. The survivor begins to take such chances as trusting others, joining social activities, and appreciating selected memories. Concentration improves and painful or energy-sapping ruminating decreases. Also, the survivor begins to feel improved physical well-being.

The family experiences the restoration of mutually need-satisfying relationships that had been blocked by grief work following the suicide (Jensen & Wallace, 1967). There is intermittent comfort with new roles and with new rules. The family appears to have redistributed the responsibilities of the suicider. While an adolescent may resist an uncomfortable role "assignment" such as a parenting role, this is a normal, healthy response. For the most part, family members enjoy increased closeness, experience healthier communications, and are less hindered by testing behaviors.

Family members may re-establish a link with the deceased. An object such as a piece of jewelry may communicate, "yes, I cared." Grievers recall positive and negative aspects of the lost relationship. New relationships may also be initiated.

Individuals often reassess their values and attain a different perspective following a suicide. Material possessions take on a different significance. The family that survived the ordeal together seems all the more valuable. Prior concerns such as looks or clothes seem petty. Adolescents may find the preoccupations of their peers insignificant.

Socially, adolescents may continue to have a difficult adjustment, but, with family support strengthening, this is not as potentially destructive as it might have been. Indeed, adolescents may draw upon rejuvenated energies to plan and implement new-found life choices, such as career decisions. It is likely that these adolescents will be more aware than their peers of the spectrum of opportunities and network of community resources available to them.

A THERAPEUTIC ENVIRONMENT
FOR ADOLESCENT SUICIDE SURVIVORS

Creating a Safe, Therapeutic Context
for Grief and Mourning

Because of the stigma of suicide, a therapeutic environment needs to allow the adolescent to explore repeatedly why the deceased committed suicide, to understand the meaning of a suicidal death, and to have a relationship based on trust and acceptance. A therapeutic environment allows the free expression of anger, joy, sadness, or shame without fear of judgment. The adolescent will examine "Why did Grandpa commit suicide? Why didn't he let us help him feel better?" He or she will also go on to ask in thousands of ways: "Why didn't I do something that prevented this death?" The adolescent may hide the fact that these questions are painful to consider and even more painful to share. Yet, bottling up even more frightening questions (such as "Could I ever commit suicide?") often leaves the adolescent confused and vulnerable. Because well-meaning friends and family simply cause more pain when trying to be helpful by saying, "You'll get over it. Just be glad it's over," or, "Well, just think—it could be worse, look on the bright side," the adolescent may resist sharing pain and fear. For the adolescent, the suicide may be shattering, but hiding pain and confusion may cause even more severe damage and loss of support.

Before trusting someone to understand and be supportive, adolescents may want to see that they will not be blamed for how they are feeling and will not be given the impression that their feelings are wrong or unimportant. Adolescents will trust someone who respects their own style of grief, honors confidences, does not simply offer advice about what they should do or feel, and is sincerely interested in their concerns.

Being therapeutic also implies understanding and setting limits on destructive behavior as well as helping the adolescent set limits on self-punishing or self- destructive behavior. The adolescent who feels vulnerable to loss of control needs to know that a trusted adult will help protect safety and help control destructive impulses such as drinking excessively or threatening suicide.

Any suicide threat should be considered seriously as a cry for help. Nothing that threatens life or safety should be kept confidential. Because the adolescent survivor tends to think no one understands this experience, it is often therapeutic for a listener to disclose his or her own feelings relating to what the adolescent is experiencing. But it is important that this self-disclosure does not take attention away from the adolescent. It need only communicate understanding and briefly model a way to share feelings. Adolescents who are struggling to learn how to put feelings into words can benefit from a relationship where the other person emphasizes the importance of feelings. This can be done in a variety of ways. One approach is to say: "If that had happened to me, I would probably feel numb, hurt, or confused. I wonder how you feel?"

A therapeutic relationship encourages the adolescent to feel understood and to risk sharing feelings. Another way of offering support is to recognize the positive ways in which the adolescent is coping. When denial is the major coping strategy in use, then it is usually necessary to support denial and to explore what may *not* be denied. For instance, one 16-year-old boy was traumatized by finding his father who had just shot himself. He was frozen with fear and for months later kept saying, "I'm fine," while he looked miserable. In this case, the adolescent expressed concern about school work and trouble falling asleep. So it was important to focus on these areas of concern. Adolescents who are grieving also wish to be recognized as individuals who have hobbies, school work, goals, and values. It is as if the adolescent survivor believes that because of the suicide, "I'm no good and I don't deserve to live." A therapeutic relationship helps the adolescent regain the image of being a worthwhile person.

A supportive person who believes that the adolescent is worthwhile and is not the same person as the suicider can have tremendous impact on helping the adolescent consider these thoughts and feelings. With such support, the adolescent can confront the reality that no one can keep another person alive, and nobody's self-worth depends on pre-venting suicide. Often *giving* another person a "reason to live" is more than any one individual can do. Whether or not therapeutic support is successful rests on its ability to help the adolescent explore the feelings and fears behind thoughts such as these, to understand the messages of suicide, and to plan constructive ways of coping with disturbing feel-ings. The therapeutic message must be that suicide is a permanent solu-tion to what is often a temporary problem—and that the adolescent can develop more productive ways to solve problems.

Respecting the Needs of Adolescents

Each person experiences grief in a unique way. Appreciating and sup-porting the adolescent requires knowing that there is no way that he or she *should* feel at any one time—and that what adolescents can do is to respect the feelings they have. It helps the adolescent to hear that every-one at some time wants to be taken care of or held or nurtured. Adoles-cents receive confusing messages about what grief should be and how long it should last, so it is usual for the adolescent to imagine that it is wrong or bad to have feelings such as anger, sadness, or joy. Often, the adolescent's need to be rebellious, aloof, difficult, or volatile is hard to understand and respect. This is especially true when the inner pain of grief prompts the adolescent to strike out and hurt those nearby trying to be helpful. Sometimes being angry at those around is the way the ad-olescent is trying to maintain control.

Monitoring Symptoms
of Self-Destructive Behavior

After a suicide, survivors wonder if they have enough reason to go on living. Many survivors choose to punish themselves by self-destructive behavior. Self-destructive behavior may come in many forms, from ob-vious suicide threats and attempts to drunk or reckless driving, sub-stance abuse, or eating disorders. If there is any hint of these behaviors or of the idea that the adolescent may think life is not worth living, then it is important to ask about suicidal thoughts and whether there is any plan for carrying out such ideas. If so, the adolescent should see a professional suicide prevention counselor and should be asked to promise that nothing dangerous will be done before talking with the counselor, a supportive adult, or the suicide prevention center.

What more frequently occurs is that adolescents increase their drinking or drug use as they try to cope with the pain of grief. In these cases, it is important to understand that moderate increases are ways of coping. However, what is equally important is to plan with the adolescent for safe precautions, for example, promising not to drive after drinking and agreeing to discuss how much drinking or drug use is increasing over what periods of time. Often, adolescents will set their own limits about how much liquor or how many sleeping pills are too much. Any increased drug or alcohol use should be explored for a hidden wish to die or just to not wake up again. Most often, adolescents are reassured that someone is concerned about their safety if they drink or use drugs. If the problem is sleep disturbance or appetite disturbance, then depression may be the underlying issue. When such symptoms continue, a complete examination for physical and psychological causes is indicated. All physical symptoms should also be monitored. It is routine to ask about nightmares, sleeping, appetite, and any aches or pains. The symptoms of grief should be acute for the first few months and then they should generally begin to subside. One indication that grief is proceeding in a normal pattern, however, is the ability of deep feelings of loss and sadness to be triggered suddenly. In the grief after suicide, it is not uncommon to have episodic resurgences of acute grief for 1 to 2 years after the suicide.

Indications for Referral

For the adolescent suicide survivor, suicide threats or attempts or other self-destructive behavior should indicate a referral to a professional counselor trained in suicide and bereavement. Symptoms of depression, such as sadness or weight loss (of more than 10 pounds) that continues and is accompanied by a sense of worthlessness and thoughts of death, should suggest the need for a referral.

Mourning is a normal process, but grief after suicide has potentially serious complications. An adolescent should thus be encouraged to talk with a counselor if he or she has no social support system available, no peer or adult with whom to share confidences, or prolonged difficulty functioning with school work, peers, and the family. Another reason for referral would be increased use of drugs or alcohol that continues for long periods. It is reasonable to expect that symptoms of grief during the first 6 weeks to 3 months may include some sleeplessness, dejected mood, and sadness. When symptoms become severe and the adolescent cannot eat, sleep, or concentrate in school, then a referral is indicated. Other behavior problems, such as truancy, aggression, or increased sexual acting out, may also indicate that the adolescent needs help to cope with emotions and the pain of loss.

Sometimes families who feel their resources are strained simply decide that adolescents should have a supportive counselor available during the mourning process to explain what happened and what suicide means. One of the most frightening thoughts to a family is that another person might die by suicide—so counseling as a preventive measure is one way to support family self-esteem and coping.

Issues for Significant Others

Those who offer support to or work with an adolescent suicide survivor are likely to experience several feelings. First, such a person is tempted to think that he or she simply does not know the right thing to say in order to help anyone who is experiencing such acute grief. However, for those who are grieving, what is of critical importance is not the "right" or "correct" word but the presence and concern of a caring human being and the effort to listen without offering a judgment or a criticism. When the right word does not come to mind, it is often best to say, "I feel for you, but I simply don't know what to say to offer comfort." Second, there is the magic wish or hope that simply by caring a person can help the adolescent feel better. There are many times when what the adolescent survivor needs is someone who tries to understand his or her feelings—not someone who "needs" him or her to feel differently or to feel better. The pain of loving and losing someone is a very real pain; no one can take that pain away. But having someone who cares enough to listen does help.

Third, listening to the adolescent survivor's pain and questions about suicide and death is likely to evoke in the helper questions about life and death and suicide. Adolescents are likely to ask those who offer help if they have ever considered suicide, and they may depend on an adult as a role model who will counterbalance the role model they already have for suicide. It is important that the helper is honest about his or her values, and it is also important that he or she has a commitment to nonsuicidal coping strategies in advising an adolescent to choose life-enhancing strategies. In any case, it is advisable for the helper to think about his or her values regarding suicide and death before a vulnerable survivor puts him or her on the spot and expects a quick answer. Finally, because supporting a suicide survivor may be rewarding as well as exhausting, helpers need to respect their own needs and limits as well as those of adolescents. Hence, consultation is one approach to consider that will help a supporter maintain objectivity and be a constructive helper. Most suicide prevention counselors depend heavily on consultation. The consultant should be a colleague or professional counselor who provides support for the caregiver and helps the caregiver understand and cope with his or her own needs, feelings, and difficulties.

SUMMARY AND CONCLUSIONS

The need for research is evident to explore normal and disturbed grief after suicide and the impact of this grief on survivors in early, middle, and late adolescence. Because adolescents are, simply by virtue of age and developmental status, at high risk for suicide, and because suicide survivors are also at increased risk for suicide, a research description of adolescent needs and experiences is critical as a guide for parents, friends, and counselors who wish to help adolescents cope with suicide bereavement in a positive manner.

Healing following any loss of a loved one is a long, painful process. Adolescent survivors of suicide have a particularly difficult task. They must move through the mourning process at the same time as they experience the difficult challenges that all adolescents face. Since the risk of suicide by the adolescent is increased the longer this process is delayed, it is especially hoped that the adolescent moves smoothly into the reorganization phase of bereavement.

REFERENCES

Bowlby, J. *Attachment*. New York: Basic Books, 1969.

Cain, A. C., & Fast, I. Children's disturbed reactions to parent suicide: distortions of guilt, communication, and identification. In A. C. Cain (Ed.), *Survivors of suicide* (pp. 93–111). Springfield, IL: Charles C Thomas, 1972.

Duszynski, K. R., Shaffer, J. W., & Thomas, C. B., Neoplasm and traumatic events in childhood: Are they related? *Archives of General Psychiatry*, 1981, 38, 327-331.

Hatton, C. L., & Valente, S. M. *Suicide: Assessment and intervention* (2nd ed.) Norwalk, CT: Appleton-Century-Crofts, 1984.

Jensen, G. D., & Wallace, J. G. Family mourning process. *Family Process*, 1967, 6, 56–66.

Lindemann, E., & Green, I. M. A study of grief: Emotional responses to suicide. In A. C. Cain (Ed.), *Survivors of suicide* (pp. 63–69). Springfield, IL: Charles C Thomas, 1972.

McIntyre, M. S., & Angle, C. A. *The child's concept of death.* Paper presented at Workshop in Methodology, Ambulatory Pediatric Society, Atlantic City, NJ, April 1970.

Richman, J. Family and environmental aspects of suicide. In B. Danto & A. H. Kutscher (Eds.), *Suicide and bereavement* (pp.119–123). New York: MISS Information Corporation, 1977.

Rudestam, K. E. Physical and psychological responses to suicide in the family. *Journal of Counseling and Consulting Psychology,* 1977, 45, 162–170.

Schuyler, D. Counseling suicide survivors: Issues and answers. *Omega,* 1973, 5, 313–320.

Warren, M. Some psychological sequellae of parental suicide in surviving children. In A. C. Cain (Ed.), *Survivors of Suicide* (pp.112–120). Springfield, IL: Charles C Thomas, 1972.

BIBLIOGRAPHY

Calhoun, L. G., Selby, J. W., Redeschi, R. G., & David, B. The aftermath of suicide: An instrument for measuring reactions to the surviving family. *Journal of Psychiatric Treatment and Evaluation,* 1981, 3, 99–103.

Cook, J. A. A death in the family: Parental bereavement in the first year. *Suicide and Life Threatening Behavior,* 1983, 13, 42–61.

Dorpat, T. L. Psychological effects of parental suicide on surviving children. In A. C. Cain (Ed.), *Survivors of suicide* (pp. 121–142). Springfield, IL: Charles C Thomas, 1972.

Hatton, C. L., & Valente, S. M. Bereavement groups for parents who survive a suicidal loss of a child. *Suicide and Life Threatening Behavior,* 1981, 11, 141–150.

Welch, T. A. This is a safe place. *Omega Report,* 1980, 1, 2–3.

PART IV

Prevention, Intervention, Postvention

Chapters 11, 12, and 13 address interventions by adults and other helpers that take place before, during, or after a death-related experience and that are designed to help adolescents cope with that experience. In turn, these three chapters consider constructive roles for parents and peers, educators, and counselors. By focusing on the people who might help rather than the places where help is offered (for example, home, school, church, synagogue, etc.), these chapters are able to identify opportunities, suggest strategies, and propose concrete guidelines that will be applicable to innumerable helpers and to a variety of situations.

A fundamental principle is that intervention is most naturally undertaken and most likely to be productive when it occurs prior to a crisis. As Joan McNeil makes clear in Chapter 11, it is in the ordinary exchanges among family members and friends that ideas are originally developed, feelings shared, behaviors modelled, and values formed. The question is not whether this will take place, but how effectively it can be carried out. Learning to cope with the minor losses of childhood within the security of one's own family and close peer group is the best preparation that we know of for responding in a mature manner to more significant death-related issues in adolescence. McNeil's identification of the central factors involved in communications among adolescents, their parents, and their peers reveals why interactions related to death are often difficult and shows how they might be made more effective.

Informal death education within families is a secure foundation upon which to engage in formal programs of study within a school setting. Adults who wonder whether or how to teach adolescents about death have only to consider the very practical advice on these matters that is offered by Nina Rosenthal in Chapter 12. Rosenthal outlines three primary aspects of death education —information, self-awareness, and skills for helping—in a way that will fit any balanced course of study. She also offers detailed examples of pedagogical topics, objectives, materials, methods, and procedures for evaluation under each of these primary headings. All of this can be applied easily by individual educators to the particular adolescents they are teaching and to their own special curricular situations.

Prevention becomes postvention in the wake of a death-related experience, a time when adolescents look to family members, peers, or other adults to help them in coming to terms with what has happened. Chapters 11 and 12 do not neglect such retrospective intervention, but it is most fully considered here in Chapter 13 in the context of what Suzanne Calvin and Inez Smith have to say about counseling adolescents in death-related situations. For Calvin and Smith, the term "counseling" covers a broad range of relationships and a wide variety of activities. It can be the work of many kinds of individuals—professionals and lay persons alike. The key point is that counselors must not do the work for adolescents. They should not and need not pretend to have answers for all problems. Instead, the very distinctive and often quite indispensable role for counselors is one of helping adolescents solve their own problems. Anyone familiar with the common adolescent demand for independence will realize how important it is to support this legitimate need for autonomy. As Calvin and Smith point out, counseling strives to foster an atmosphere of safety and clarification in which adolescents can resolve what may be a very wide range of intra- and interpersonal difficulties. In this way, counselors enable adolescents to improve their own lives in the short run and to acquire the skills needed for further growth over the longer haul.

11

Talking About Death: Adolescents, Parents, and Peers

Joan N. McNeil

I don't remember much about my mother, or how she died, or anything. I was about five years old, and my Dad has never mentioned her again, not since the day she was buried. There aren't even any pictures of her around the house! I wonder about her a lot. But I guess I'll never find out—he just doesn't like to talk about her.

Death is *not* talked about in our house! I wish it would be—at least once in a while. There are some things I'd like to know about. You know, why people have to die . . . and what we can do about wars and killing and stuff. And how everyone feels about things like dying. But I've always understood it wasn't a good idea to ask questions about such things, so I never have. (McNeil, 1984b)

These comments from young people are, unfortunately, not imaginary or even unique. They appear to be representative of some family situations in which the dilemmas of death occur and that require —but do not always provide— some measure of understanding between parents and children.

Although death is often encountered in various ways throughout childhood, actual preparation for dealing with death events often may not be achieved in family settings, as various authors have pointed out (for example, Gordon & Klass, 1979; McNeil, 1983). By the time the average young person reaches adolescence, family patterns of communication about both "acceptable" and "unacceptable" topics are usually well established. Interactions both with parents and with peers tend to be the primary sources for acquiring attitudes about most taboo subjects such as sex (Hass, 1979; Sorenson, 1973). Is this also true for the subject of death? I would suggest that it is indeed a comparable form of socialization, and that parents and young people need to be aware of the importance of open, helpful discussions of death concerns in family settings.

This chapter will examine recent literature concerning adolescent-parent relationships, particularly as these studies can reveal insights into some general attitudes and communication themes in families of adolescents. Additional clues to the socialization of young people in Western society are provided in selected studies of adolescent peer relationships. A report of a recent exploratory study will emphasize further the ways adolescents tend to talk about their death concerns. Finally, implications of these studies will be formulated since they may encourage parents and young people to develop more useful and meaningful communication skills—a primary concern in talking about death.

PARENT-ADOLESCENT COMMUNICATION

Humor columnist Erma Bombeck has written in "Talk to Me—I'm Your Mother" (1973):

> Communication has always been a problem among families. . . . We have a son who speaks only four words a year. One day as I was separating an egg, the whole thing cracked and slid to the floor. He looked at me and said, "Way to go, Mom." I have always been envious of the mothers of children who talk. What good times they must enjoy . . . the intimate laughter, the first blush of a shared secret. Our relationship is a lot like the President and Congress. Getting through to kids is not easy for parents. (pp. 28–40)

Parents who can share this problem may feel, like Erma Bombeck, a bit envious of families who seem to handle the traumas of life with adolescents smoothly and baffled by the changes occurring in their own families as their children grow toward adulthood. Although the nature of interpersonal relationships varies from family to family, the one essential ingredient for soothing the inevitable sore spots as families experience the ups and downs of growth and development of individual members is undoubtedly *open communication* (Barnes & Olson, 1982).

Kastenbaum (1981) has suggested that the general level of communication established early by parents influences a child's ability to talk about any topic of concern and thus his or her eventual attitudes toward life and death. This process is affected by the mutual influences of parents and children interacting within the family system. Thus it is appropriate here to consider general characteristics of *both* adolescents and their middle-aged parents, as they may influence each other and the unique quality of relationships in their families.

Adolescent Characteristics

The common-sense notion that it is more difficult to communicate with someone of another generation contains some truth. American teenagers are often caught up in what Sorenson (1973) has termed "generational chauvinism," seeing themselves as part of a special group of people their own age, a group that is better than any other. Comparing themselves with people in their forties and fifties, adolescents consider themselves more idealistic, less materialistic, healthier sexually, and better able to understand friendship and the important things in life (Sorenson, 1973). This attitude is obviously one that can cause some resentment and defensiveness on the part of their elders, and is not likely to enhance communication.

A second characteristic that can inhibit effective communication is the inconsistency that adolescents often display in their responses toward their parents; it may be difficult for parents to know what to expect. One day the teenage daughter will talk enthusiastically with her mother about her friends and her feelings about life in general. The next day, she will appear very secretive and complain that her mother asks too many questions. Or the teenage son will resort to a "closed door" policy (as illustrated above) and allow his parents entry only after repeated attempts to urge his cooperation. Such inconsistent behavior among early adolescents is common, as they vacillate frequently and unpredictably from adult behavior to child behavior. Although they may display increased self awareness as they leave their elementary school years, adolescents are often so engrossed in their own complex changes that they cannot pay adequate attention to adult feelings (Gibson, 1983).

Young people frequently feel conflict between wanting to be independent of their parents and realizing how dependent they actually are. In the pursuit of independence, adolescents often repulse their parents' attempts to guide them, dismiss their opinions as hopelessly out of date and irrelevant, and deliberately say and do things to shock them. Erikson (1950), whose ideas on the adolescent search for identity are commonly accepted, says:

> In their search for a new sense of continuity and sameness, adolescents have to refight many of the battles of earlier years, even though to do so

they must artificially appoint perfectly well-meaning people to play their roles of adversaries. (p. 261)

Some display of rebelliousness is normal in adolescence, especially during the emotional midteens, although marked or persistent rebelliousness appears to be more of a defensive response reflecting the teenager's frustrations in attaining autonomy in an unsupportive environment. In one study (Clemens & Rust, 1979), feelings of rebellion and alienation were positively correlated with parent-adolescent disagreement about how the adolescent should be reared, as well as with the adolescent's negative attitude toward school. Adolescent rebelliousness decreased somewhat with higher levels of parent education. Rebellious tendencies are also associated with extremely restrictive or extremely permissive child-rearing practices, or with homes in which parents have an unhappy marriage (Balswick & Macrides, 1975). Whatever the cause, this characteristic in one's growing child is not likely to facilitate patience and forbearance in normal parents.

In spite of recent societal openness toward "taboo" topics, communication about sex and death still remains a problem for most parents and teenagers. Young people generally want to be able to talk freely with their parents about problems in these areas, but do not for many reasons. Hass (1979) reports that teenagers say they cannot be open with their parents because their parents are not open with them; because their parents' views are so different and would therefore exclude any possibility of understanding; because they are afraid of their parents' disapproval, lectures, or punishment; because they are embarrassed; or occasionally, because of their own desire for privacy. Inexperience in talking with adults or anyone else about potentially emotional topics may arouse defensive behaviors in immature young people, such as sarcasm, joking and "horsing around," or stubborn silence. Such behaviors are undoubtedly strong blocks to helpful communication between adolescents and their parents.

At the same time that adolescents appear to be uninterested in their parents or even scornful of their ideas, they frequently are still using their parents as models in their day-to-day behaviors. This fact can be both a positive and a negative aspect of parent-adolescent relationships. On the negative side, parents may often complain about the way their adolescents talk to them, although adolescents have learned their basic style of communication by imitating their parents. Parents who adopt a "do what I say" rather than a "do what I do" policy are often surprised to find that adolescents have obeyed their parental behavior instead of their words. Defense-producing statements from mothers and fathers, such as "Do what I tell you" or "Shut up," are sometimes thrown back at them when their children become adolescents.

On the positive side, numerous studies have shown that parents' political, religious, educational, and vocational opinions and values have a powerful impact on adolescents. Most young people, for instance, favor the same candidate for president and attend the same church as their parents. Devereux (1972) demonstrated that a clear indicator of adolescent values is the behavior and attitude of parents toward moral issues. A survey asking parents and adolescents what values (such as peace, wisdom, honesty, salvation) they esteemed found many similarities between the generations. Daughters were even more similar to their parents than sons were (Feather, 1980).

Lerner (1975) reported that while high school students and their parents differed on more than half of a large group of opinion items, the majority of these differences consisted of the intensity of the attitude rather than a basic difference in attitudes. Both adolescents and their parents in Lerner's study tended to misperceive their attitudinal differences, with adolescents *overestimating* the number of major differences between themselves and their parents, and their parents *underestimating* the differences. This misperception indicates another possible communication snag between the generations.

Parent Characteristics

A first point to observe about parents is that their attitudes clearly have an effect on adolescent behavior, just as adolescent attitudes have an effect on parents. That is, in most families there is a natural system of mutual influences (McGillicuddy-Delisi, 1980). Thus, when parents begin to recognize the adolescent's ability to behave as a competent adult, the young person tends to reciprocate. Also, research has shown that parents who are detached and hostile are more likely to have teenagers who get into trouble and exhibit hostile rather than trusting behavior, and that parents who are warm and attentive tend to have adolescent children who have less difficulty in adjusting to the changes of this age period (Snoek & Rothblum, 1979).

Second, assuming that the majority of parents who have adolescent children are themselves middle-aged, this factor alone may be responsible for some parent adolescent conflicts. For example, at least one study has shown that age differences are consistently accompanied by value differences as well (Fengler & Wood, 1972). Because education affects one's personal values, we might also expect adolescents' values to change as they acquire more education. One study showed that the more education individuals receive, the greater the difference in personal values between themselves and their parents (Bengston, 1975). These differences in values may further diminish effective communication between adolescents and their parents.

A third important source of parent-adolescent conflict lies in parents' unwillingness to "let go" of their growing children. Atwater (1983) comments:

> Having invested so much of themselves in their children's lives for so many years, even the healthiest parents experience mixed feelings about their adolescents' growing independence, especially in a fast-moving permissive society. So the more unfulfilled or frustrated parents are in their personal or marital lives, the more reluctant they may be to let go of their adolescents. . . . Such problems may become even more intricate when there has been a divorce or a remarriage, with the resulting complications of the parent-adolescent relationship. (p. 118)

Parental "holding on" can result in rebellious behaviors on the part of their children and in an increase in negative interactions in the family.

Fourth, conflicts often arise in families because adolescents and their parents are at different developmental stages. Physically and psychologically, adolescents have boundless energy and are eager to explore their potentials. At times, this intensity seems to burst forth in all directions at once. However, their middle aged parents are at the stage of life when they have less physical energy and more stress-producing responsibilities. Within the family, middle-agers often feel caught between generations. They are increasingly concerned with providing an education for their young and with taking care of their aging parents. Moreover, many are involved in work roles of increased power and competence, at the peak of their creative productivity and career experience, or involved in changes in life goals. Physical changes and general health problems also tend to develop in midlife.

All these contrasting psychological and physical states in young people and their parents can be intensified by differences in expectations. Parents often presume that their budding adolescent children are more emotionally mature than they really are (because they *look* grown up!) and sometimes parents may demand in exasperation, "Why don't you grow up!" Adolescents, still in the clutches of adolescent egocentrism, may expect their parents to give complete attention to their every problem or enthusiasm, and may complain, "Why don't you understand!" Each then experiences disappointment at the seeming lack of unconditional appreciation on the part of the other. And communication between them may from time to time deteriorate to criticisms, commands, and mutual resistance.

The subject of death undoubtedly has different meanings for middle-aged parents and for their adolescent children. From the unique experiences of their own growing-up years, their present concerns about their elderly, ill, or dying parents, and perhaps the deaths of their own peers, people in midlife become more aware of life's realities. Research does show that middle-aged adults say they are less fearful of death and dying than are younger adults (Kalish & Reynolds, 1981), but they also give more thought to their own eventual death. People in midlife gradually move from thinking in terms of the time they have already lived, to thinking in terms of the time they have left to live, for they "know more deeply than ever before that [they are] going to die" (Levinson, Darrow, Klein, Levinson, & McKee, 1978, p. 205).

These parental perceptions may include both a deeper awareness of the purposes of their own lives and a greater desire to avoid the pain of loss experiences. Also, their need as parents to protect their young from the knowledge and discomfort of loss and grief is understandable. However, as adolescents display a growing curiosity about death and actively seek life-risking behaviors, they play on the fears of their parents, thus complicating the communication between them.

PEERS AND PARENTS

Many parents, particularly upper- and middle-class parents, place a great emphasis on popularity and success for their children. They may complain about the amount of time and energy their children devote to their peers, but their own affirmation of the importance of popularity with peers may strengthen the adolescent's desire to conform to peer expectations. Some parents are uncertain about the behaviors they should expect from adolescents, and tend to see the influence of their children's age-mates as more powerful than their own, which may easily become a self-fulfilling prophecy (Conger & Petersen, 1984).

Friends become vitally important during the adolescent years as young people pursue the task of separating from their families, seeking their own identities, and, in the process, looking for kindred spirits with whom to relate. There is no single peer group for all teenagers. The subgroup they are drawn to depends partly on socioeconomic status, partly on the values picked up from home, and partly on their own personalities. The desire to be accepted by the crowd is strong during adolescence, but not all adolescents run with the herd. Some are independent and individualistic. Some are pursuing life goals that keep them too busy. And some prefer fewer but more intimate friendships. In most cases, friends give each other the emotional support that adolescents need but often can no longer accept from their parents.

However, as important as peers are to the adolescent, in most cases they serve to supplement, rather than undermine, parental influence (Sorenson, 1973). In fact, at the beginning of adolescence, both parents and peers are important sources for psychological support, and as adolescence continues, the young person develops autonomy in relation to both. The common belief that parental and peer-group values are incompatible, and that teenagers' dependence on their friends indicates a sharp decline in parental influence is untrue for most adolescents. Conger and Petersen (1984) point out that there is usually considerable overlap between the values of the adolescent's parents and his or her peers because of their common backgrounds. A teenager's parents and his or her friends usually belong to the same or similar social, economic, geographic, educational, and religious groups. So peers may actually reinforce parental values on many issues.

Neither parental nor peer influence extends to all areas of adolescent decision making and behavior. The opinions of parents or peers carry different weights in specific situations. For example, peer influence is likely to be more important in such matters as attitudes toward school subjects or teachers, fashions in clothing and language, tastes in music and entertainment, and patterns of social interactions with the same or opposite sex. Parental influence is more likely to dominate in such matters as basic moral and social values, and in an understanding of the adult world (Larson, 1972).

Adolescents who are strongly peer-oriented have been found to be more likely than those who are adult-oriented to hold negative views of themselves and their peer group. They see themselves and are seen by teachers and their peers as less dependable, more subject to peer group pressure, "meaner," and more likely to disobey adults. They tend to lack positive self esteem and to take a somewhat gloomy view of their futures. Peer-oriented adolescents are also less interested in and less effective in academic work (Condry & Siman, 1974).

The parents of adult-oriented adolescents have been seen as being more "active," that is, more nurturant, demanding, giving of companionship and discipline, and more consistent in these qualities. This was especially true in the case of boys. Apparently, parents of the peer-oriented adolescent leave their child to seek approval and affection outside the home, so that "he turns to his age-mates less by choice than by default" (Bronfenbrenner, 1970, p. 96).

In the case in which parents have not chosen to help an adolescent deal with a death-related problem, interested peers may serve as a necessary source of understanding and support, as a young girl's comments in a recent interview illustrate (McNeil, 1984b):

> I keep thinking, this is my senior year, it's supposed to be happy! But there's that old dark cloud hanging over, with Jerry so sick and everyone so busy, too busy to talk, it seems. What would I do without my pal Sal, who listens and listens and mops up my tears and loans me Kleenex and gives me hugs when I need 'em so bad. I just can't cry at home, seems like it's a selfish thing to do, but have to keep cheerful and help get supper and do up the dishes without complaining. I do try hard, but it's such a relief to run to Sally's where I can be free for a while, and just give in.

DEATH AND DEFENSIVENESS

It seems likely that, given the potentially difficult nature of the subject of death and dying as well as the generally unpredictable quality of many adolescent-parent relationships, a certain amount of tension can evolve, creating barriers to communication—especially in emotionally affecting situations.

When a young person encounters a personally involving death event, his or her ability to control emotions may be threatened, and developing skills used to order thoughts and actions may be shaken (see Chapter 2). Such an adolescent may feel it necessary, in order to protect or bolster self-esteem, to react with defensive humor, blank stoicism, or sometimes with aggression. All of these behaviors can easily be misunderstood by others. An example of this is the case of 16-year-old Alan, who related his struggles to find solace and release after his father's unexpected death (McNeil, 1984b):

> We had a big basketball game a couple nights after Dad's funeral, and I was on the team. My Mom didn't want me to go. In fact, she ordered me to stay home. But I just had to get out of the house. I told her I didn't *care* what people said, I was going to play ball! So I went anyway, played the roughest game of my life, scored 20 points, and got in a fight on the court and fouled out. Then I drove home down that country road in the dark and just bawled my head off. It was the first time I'd cried since Dad died—it felt good. But Mom never understood why I went to play ball.

Alan's mother was obviously also under great stress during this period, and her competence in handling her son's "inappropriate" behaviors seemed to be undergoing a difficult test. After all, she was sorely missing her spouse who might have been able to enforce discipline with Alan, so her confidence in her own ability to be a "good" parent was shaken, and her natural reactions to Alan were defensively authoritative in nature.

Even when personal death events are not the focus of concern, the subject of feelings and thoughts about death and loss is not likely to be brought up in most everyday family conversations. There is a strong tendency to avoid ideas that are too stressful to contemplate. As Kalish (1985) says,

> In our society we are uncomfortable in the face of certain kinds of failure, certain kinds of intimacy, certain kinds of loss, and we are led to believe that others are similarly uncomfortable. Therefore, we avoid topics that we feel would bring discomfort to them or to ourselves. Our attitudes toward death are such that, in certain contexts, we perceive it as a failure, as intimacy, and as loss. (p. 87)

Such avoidance differs from but is related to *denial*, which is unconscious and, according to Kalish (1985), occurs because:

> since we can't fully obliterate the knowledge that death is real, we unconsciously find ways to insulate ourselves from the emotional impact of this knowledge. . . . If I don't talk about it or read it, then it isn't there, and it can't happen to me. (p. 86)

Defensive behaviors may result from such denial or avoidance of stress and vulnerability, and as Gibb (1961) found in his early studies, as a person becomes more and more defensive, he or she becomes less and less able to perceive accurately the motives, the values, and the emotions of another in a relationship. Such defensiveness is *reciprocal*, Gibb learned, in that when Person A in a relationship becomes threatened and begins to use defense mechanisms and pretenses to protect himself or herself, much of the time this behavior will begin to cause Person B also to begin putting up defenses. This in turn threatens Person A even more, and so a spiraling defensive cycle is started, making communication more and more difficult. Defensiveness has been termed "the greatest single barrier to effective interpersonal communication" (Adler & Towne, 1978, p. 138).

Fortunately, just the opposite is also true. Gibb also found that when Person A behaves in a *supportive* way, Person B has less cause to feel threatened and so usually lowers defenses. In turn, this openness causes Person A to become even less defensive, resulting in a more open, spontaneous, and empathic relationship.

Adolescents—who are commonly searching for who they are and what they are able to do and become—when given support for *searching* and *becoming,* will surely mature in more positive ways, trusting in others and in themselves. Jourard's (1964) lifelong work with patterns of human self-disclosure led him to believe firmly that:

> no man can come to know himself except as an outcome of disclosing himself to another person. . . . The person will disclose himself, permit himself to be known, only when he believes that his audience is a man of good will. . . . Self-disclosure follows an attitude of love and trust. (p. 3)

However, Jourard found that often a paradox exists within the family, where traditionally love is expected to prevail and people should be able to relax and be themselves. Instead, there is often a lack of mutual disclosure. "Children do not know their parents; fathers do not know what their children think, or what they are doing. Husbands and wives often are strangers one to the other to an incredible degree" (Jourard, 1964, p. 5). The growing child learns that his or her spontaneous disclosures meet a variety of responses: some disclosures are ignored, some rewarded, and some punished. "We are punished, in our society, not only for what we actually do, but also for what we think, feel, or want. Very soon, the growing child learns to display a highly expurgated version of his self to others" (Jourard, 1964, p. 6).

Thus, it is little wonder that many adolescents and parents learn to hide their true feelings from each other and to avoid discussions that might lead to self-disclosure, with the aim of protecting their own apparent weaknesses from exposure.

TALKING ABOUT DEATH IN FAMILIES

In a recent exploratory study of adolescents and parents (McNeil, 1984b), 335 young persons from 12 through 18 and 50 parents of adolescents reported their views on life, death, and families, as well as their perceptions of family communication patterns. Students completed questionnaires and discussed them in small groups.

Consistent with other studies of teenagers and peers, the majority of this sample reported that they disclosed more to their *friends* than to their parents on items relating to feelings about themselves, personal worries, and attitudes and opinions on love, sex, school, and friendships. However, the majority of these students also preferred to disclose their feelings and thoughts to their *mothers* more than to their peers or their fathers on questions of: family events, family rules, money matters, personal health concerns, future goals and ambitions, attitudes toward war and peace, ideas about "the meaning of life and death," and concerns about "what happens when you die." Thus, it appears that most of these young people perceived at least one of their parents as open to talking about the subject of death.

In evaluating their perceptions of their parents' responses to specific death-related situations such as a grandparent dying, a young friend being killed in an accident, or a television show about nuclear war, 40% of the adolescents in this sample thought their parents would behave in ways judged to be "supportive, concerned about my feelings." The remaining 60% considered that their parents would probably be "instructive and advice-giving" or "protective," or "not interested" in the adolescent's concerns about the situations.

Fathers were seldom confided in to any great degree on any subject, but less especially on those subjects with emotional connotations. Girls tended to disclose themselves to *both* parents more than boys did, and some were concerned about their lack of interaction with their fathers. One girl remarked after completing her questionnaire (McNeil, 1984b): "I didn't realize before how little communication I have with my dad. It seems we hardly talk about anything really important. I'd like to change that, if I can!" This apparent sex-role difference reinforces the stereotype of female openness and male reticence, and indicates a special problem in some parent–adolescent communication.

Thirty percent of the entire sample of young people expressed the wish that they could talk *more* about death-related subjects with their parents than they do now. Parents, when interviewed, revealed a similar desire, but many thought that talking about death would require some sort of "special occasion" and confessed their feelings of inadequacy about discussing any aspect of this subject.

This pilot study appears to indicate that both the "typical" adolescent and the "typical" parent may need to find opportunities to develop their skills in verbalizing thoughts and feelings about death—*before* a significant death event occurs. This does not require waiting for an emotionally affecting situation, but can be a part of an everyday conversation, such as discussing an item on the television news or the death of a community acquaintance. In such casual, nonthreatening ways, misconceptions about death can be clarified, emotional reactions can be validated, and family closeness can be enhanced, providing a basis for further explorations and deeper sharing when the need arises.

Perhaps awareness of these needs is the first step, as Fleming and Adolph point out in Chapter 6. Then recognizing the specific qualities of one's family communication patterns can follow (McNeil, 1984a), with an attempt to correct negative aspects and to promote positive characteristics.

Most of us need to learn more about how to foster growth and security, even though we are vulnerable to loss and change, sadness and death; how to work together in families to help each other; how to help even when acknowledging limitations, inadequacies, and lack of "answers"; and how to do better in normal, everyday family interactions.

SUGGESTIONS FOR IMPROVING COMMUNICATION ABOUT DEATH

Certainly it takes a great deal of patience and practice to be constantly aware of the interpersonal needs of others, especially in family life where we may tend to take each other for granted. Human nature is stubbornly imperfect in such matters. However, the people who make the greatest strides in improving their communication habits are those who will accept the risks involved in discarding their defenses and responding positively to others' needs for encouragement and confirmation.

Some guidelines for improving family communication are offered here, as suggestions and not panaceas, for adolescents and their parents, as well as for those who may provide professional counsel to families:

1. Adults must usually take the lead, at least in heightened awareness of the teenager's concerns about death and in openness to discussion of anything the adolescent feels like exploring. Sometimes feelings about death are not easy to reveal or to articulate. So it is wise to be alert to an adolescent's nonverbal behaviors, especially when a death-related situation has occurred. For example, is she silent and moody more than normally? Is he unusually angry and aggressive? Is she withdrawing to her room or running off to be with friends more often than usual? Or is he lingering near and striking up inconsequential conversations that may be attempts to catch your attention?

2. Listen actively and perceptively, keeping your attention on the other person and the apparent feelings underlying his or her words. "Pseudolistening" (Adler & Towne, 1978, p. 194) or pretending to listen while thinking about one's own concerns or an answer to the other's ideas is all too common. But while this practice can give an appearance of interest, it is easily detected as a not so subtle sign of indifference, and can turn off any potential confidence.

3. Accept the other's feelings as real, important, and "normal." This nonjudgmental attitude is one that allows the other person the right to

his or her own ideas and feelings, without imposing your own views on that person. Resist the temptation to plunge into stories of your own experiences, or to evaluate the teenager's opinions as "right" or "wrong." Gordon (1970) has proposed an effective communication model in which he claims that much of our spontaneous, habitual way of responding to others is judgmental because we tend to advise, praise, warn, criticize, or question without fully realizing what we are doing. Yet such responses are self-defeating and especially tend to put sensitive adolescents on the defensive.

4. Use supportive responses that reflect your acceptance and understanding of what the teenager is trying to say. You might respond to a son or daughter's statements or questions by paraphrasing them, or giving an example of the underlying feelings you detect, such as, "You sound worried about Grandmother." Such feedback can help the young person to continue to express his or her feelings because it is felt that you are really listening, and it can help you to identify the problems that are bothering the adolescent. Nonverbal messages can be even more helpful than verbal messages in communicating empathy. Tone of voice, eye contact, touch—all these are powerful communicative tools that are the most natural ways to show trust, love, and caring between parent and adolescent. None of us outgrows the need for these important messages that assure us we are valued and significant individuals.

5. Project a belief in the other person's worth by indicating that you are not attempting to solve his or her problems, but are instead trying to help the adolescent find his or her own solutions. While it may be difficult to say, "I don't know," or "I wish I knew the answers to this," such honesty shows an attitude of equality and a willingness to generate and evaluate solutions together, settling on one that is satisfactory to both. As a part of this interaction, parents must respect confidences revealed in private. Adults who tell other relatives or friends what they have been told by their children or who discuss their opinions about the teenager's problems with others are not likely to promote trust on the part of their child or to gain further confidences.

6. Be willing to take time to enjoy each other's company and to provide frequent opportunities for talking together. According to one study (Burke & Weir, 1978), the more satisfied adolescents were with the communication and help received from their parents, the higher their self-esteem. It is important to encourage teenagers to participate in family decisions, to seek their opinions, and to praise their ability to handle responsibility in mature ways. Most of all, sharing mutual concerns about life and death matters can enhance and deepen bonds of love and support in parent-adolescent relationships.

SUMMARY

Although they may have many attitudes and values in common, communication between most parents and their adolescent children may not be a smoothly operating process. Family interaction can be affected by the personal characteristics of individual adults and teenagers, as well as by the general developmental crises of their particular age groups. For many adolescents, parents serve as models for beliefs and attitudes on politics, religion, education, vocations, and a wide variety of other moral and social values. Peers, also important influences in adolescent daily life, tend to serve primarily as sharers of common experiences who can support and reinforce the individual teenager's competence and self-worth.

A young person searching for a confidante may look either to parents or to peers, depending on the type of situation and on his or her perception of the attention and empathy that might be encountered. Often when peers play an especially dominant role in the lives of teenagers, it may be due to the lack of attention or genuine concern at home more than to the inherent attractiveness of the peer group.

The subject of death can be a "touchy" topic in any family, and when a death situation arises, a helpful discussion of thoughts and feelings may be hindered by the complex defensive reactions of both adolescents and their parents. When adolescents are queried about their family life, they report that parental responses to their self-disclosures are often concerned with instruction about appropriate behaviors and attitudes, or overprotectiveness and avoidance of emotional issues, rather than with supportive listening. Parents, too, find it difficult to know what to say or when to say it, with regard to death-related events. Nevertheless, it is obvious that parents and adolescents can learn to communicate more openly and empathically on death-related topics, just as they do on all other subjects. When this is achieved, anxieties about life and death issues can be alleviated, grief from unresolved losses can be eased, and the emotional development of young people can be significantly enhanced.

REFERENCES

Adler, R., & Towne, N. *Looking out/looking in: Interpersonal communication* (2nd ed.). New York: Holt, Rinehart & Winston, 1978.
Atwater, E. *Adolescence*. Englewood Cliffs, NJ: Prentice-Hall, 1983.
Balswick, J. O., & Macrides, C. Parental stimulus for adolescent rebellion. *Adolescence*, 1975, *10*, 253-266.

Barnes, H., & Olson, D. H. Parent-adolescent communication. In D.H. Olson, H. I. McCubbin, H. Barnes, A. Larson, M. Muxen, & M. Wilson (Eds.), *Family inventories* (pp. 33–48). St. Paul, MN: University of Minnesota Press, 1982.

Bengston, V. L. Generation and family effects in value socialization. *American Sociological Review*, 1975, 40, 358-371.

Bombeck, E. Talk to me—I'm your mother. In E. Bombeck, *I lost everything in the postnatal depression*. (pp. 28–40). New York: Doubleday, 1973.

Bronfenbrenner, U. *Two worlds of childhood: U.S. and U.S.S.R.* New York: Russell Sage Foundation, 1970.

Burke, R. J., & Weir, T. Benefits to adolescents of informal helping relationships with their parents and peers, *Psychological Reports*, 1978, 42, 1175–1184.

Clemens, P. W., & Rust, J. O. Factors in adolescent rebellious feelings. *Adolescence*, 1979, 14, 159-173.

Condry, J., & Siman, M. L. Characteristics of peer- and adult-oriented children. *Journal of Marriage and the Family*, 1974, 36, 543-554.

Conger, J. J., & Petersen, A. C. *Adolescence and youth: Psychological development in a changing world*. (3rd ed.). New York: Harper & Row, 1984.

Devereux, E. Authority and moral development among German and American children: A cross-national pilot experiment. *Journal of Comparative Family Studies*, 1972, 3, 99-124.

Erikson, E. H. *Childhood and Society*. New York: Norton, 1950.

Feather, N. T. Values in adolescence. In J. Adelson (Ed.), *Handbook of adolescent psychology*. New York: Wiley, 1980.

Fengler, A. P., & Wood, V. The generation gap: An analysis of attitudes on contemporary issues. *Gerontologist*, 1972, 12, 124-128.

Gibb, J. Defensive communication. *Journal of Communication*, 1961, 11, 141-148.

Gibson, J. T. Adolescents in their environments, In J. T. Gibson, *Living: Human development through the lifespan* (pp. 344-377). New York: Addison-Wesley, 1983.

Gordon, A. K., & Klass, D. *They need to know: How to teach children about death*. Engelwood Cliffs, NJ: Prentice-Hall, 1979.

Gordon, T. *Parent effectiveness training*. New York: Peter H. Wyden 1970.

Hass, A. *Teenage sexuality: A survey of teenage sexual behavior.* New York: Macmillan, 1979.

Jourard, S. M. *The transparent self*. New York: Van Nostrand Reinhold, 1964.

Kalish, R. A. *Death, grief, and caring relationships*. (2nd ed.). Belmont, CA: Brooks/Cole, 1985.

Kalish, R. A., & Reynolds, D. K. *Death and ethnicity: A psychocultural study*. (2nd ed.) Farmingdale, NY: Baywood, 1981.

Kastenbaum, R. *Death, society, and human experience*. (2nd ed.). St. Louis: Mosby, 1981.

Kennell, J. H., Slyter, H., & Klaus, M. H. The mourning response of parents to the death of a newborn infant. *The New England Journal of Medicine*, 1970, 283, 344.

Larson, L. E. The influence of parents and peers during adolescence. *Journal of Marriage and the Family*, 1972, 34, 67-74.

Lerner, R. M. Showdown at generation gap: Attitudes of adolescents and their parents toward contemporary issues. In H. D. Thornburg (Ed.), *Contemporary adolescence: Readings* (2nd ed.). Monterey, CA: Brooks/Cole, 1975.

Levinson, D. J., Darrow, C. N., Klein, E. B., Levinson, M. H., & McKee, B. *The seasons of a man's life.* New York: Knopf, 1978.

McGillicuddy-Delisi, A. V. The role of parental beliefs in the family as a system of mutual influences. *Family Relations,* 1980, *29,* 317–323.

McNeil, J. N. Young mothers' communication about death with their children. *Death Education,* 1983, *6,*323–339.

McNeil, J. N. Death education in the home: Parents talk with their children. In H. Wass & C. A. Corr (Eds.), *Childhood and death* (pp. 293–313). Washington, DC: Hemisphere, 1984a.

McNeil, J. N. Unpublished interviews with adolescents and their parents, 1984b.

Snoek, D., & Rothblum, E. Self-disclosure among adolescents in relation to parental affection and control patterns. *Adolescence,* 1979, *14,* 333-340.

Sorenson, R. C. *Adolescent sexuality in contemporary America.* New York: World, 1973.

12

Death Education: Developing a Course of Study for Adolescents

Nina Ribak Rosenthal

Adolescence is a time for growth, for change, for life, not death. Why teach and talk about death at this stage of life? Why? Because, regardless of age, one cannot escape the inevitability of death. In fact, Getson and Benshoff (1977) point out that in a school district of 6,000 students, at least three children will die each year, and Jones (1977) states that 20% of all students will experience the death of a parent by the time they reach 16 years of age. If one adds the possible death of a friend's parents plus the possible death of relatives such as aunts and uncles, the adolescent's experience with death and grief becomes even more encompassing.

Yet, as with the area of sexuality and other taboo topics, adolescents frequently have little information and in many cases possess only distorted information about death. In many instances, they gather knowledge from their peers, and such knowledge contains little more than superstitions, fears, and "horror" stories. Acting on this lack of information or misinformation, the young person's ability to deal with grief and/or to support others is hindered. Despite the fact that peers may experience loss, adolescents frequently act as if nothing had happened. They avoid contact with their bereaved friends. They fear bringing up the topic because they "don't know what to say," or they believe changing the subject will make their friend(s) feel better.

It is obvious that we need to teach adolescents about death, dying, and the grieving process. In place of no information and misinformation, we need to assist young people in the pursuit of knowledge. In place of fears and superstitions, we need to help young people become aware and thus gain a better understanding of themselves and others. In place of avoidance and lack of support, we need to enable young people to acquire the skills necessary to help their peers in times of grief and death.

Three primary aspects or concerns in death education for adolescents are: 1. information; 2. self-awareness; and 3. skills for helping. Integration of all three elements is important for a "balanced" course of study. In each area, teachers need to decide on possible topics, develop objectives, choose the materials and methods to be used, and then develop evaluation procedures to assess the effectiveness of their efforts. Suggestions for performing these tasks are offered below.

INFORMATION

This aspect includes presentation of specific facts related to the general topic of death and dying. Generally, this involves the cognitive domain and helps students obtain a base of information from which they can develop accurate concepts, make decisions and take positive action.

Topics and Objectives

Initially, one needs to decide what information should be incorporated into a course on death and grief. Although he was not writing specifically for adolescents, Knott (1979) suggests that topics such as bereavement and grief, religious and cultural expression of death, life expectancy, and causes of death may be included in a death education class. Wolowelsky (1981), in his description of a death education course taught in a parochial high school, lists legal (wills, organ donations) and financial (funeral costs) concerns as well as available social services (support groups) as important factual information. Corr (1978), in his article "A Model Syllabus for Death and Dying Courses," lists units that include the following: historical and demographic background; defining and determining death; euthanasia; suicide; socially approved deaths; body disposal, funeral practices, and other practical consequences; children and death; life, death, and human destiny. Recently, Leviton and Wendt (1983) suggested that we "educate to prevent apocalyptic deaths" (p. 370). They hypothesize that awareness of such events can prevent their recurrence. Following Leviton and Wendt's suggestion, one might include horrendous death such as death caused by war, homicide, holocaust, terrorism, starvation, and destruction of the environment in a course on death education.

Information and topics for a death education course are plentiful, and one has a large list from which to choose. It is important, however, to formulate different goals and objectives for different students who may have different needs. Therefore, a course may vary from one section to another and/or from one semester to the next. How, then, might the teacher decide from among the various possibilities? Initially, the instructor might:

1. use a pretest and assess what students know prior to the class;
2. construct a needs assessment or survey instrument; or
3. ask students to write down the topics/areas in which they desire added information.

Results of one such open-ended request for topics from sophomore and junior high school students enrolled in two death education classes produced the following requests for topics: the murdering mentality; prolonged death (terminal illness); extending life with machines; life after death; suicide; funeral preparation and customs; emotional stress on the family; how to react to death in the family; family preparation for a death; cancer; how to tell a person he or she is going to die; legal/medical definition of death; legal aspects; abortion; what physically happens when a person dies; and explaining death to children.

In answering the question of what to include in a death education course, Noland, Richardson, and Bray (1980) used steps developed by Green (1975) to plan and evaluate a death education unit for ninth-grade girls. These included:

1. conducting a needs assessment;
2. writing objectives to meet the needs;
3. developing a program in accordance with the stated objectives; and
4. evaluating the course with cognitive, affective, and behavioral measures.

Eddy and Alles (1983) suggest the additional step of consulting with community representatives when developing curriculum for school-aged children. By combining that which adolescents describe as needed with suggestions from community resource persons and topics delineated by "experts" in the field, teachers can develop objectives that adhere to the general goals of helping young people become aware of basic information and that also meet the specific needs of their students. In so doing, teachers may help adolescents to cope better with their own death-related concerns and also assist others in times of death and grief.

Materials

Since death education is interdisciplinary in nature, it may be difficult to determine which materials to use. Materials may be selected from such diverse fields as English, science and medicine, art, music, social studies, psychology, and law (Berg & Daughtery, 1973). Another complicating factor is the fact that increased interest has led to a rapid proliferation of materials and little in the way of quality control. Fortunately, some effective resource guides are now available in this broad field (for example Wass, Corr, Pacholski, & Sanders, 1980; Wass, Corr, Pacholski, & Fortfar, 1985). Nevertheless, it is essential that the death educator preview and choose materials carefully. Gideon (1977) developed a set of criteria for use in evaluating death education materials. The criteria include assessing:

1. the accuracy of content;
2. the technical and educational quality of the material;
3. the cost and availability of the material;
4. whether guidelines for using the material are included;
5. whether results of the use of the material are given; and
6. whether there are references and bibliographies that accompany the material.

A death educator might find it worthwhile to develop a simple check sheet that includes each of the criteria described by Gideon. Such development and use of the check sheet might help ensure that only quality materials are used.

Methods

Use of lecture, discussion groups, and report writing is common when teaching adolescents. Such methods are easily incorporated into a course dealing with death, dying, and bereavement. Other methods might include: inviting guest speakers, such as funeral directors, counselors, clergy, lawyers, and doctors; reading relevant literature, for example, Langone's *Death is a Noun* (1972); and, if possible, taking field trips to cemeteries, crematoria, and other death-related places (for example casket companies, florists, monument makers). In addition to using both didactic and experiential methods to help students acquire information, the death educator needs to develop sensitivity to the needs and reactions of the students, and thus be willing to allow students to opt out of ANY assignment. Because of the nature of the content, individual students need to seek their own level of involvement, and teachers need to be flexible in order to permit this to occur.

Evaluation

Cognitive instruments may be the basis for evaluation of the informational aspect of death education for adolescents. The instrument could be similar to those used to assess other subjects taught by the teacher. The instrument should be used to assess the knowledge of individual students, and items need to correlate with course objectives. Pre- and posttesting are appropriate for this aspect of the course. Multiple choice, true/false, short answer, and essay-type questions are applicable. Suggestions for developing assessment instruments dealing with death and dying may be found in Eddy and Alles' (1983) death education text.

SELF-AWARENESS

The self-awareness aspect of death education includes examination of one's own thoughts, feelings, attitudes, and opinions related to death, dying, and bereavement. Generally, this involves becoming aware of personal reactions to the information presented and the ideas and actions of one's peers and family members, as well as listening to others and talking about death-related concerns.

Topics and Objectives

Many of the topics included in a death education course arouse emotions. These emotions frequently are based upon attitudes, thoughts, and feelings held by the students—who may be unaware of them. Therefore, goals and objectives in this aspect of death education might include becoming aware of one's own attitudes, thoughts, feelings, and reactions related to death, dying, and bereavement. In the affective domain, Hollis (1975) suggests that death education might:

1. ease the fear of one's own death;
2. lessen feelings of guilt; and
3. develop attitudes that facilitate a better understanding of life.

Gibson, Roberts, and Buttery (1982) list awareness goals as follows:

1. to improve the quality of life through consideration of personal values and priorities;
2. to enable youth to deal with feelings; and
3. to assist in clarifying values.

One other objective might involve trying to dissolve commonly held beliefs based on myths.

Materials

Much of the material chosen for informational purposes can be used to help young people gain greater self awareness. A few well-placed questions may elicit some interesting results and help adolescents gain greater understanding and awareness. Feature films, such as *Love Story* (1970) and *Ordinary People* (1980), can be used to help students not only to learn about the process of dying and grieving, but also to help them become aware of their own reactions to death. A wide range of other audiovisual resources is given in Chapter 16. Newspaper articles that deal with moral dilemmas (for example, mercy killing, abortion, assisting a handicapped person starve to death) can be used to explore the values youngsters have in this area. Further, using death-related incidents and events as portrayed on television may prove effective for helping adolescents become aware of the media's influence on young persons' thoughts and opinions. Helpful curriculum guides are available, such as the one developed by Mills, Reisler, Robinson, and Vermilye (1976) or the book by Gordon and Klass (1979), both of which contain a section for use with high school students. Similarly, Stanford and Perry's (1976) curriculum guide offers useful suggestions and values clarification techniques. *Thanatopics*, by Knott, Ribar, Duson, and King (1982) and *Death: The Experience*, by Meagher aand Shapiro (1984), contain a plethora of materials that might be used in self-awareness activities.

Methods

As stated previously, the use of affective questions may facilitate self-awareness of students. In addition to discussing what happened in a story, questions such as "How would you feel in such a situation?" or "Which character is most like you?" will personalize the story and also help students learn more about themselves. Attitudinal and affective questionnaires can be developed by a teacher and used to stimulate discussion and self-exploration. Activities such as role playing, values clarification, and decision-making exercises also are useful in this area. Having students read relevant death-related stories (for example, those in the collection *We Are But a Moment's Sunlight*, edited by Adler, Stanford, & Adler [1976]) and develop position papers, along with writing poems, obituaries, and wills, have all been used successfully. Guided imagery (cf., Galyean's *Mind Sight: Learning Through Imaging* [1983]) and simulation techniques also might be incorporated. Using methods like these enables students to relate information to their own lives, to learn about themselves and their own values, and to learn about the thoughts, feelings, and attitudes of their peers.

Evaluation

One might use the same questionnaires used for stimulating discussion (mentioned previously) as a pre- and postassessment instrument for attitude change. Teacher-made instruments might include statements such as, "I am aware of my attitudes toward death" and "I feel comfortable talking about death," to which students respond by indicating their degree of agreement or disagreement on a four or five-point scale. Sentences should include statements that correlate with the written objectives in this area and that are easily understood by students.

Another area for assessment involves death anxiety. Reduction of such anxiety is frequently listed as a reason to teach about death and grief in the school. Yet, research in this area is sparse and conflicting, with both increased and decreased anxiety being reported (Bailis & Kennedy, 1977; Mueller, 1975, 1976; Rosenthal, 1979). Furthermore, it is important to assess the pattern of increasing or decreasing anxiety, and it is advisable to do so at periodic intervals (for example, 4, 8, and 12 weeks into the course). Such assessment enables teachers to be better aware of the effects of their methods, and to make plans and changes as necessary. Reliable and valid instruments, such as Nelson's (1978) Death Attitudes Scale and Templer's (1970) Death Anxiety Scale, could be used. In addition, Hardt's (1975) scale has been validated and constructed specifically for use with adolescents.

SKILLS FOR HELPING

The skills needed for helping oneself and others involve acquiring an understanding and acceptance of varying points of view, a desensitization to emotionally laden language, and the possession of good communication skills.

Topics and Objectives

Performance objectives geared toward acquiring or enhancing basic listening and communication skills should be developed. These might include the ability to:

1. act attentively;
2. demonstrate interest and concern;
3. delay responses;
4. encourage communication;
5. listen and reflect content and feelings;
6. assess nonverbal and verbal behavior;
7. recognize effective and noneffective communication;
8. ask open-ended questions; and
9. comfort family and peers.

Materials

Several resources have been developed to help adolescents acquire or enhance their communication skills. *Innerchange* (Palomares & Ball, 1977) contains an excellent unit on communication stoppers (for example, advising, dominating, put-downs, interrogating, interrupting, interpreting) and communication helpers (for example, paraphrasing, silent listening, good eye contact). The Stanfords' book, *Learning Discussion Skills Through Games* (1969), contains a series of exercises (games) that help enhance students' abilities to listen, share, and accept ideas. Gordon's (1980) *Leader Effectiveness Training* has been used successfully and contains many excellent ideas in this area. Furthermore, the curriculum guides previously mentioned in this chapter contain exercises to enhance listening and communication.

Methods

Initially, adolescents need to become aware of the effect and prevalence of euphemisms used to describe death and grief. Using euphemistic expressions (for example, "slumber room," "expired," "passed on") helps to increase denial and delay acceptance of the reality of death. However, many young persons may need practice in using accurate death-related terms, and desensitization to words may be necessary. The death educator can help students by using only accurate terminology (for example, "died" rather than "passed away"; "dead" rather than "expired") and thus model more helpful ways of interacting and increasing the likelihood of acceptance of death.

After students become more comfortable with using accurate death-related terms, the teacher should start communication exercises. In the beginning, use of skits or specific role-playing scenarios might help students become aware of how certain responses thwart communication. In addition to demonstrating the typical communication stoppers as defined by Palomares and Ball (1977), clichés used frequently in the presence of the bereaved, such as "The Lord works in strange ways," and "Time heals all wounds" might be incorporated into role-play situations. By using these clichés and discussing their effects, adolescents become aware of the fact that such responses may cut off communication rather than make a bereaved person actually feel better. Frequently, the bereaved person will change the topic or become silent, not as a result of being helped but as a result of being aware that the other individual does not want to talk about the death.

Once students gain awareness of the effects of negative communication, they are ready to begin to practice facilitative responses, such as reflection of feelings, comforting, and clarifying. Modeling and role playing should be used during this phase (see Rosenthal, 1978). For students who need less structure, open-ended roles with just a few suggestions for topics can be used. Working in triads, participants rotate the roles of speaker, listener, and observer so each individual has a chance to experience and observe the interactions.

Evaluation

Feedback given in triads by the observer to both the listener and speaker helps participants evaluate their abilities and modify their behavior where appropriate. Another useful technique for evaluation involves audio- or video-taping the role-played interaction and then analyzing and reviewing it. A check sheet can be developed and used to assess objectively the occurrence of positive and negative communication. If a more formalized evaluation is desired, the teacher might develop performance tests in which students are required to make specific responses and then are evaluated on their ability to do so. This, however, may stultify participants and increase anxiety and feelings of "unnaturalness." The real "test" will come when the students use their skills in actual situations. However, this is a "testing" of death education which might not occur immediately.

INTEGRATING INFORMATION, SELF-AWARENESS, AND SKILLS

In developing a course in death education, a word of caution is necessary. The three aspects outlined above—information, self-awareness, skills development—should not be seen as discrete units; rather, these areas should be seen as interrelated, with information influencing self-awareness and, in turn, enabling better communication skills. Despite the fact that the teacher may deal with one area at a time, interaction will take place and integration of information, self-awareness, and skill development should occur.

TEACHER REQUIREMENTS

Although at the present time teachers do not need special certification to be permitted to teach death education courses, certain criteria should be met. Leviton (1977) suggests that teachers should:

1. be aware of their own feelings and reactions to death, dying, and grief;
2. know the subject matter thoroughly;
3. use the language easily;
4. know the developmental stages of life; and
5. be aware of social changes.

It seems logical to assume that, at the very least, death educators should possess the three competencies (knowledge, self-awareness, and communication skills) that they are trying to help their students obtain.

In dealing with the informational aspect, teachers need to know facts related to their objectives. By reading books, attending seminars, viewing films, and the like, teachers may acquire this necessary information. Furthermore, persons planning to teach about death might benefit from asking themselves the following questions (cf. Rosenthal, 1980):

1. Will I have enough knowledge to answer factual questions and have an understanding of what is happening in the subject area of death and dying? If I do not know the answers to questions, do I know the resources available to obtain the answers?
2. Will I have time to preview all materials that I plan to use and evaluate the worth of these materials? Do these materials help to achieve my

objectives? Will I be willing to plan and use alternative exercises for those students who do not want to participate in the experiences planned for the day?

3. Will I be willing to go to all field-trip sites before taking my class there? Will I go to the cemetery, funeral home, etc., so that I know what the students may expect to encounter?

In addition to this knowledge, teachers need to become aware of their own attitudes, beliefs, values, and feelings regarding death and grief. Questions such as the following, similar to those posed by Rosenthal (1980), may assist in obtaining greater awareness:

1. How will I feel when students ask me difficult questions? Am I willing to share my points of view? Do I accept varying opinions on topics such as abortion, suicide, euthanasia, and can I teach both sides of such issues?

2. How will I feel if students seem quite upset when discussing death? Will I change the topic? Will I get depressed? What will my feelings be toward a student who directs hostility at me and at the course?

3. How will I feel when a student expresses suicidal thoughts? Will I feel responsible? Will I be able to help a student who sobs uncontrollably? Will I be able to talk to a student whose mother is dying?

In the third area of competence, skill development, the death educator needs basic listening and communication skills. Open and honest communication is essential. The following questions, an earlier version of which appeared in Rosenthal (1980), might help in assessing such skills:

1. Am I able to talk about death without using euphemisms? Can I respond to students without using clichés?

2. Am I able to listen and not try to "cheer up" the person? Can I respond with empathy or just remain silent when appropriate?

3. Am I able to express the fact that I care? Am I more concerned with what I might say rather than how I might help? Do I realize that sometimes a touch on the shoulder or hand of the student may be all that is needed to help?

Death education deals with the end of life, yet it can be a beginning. Through a course on death, adolescents can begin to learn more about death and grief, more about themselves, and more about ways to help others. Adolescence is a time for growth, for change, for life, and, yes, for learning about death.

REFERENCES

Adler, C. S., Stanford, G., & Adler, S. M. *We are but a moment's sunlight.* New York: Pocket Books, 1976.

Bailis, L. A., & Kennedy, W. R. Effects of a death education program upon secondary school students. *Journal of Education Research,* 1977, *71,* 63–66.

Berg, D. W., & Daugherty, G. G. Teaching about death. *Today's Education,* 1973, *62,* 46–47.

Corr, C. A. A model syllabus for death and dying courses. *Death Education,* 1978, *1,* 433–457.

Eddy, J. M., & Alles, W. F. *Death Education.* St. Louis: Mosby, 1983.

Galyean, B. *Mind sight: Learning through imaging.* Long Beach, CA: Center for Integrative Learning, 1983.

Getson, R. F., & Benshoff, D. L. Four experiences of death and how to prepare to meet them. *School Counselor,* 1977, *24,* 310–314.

Gibson, A. B., Roberts, P. C., & Buttery, T. J. *Death education: A concern for the living.* Bloomington, IN: Phi Delta Kappa Educational Foundation, 1982.

Gideon, M. E. Criterion for evaluating curriculum materials in death education from grades K-12. *Death Education,* 1977, *1,* 231–234.

Gordon, A. K., & Klass, D. *They need to know: How to teach children about death.* Englewood Cliffs, NJ: Prentice-Hall, 1979.

Gordon, T. *Leader effectiveness training.* New York: Bantam, 1980.

Green, S. S. *Continuing professional education: A comparative analysis of the program development process in business administration, educational administration, and law.* Unpublished doctoral dissertation, University of Illinois at Urbana/Champaign, 1975.

Hardt, D. Development of an investigatory instrument to measure attitudes toward death. *Journal of School Health,* 1975, *45,* 96–99.

Hollis, J. The relevance of death. *Chronicle of higher education,* 1975, *10,* 24.

Jones, W. H. Death-related grief counseling: The school counselor's responsibility. *School Counselor,* 1977, *24,* 315–320.

Knott, J. E. Death education for all. In H. Wass (Ed.), *Dying: Facing the facts* (pp. 385–403). Washington, DC: Hemisphere, 1979.

Knott, J. E. Ribar, M. C., Duson, B. M., & King, M. R. *Thanatopics: A manual of structured learning experiences for death education.* Kingston, RI: SLE Publications, 1982.

Langone, J. *Death is a noun.* New York: Dell, 1972.

Leviton, D. The scope of death education. *Death Education,* 1977, *1,* 45–56.

Leviton, D., & Wendt, W. Death education: Toward individual and global well-being. *Death Education,* 1983, *7,* 369–384.

Meagher, D. K., & Shapiro, R. D. *Death: The experience.* Minneapolis: Burgess Publishing, 1984.

Miller, A. (Director). (1970) *Love Story* [Film]. Los Angeles: Paramount Pictures.

Mills, G. C., Reisler, R., Robinson, A. E., & Vermilye, G. *Discussing death: A guide to death education.* Palm Springs, CA: ETC Publications, 1976.

Mueller, M. L. Fear of death and death education. *Notre Dame Journal of Education,* 1975, *6,* 84–91.

Mueller, M. L. Death education and death fear reduction. *Education,* 1976, *97,* 145–148.

Nelson, L. D. The multidimensional measurement of death attitudes: Construction and validation of a three factor instrument. *Psychological Record,* 1978, *28,* 525–533.

Noland, M., Richardson, G. E., & Bray, R. M. The systematic development and efficacy of a death education unit for ninth-grade girls. *Death Education,* 1980, *4,* 43–59.

Palomares, U. H., & Ball, G. *Innerchange: A journey into self-learning through group interaction.* La Mesa, CA: Human Development Training Institute, 1977.

Redford, R. (Director/Producer). (1980). *Ordinary People* [Film]. Los Angeles: Paramount Pictures.

Rosenthal, N. R. Teaching educators to deal with death. *Death Education,* 1978, *2,* 293–306.

Rosenthal, N. R. Adolescent death anxiety: The effect of death education. *Education,* 1979, *101,* 95–101.

Rosenthal, N. R. Death education: Help or hurt? *Clearing House,* 1980, *53,* 224–226.

Stanford, G., & Perry, D. *Death out of the closet: A curriculum guide to living with dying.* New York: Bantam, 1976.

Stanford, G., & Stanford, B. D. *Learning discussion skills through games.* New York: Scholastic, 1969.

Templer, E. I. The construction and validation of a death anxiety scale. *Journal of General Psychology,* 1970, *82,* 165–177.

Wass, H., Corr, C. A., Pacholski, R. A., & Forfar, C. S. *Death education II: An annotated resource guide.* Washington, DC: Hemisphere, 1985.

Wass, H., Corr, C. A., Pacholski, R. A., & Sanders, C. M. *Death education: An annotated resource guide.* Washington, DC: Hemisphere, 1980.

Wolowelsky, J. B. Death education in parochial high schools. *Death Education,* 1981, *5,* 67–73.

13

Counseling Adolescents in Death-Related Situations

Suzanne Calvin and Inez M. Smith

COUNSELING ADOLESCENTS: OPPORTUNITIES AND LIMITATIONS

"Help me, I hurt" is a plea expressed in many ways. Sometimes it is said directly. In other instances, we may hear the plea in door slamming or tire screeching, quiet tears or heavy sobs, raised voices or silent withdrawal. Adolescents may disguise their need in behavior patterns of truancy, failure, belligerence, substance use and abuse, and promiscuity. Messages of "help me, I hurt" often signal a need for counseling.

A counseling situation exists when an individual expresses to a listener or responder personal information regarding problematic behavior, feelings, thoughts, and situations. Counseling is considered formal counseling when the listener or responder is a trained professional, and it is considered informal counseling in all other situations. Counseling situations might include relationships adolescents experience with parents, teachers, coaches, social workers, psychologists, medical personnel, or clergy. The material that follows in this chapter is based upon formal counseling in an educational context, that is, adolescent and school counselor interchanges, but we believe the principles and guidelines suggested can be applied in other trusting or confidential situations.

When we care about someone, it is difficult to see them hurting. Our impulse is to offer a quick remedy that eliminates the source of the pain. However, while comforting and consoling are natural and appropriate responses, we need to realize our limitations in taking over and managing the lives of others.

Adults often forget that teenagers have passed through the childhood belief that grownups can make everything all right. Unlike children, adolescents seeking help are not asking the listener or responder to solve their problems. Rather they are asking for assistance in the problem-solving process. They are seeking counsel.

Counseling is not an automatic response. Counseling is a reflecting, clarifying, problem-solving process calling for listening and questioning skills. Certainly, the trained professional who counsels in a formal setting can be expected to have more specialized skills and academic tools than persons approached in informal counseling situations. Nevertheless, it is essential that those who are sought out as counselors on the basis of mutual caring remember that their function is not to solve the problem but to assist in the problem-solving process.

COUNSELING AND DEATH-RELATED CONCERNS

Death-related concerns lend themselves to the counseling process because ordinarily they are distinctively individual and personal. Seldom does anyone have ready-made answers or quick solutions for themselves or others to the problematic feelings, thoughts, and behavior prompted by the impact of death.

Any isolated event or series of events may create the need for death-related counseling. For some adolescents, thoughts and feelings about death may be triggered by death-related social phenomena. Such phenomena might include armed conflict of military troops on foreign shores. To many adolescents, such activity half way across the world would mean nothing. Yet to those who have friends or family in the military or in the foreign country, the conflict may have great personal significance.

Study, discussion, or media productions about the potential destructiveness of nuclear war may initiate personal questioning about death. Such exposure may stimulate fears of one's own death, the death of significant others, or the pain of dying.

Media coverage of teenage victims of murder, kidnapping, abuse, incest, or fatal accidents can stimulate thoughts of mortality in adolescents. Likewise, the news of the death of an idol or mentor may have a stark, startling effect on adolescents. On these occasions, some adolescents realize for the first time that even superstars die. While such social phenomena are not always personal at the onset, many adolescents experience personal relevance that prompts death-related concerns.

Death education classes sometimes spur the need for death-related counseling. A classroom interchange can be the catalyst causing unresolved grief to surface.

Teenage pregnancies are common. So are teenage abortions. While abortion is a uniquely personal experience, it is also a highly visible moral and social issue. The controversies surrounding abortion, as well as the act itself, may create the need for death-related counseling.

Personal loss situations may evoke death-related concerns. The adolescent who upon the breakup of a romance declares, "I don't think I can go on living without her," may or may not have suicidal thoughts. Nevertheless, this adolescent is making a statement about the effect of loss on self-esteem. Thus, out of 100 teenagers participating in a self-response class exercise, 91% selectcd "loss of your boyfriend or girlfriend" as a significant loss, compared to 81% who selected death of a loved one.

Illnesses or handicapping conditions often precede death-related counseling concerns. Frequently, such long-term conditions give rise to depression and even despair. In such situations, it is important to invite sharing of concerns related to death, while also exploring the loss inherent in the conditions themselves.

Dog and cat lovers can identify with experiencing grief over the death of a pet. Many teenagers grieve when their pet—whether it be cat, dog, hamster, fish, bird, or rat—dies. Yet, they try to hide both their grief and the reason for the grief because many people do believe: "It was only a cat. You can get another one."

The thoughts, feelings, and behavior associated with these and a variety of other personal losses, such as parental divorce, failure, or moving, are often similar to those associated with loss through death. Moreover, in the process of dealing with other separation and loss concerns, death-related concerns may emerge.

Any circumstances in which the value of life or life's values are in question might evoke death-related concerns. However, if the concerns are not articulated explicitly and directly, they may be overlooked. For example, a teacher's baby dies. A student comments, "That's really something about Mr. Dixon's baby dying." Unless further conversation follows, one does not know if the comment is made as an informational news item or as a lead into personal death-related concerns.

The death or critical condition of a significant person in the adolescent's life is the kind of circumstance generally assumed to create counseling needs. Sometimes under conditions of this sort, "Help me, I hurt" is too difficult to express directly. The vulnerability of possible additional pain through a listener or responder dismissing or discounting the death-related concern is high. Adolescents who have perceived adults giving little regard to other adolescent-felt losses may be particularly guarded.

If a teenager says, "My father died last week," one would need to be completely insensitive to consider such a comment as merely informational news. However, such direct statements often make us feel stunned and helpless. Unless we know the person quite well, we may resort to treating such a statement as primarily informational because of our own discomfort in responding.

It is not unlikely that an adolescent would be in a situation in which he or she would be the one to give the information about a death in the family. In communities that have small social groupings, word of a death in a family travels quickly. In other communities in which social groupings such as high school enrollments and church memberships are large, personal information about others is much more limited. "My father died last week" may be the accurate statement of explanation to questions such as "How come you weren't at the party Friday?" or "Why are your library books overdue?"

INITIATING THE COUNSELING PROCESS

Counseling can be self-initiated, come about by referral, or occur as a result of one's role. In cases of *self-initiated counseling*, the adolescent would seek assistance through a direct, explicit procedure. For example, a teenager would go to a school counselor and ask for help regarding problematic feelings, thoughts, or behavior.

Referral counseling cases would be initiated by someone else on behalf of the adolescent. In some cases, the suggestion for counseling might be made to the adolescent by a concerned person who feels inadequate in the counselor role but recognizes the adolescent's need. The adolescent may then seek assistance based upon the suggestion. In other cases, the concerned person may contact someone such as the school counselor, a clergy person, or a social worker to ask that they seek out the adolescent. Such referrals are frequently made in cases of new or unusual acting-out behavior such as truancy, emotional outbursts, withdrawal, and substance abuse.

Role-initiated counseling is initiated by such persons as school, social services, or church staff. In such cases it would be a part of their professional function in their institutional setting to seek out adolescents (of whom they were aware) who had experienced the death or critical condition of a significant other.

COUNSELING GOALS:
SAFETY AND CLARIFICATION

Regardless of how the counseling process is initiated, the immediate goal is the same. The goal is to create a safe, caring environment in which the adolescent can begin to unravel his or her death-related concerns.

Adolescents who seek out counseling will very likely be ready to enter into the counseling process. When the counseling is initiated by someone else, questions such as "How are you doing?" or "How are things going for you?" may be an effective beginning point. However, such questions might bring quick, superficial responses of "fine" or "okay," followed by silence. Such responses are not uncommon.

Rhonda, a senior high student who participated in ongoing counseling after her mother died, was reluctant to talk at the onset of her referral counseling. (This example and others cited in this chapter are based on factual material. Names and some details have been changed to protect the confidentiality of the persons involved.) Rhonda gave this explanation for her reticence:

> After my mother died I didn't know if anybody wanted to listen to me. Sometimes I thought, "everybody knows but nobody mentions it!" At other times I thought, "nobody knows my mom died!" Then I wondered, how can I know who knows and who doesn't know?
>
> A few times people asked me why I did this or didn't do that. I'd tell them it was because my mom had died. Then they'd be embarrassed and uncomfortable. Sometimes I had to give them more comfort than they were able to give me.
>
> Except for my closest friends, I didn't want anybody else at school to know. I was afraid if they knew, they'd think I was different from them and they would reject me. I knew that not having a mom anymore did make me different, but I wasn't quite sure what all that meant.

Rhonda's explanation points out the importance of extending the invitation and granting permission to adolescents to express thoughts and feelings. Frequently, the thoughts and feelings include a reviewing of the circumstances surrounding the death. Such rehearsal is often impermissible with adolescent peers. One student gave this account of her reluctance to listen.

> I didn't want to listen to Cathy's story about her mother's death. I guess it was because it made death too real. Of course, I know that everybody has to die sometime, but as long as death didn't affect anybody I knew, it wasn't really real. To be reminded that Cathy's mom died was scary to me. It made me worry about my parents' dying.

Rhonda's reference to being different from her peers points to a key issue underlying death-related concerns of adolescents. The counselor's function is to help the adolescent clarify the differences.

INTERPERSONAL RELATIONSHIPS
AND DEVELOPMENTAL TASKS

The death of a significant person in the life of an adolescent does change interpersonal relationships. Death changes the social structure of survivors no matter what their age. The necessary alterations in the adolescents' roles and functions come at a time when, because of their age, roles and functions are already ambiguous. A change in social structure may have added significance to adolescents because of their developmental tasks.

Those developmental tasks include, but are not limited to, issues of: independence/dependence; peer identification; role models; physical and social self-image; social skills and bonding. Sensitivity to adolescent engagement with these tasks is crucial. Dealing with such developmental tasks is the context within which all adolescents live. Death of a significant person strongly affects the ways in which adolescent survivors respond to their developmental tasks.

Realizing the character of these developmental tasks and the ways in which death-related change impacts upon them helps the counselor recognize the adolescents' framework. However, that realization in no way gives the counselor any factual information for predicting or prescribing solutions or resolutions to the adolescent's concerns.

How adolescents appropriate the death of a significant other in relationship to developmental tasks will be individualized. It is "typical" for all teenagers to be confronted with developmental tasks. Yet, each teenager brings distinctively personal variables to those tasks.

Consider the issue of independence/dependence and how it can arise in death-related counseling. Insurance and social security benefits to which a teenager is entitled upon the death of a parent can be the focal point for independence/dependence issues. Many teenagers associate money with independence. When they learn that they are entitled to death-benefit funds, they often assume they should have free and unlimited access to those funds. But the surviving parents or guardians may need those funds to provide shelter and care for the adolescents. Even in cases in which the responsible adults are not financially dependent upon the funds, such adults may not be willing to give the adolescents access to the money. For example, they may believe that adolescents do not have the social skills needed to handle the money responsibly. In either case, money—the very thing the adolescents perceived as implying a new independence—may thrust them into a new dependency upon the adult administrators.

To some adolescents, death-benefit payments may set up real or imagined time parameters for establishing their independence. For example, some surviving parents or guardians may tell adolescents, "When you are 18 and your benefit payments stop, you are on your own." The effect of such a statement upon adolescents will depend upon the individual. To some teenagers, it may create a sense of security knowing that they have a defined time frame before they are expected to be independent. To other teenagers, a defined time frame may create a demand for establishing independence.

Some adolescents experience feelings of guilt surrounding independence/dependence issues and money. Some feel guilty when they want to gain control of money to which they are entitled only because someone has died. Because of their preoccupation with the money matters, they may question their own remorse. Some may feel guilty because they resent escalated dependence upon surviving adults.

Financial considerations following the death of a primary provider can have other spinoff effects for adolescents. When income is reduced significantly, changes in life style occur. Many adolescents may have problems in the area of peer relationships and identification if they can no longer afford such things as their usual clothing, recreational activities, transportation, and educational plans. For some adolescents, the death and accompanying changes in life style may cause them to redefine their concept of peer group. They may begin to consider as peers only those who have experienced the death of a significant other.

INTRAPERSONAL DYNAMICS

Such examples merely skim the surface of the relationship between death-related concerns and developmental tasks. Achieving developmental tasks is both an interpersonal and intrapersonal activity. Because the death of an important person will change the interpersonal social structure of adolescents, it will also change intrapersonal dynamics. That is, the intrapersonal activities of thinking, believing, feeling, and acting may change because the interpersonal social structure changes. External messages will influence internal perceptions.

Reflect again on Rhonda's explanation: "I knew that not having a mom any more did make me different, but I wasn't quite sure what all that meant." Rhonda's statement suggests that she had some notions that her mother's death made her feel different both as she related to others (interpersonally) and as she understood herself (intrapersonally). The function of the counselor is to assist people like Rhonda in clarifying how they perceive themselves to be different. Discovering the meaning of being different involves comparing *what is* to *what was*. The comparison calls for defining the roles and functions the deceased had in the life of the adolescent and clarifying the adolescent's adjustment to those role and function losses.

Since the adolescent's life is often in great flux following the death of a significant other, it may be difficult to focus on intrapersonal dynamics other than the grief itself. Frequently, intrapersonal dynamics emerge in the process of identifying the past and present interpersonal social structure. If the adolescent can identify changes in the external world, this may open the door to exploration of changes in the internal world.

FUNCTIONAL LOSS: ADDRESSING RELATIONAL NEEDS

In his work on loss and support systems, Putney (1981) points out five basic functions of interpersonal relationships in support systems. Although Putney's work was based upon separated and divorced people, we suggest that these five functions provide useful categories for death-related loss concerns because they identify ways in which people address relational needs. Putney labels the five functions as: intimacy; guidance and assistance; competency; companionship; and nurturing. We would add to this list maintenance and security functions, and define each function as follows:

Intimacy: close bonding and affection accompanied by acceptance and trust;

Guidance and assistance: providing advice and direction in choice making, values clarification, and decisions by testing ideas;

Competency: being validated for performance, judgment, or attitudes;

Companionship: enjoying time together;

Nurturing: sharing a *mutual* feeling of being needed, valued, useful, and important;

Maintenance: providing means for meeting ongoing needs such as shelter, clothing, food;

Security: trusting that one can be counted on to be there.

A survivor's sense of loss is directly related to the number of functions the deceased provided and the extent and exclusiveness to which the deceased fulfilled those functions. When counselors can help adolescents clarify functional losses, each can begin to understand what the death of the significant other means in regard to the adolescent's relationship patterns and life style.

Suppose a teenager would say about someone who had died, "He was everything to me." Such a statement is the counselor's invitation to explore the functions the deceased provided. Through such exploring, the counselee's understanding of "everything to me" becomes clarified. When the functional losses are clear, the death-related concerns become more apparent.

The exploring and examining process can be initiated by open-ended questions. Such questions might include: What kinds of things did you and your mom talk about? What do you miss about your dad? What kinds of things did you and your brother do together? How did you and your sister let each other know you cared for one another?

Sometimes the questioning is unnecessary because the clues about the functional losses will surface as the adolescent relates experiences. Cathy told her counselor of her first holiday experience following her mother's death:

> I missed my mom a lot on Thanksgiving. As soon as I walked into my aunt's I remembered so many things. I could smell the turkey cooking and it just wasn't the same smell as when my mom cooked a turkey. My mom was a good cook. She made really good dressing and now nobody has the recipe. I was always going to learn to make her dressing. I guess I thought she'd always be around to cook and to teach me.

Cathy's account alludes to some functional roles her mother had fulfilled. Mom had provided maintenance through cooking and carrying out special holiday traditions. Mom was also a person upon whose presence Cathy had depended.

Sharon's story of buying a dress for the prom points out how the functions of guidance, competency, companionship, and nurture might become apparent:

> I had to shop and shop for a prom dress this year. Last year my mom went with me and we had such a good time. My mom and I liked to shop together. We hardly ever went shopping without each other. I'd try on a dress and she'd say, "that color doesn't look good on you," or "if you buy that one you'll have to spend more money for new shoes." When she bought clothes, she was always worried that she looked too fat. She'd always ask me, "does this make me look fat? Is this too tight?"

Such accounts exemplify ways in which adolescents experience functional role losses. Counselors should not expect adolescents to identify functional losses explicitly by making statements such as: "I miss the advice and direction in choice making that my mother provided," or "My dad and I gave each other the feeling of being needed, useful, and important." Rather, counselors must be alert to the implicit losses expressed and their implications for death-related concerns.

"WHAT WAS AND WHAT IS"

Sometimes the adolescents themselves will begin to question the adequacy and appropriateness of conditions and patterns of functional role fulfillment. Such was the case with JoAnn after several weeks of counseling. JoAnn's mother died suddenly and unexpectedly from accident injuries. In the months immediately prior to the accident, JoAnn and her mother had been experiencing some difficulties in their relationship.

JoAnn described those difficulties as disagreement over her behavior. According to JoAnn, her mother was unjustly accusing her of promiscuous behavior, cutting classes, and neglecting responsibilities. JoAnn admits to developing a pattern of lying to her mother during this period. For example, she would lie about being at a friend's house because, had she admitted being there, her mother would have accused her of ditching school to be there or of being sexually active while she was there. The situation exemplified unfulfilled competency and intimacy needs.

When foster parents accused her of lying, JoAnn told her counselor about the relationship difficulties she had had with her mother. She admitted to the lying and expressed confusion about continuing the pattern after her mother's death. The lying involved telling half-truths or withholding information, as opposed to blatant fabrication. Withholding or giving only partial information or denying the truth is not uncommon to adolescents. Such behavior sometimes stems from a need to maintain the trust, approval, or acceptance of a significant other.

JoAnn's situation is yet another reminder of the necessity to take developmental issues into account in death-related counseling. Had her mother not died, JoAnn's lying may not have been confusing to her in the same way. Her mother's death cut off any opportunity to experience the feelings of competency and intimacy she had sought from her mother.

When ineffective relationship patterns are continued in new situations, the counselor might consider the possibility that such patterns are ways for the survivor to hold onto the deceased. In such cases, the counseling process clarifies what functions the deceased still fulfills.

In cases such as JoAnn's, the counselor's role is to help adolescents realize that their new situations will not ensure new ways of relating even if old ways of relating were dysfunctional. In JoAnn's case concerned with lying, the counselor's role was to confront her dishonesty, to explore consequences of the dishonesty, and to identify appropriate and effective means of fulfilling her needs.

"WHAT NEVER WAS AND NOW COULD NEVER BE"

In many instances of the death of a significant other, survivors grieve the loss of what was and what might have been. Adolescents who experience the death of an absent parent may also grieve the loss of "what never was but what they fantasized could have been." Clues to possible effects of loss of this nature can be seen in the case of 17-year-old Tina.

Tina's parents divorced when she was seven. Her mother became the full-time custodial parent. Although the father was granted unlimited visiting rights, his transient life style precluded anything but short weekend or brief holiday visits. Tina estimates that during the 10 years between the divorce and her father's sudden death, she saw him not more than two dozen times for one-day visits.

Prior to her father's sudden, accidental death, Tina had been working with a school counselor regarding some hopes she had about developing a closer relationship with her father. Her father died within a few hours following an accident in the January prior to the March in which Tina was to visit him for a week. Tina did attend his funeral. There she met for the first time her stepmother and aunts, uncles, and cousins from her father's side of the family.

A number of issues arose during the counseling that Tina initiated after her father's death. She felt so acutely the unfinished business of never having really known her father that she considered leaving her present home to live with an aunt in another state. She expressed some of her feelings and thoughts to the counselor in the following way:

> At the funeral everybody told me that my father always wanted to visit me but never did because then it was too hard for him to leave me again. I'm sad because I never got to know him. I'm mad because he never let me know that this was the reason for not carrying through on his promises to spend time with me.
>
> One of my aunts invited me to visit her and to stay for as long as I want to stay. Sometimes I think I should just pack my things, get on the bus, and move to my aunt's. It seems that since my father died, my mom and I fight all the time.
>
> Mom said I could go visit my aunt when school is out but she won't give me any help to get there. I don't think she likes it that my father's family is paying attention to me. She says things like, "Funny that they're all so inter-

ested in you now when they sure weren't before. How long do you think their new interest in you will last?"

Tina's death-related issues were interwoven and complex. Her situation was such that it prompted the counselor to ask in a professional-peer consultation, "With such a big pizza, where and how do I place a little slice of pepperoni so it will be noticed?" The task was to determine how and in what ways counseling could contribute in order to make a difference in the face of such a myriad of problems.

However, through the counseling process of question after question and reflection after reflection, Tina was able to clarify the issues and establish a perspective for her decision making. While the counselor did not make a personal judgment as to whether Tina should or should not move, the counselor did make professional judgments about areas to probe and pursue with Tina. One of those areas selected was the account of the interactions and conversations at the funeral.

Tina had reported that "*everybody* told me that my father *always* wanted to visit me but *never* did. . . ." The counselor chose to probe this area because of previous experience with adolescents' tendencies toward grandiose generalization to make a point. For example, it is common for teenagers to make statements such as "everybody is going to the party" or to describe a 2-week friendship as "we've been best friends for a long time."

Adults quickly realize that "everybody" in such statements is not universal or all inclusive. However, in Tina's situation the counselor considered it important that Tina move from generalizations to specifics in her account. Such clarification enabled Tina to redefine her grief in more concrete terms.

Questions such as "Who are the people you refer to when you say 'everybody'?" helped Tina reframe the conversation as follows: "My stepmother told me my father wanted to call me when he was here last Christmas but didn't because he knew he would have to leave me again." This revised account provided an entry for Tina to express regret that she had not known her father well enough for him to express to her directly his reasons for his limited relationship with her. Similarly, the aunt's invitation to "stay for as long as I want" was redefined as "come and spend some time with us this summer and we will see how it works out."

In this process of clarification, Tina began to wonder about both her verbal and mental exaggerations. She began to question if the attractions to her father's family and the attractiveness of moving was based upon continuing the fantasy of a good relationship with him.

Tina's response to her father's death and to the sudden and unexpected overtures by his family increased already existing tensions and created new problems between Tina and her mother. One of these problems concerned Tina's expression of grief for her father. Tina felt her mother was becoming impatient with her grief. In contrast, Tina felt that she had not yet properly grieved because she had not cried at or since the funeral.

Tina said she felt sad, but the sadness did not seem to be the same as that felt by other relatives. When the others talked about what they would miss about her father, she could not enter into or identify with the conversations. She felt like her father's family expected her behavior to be more like theirs. Her inability to express her loss caused her to question the sincerity of her grief.

Through lengthy exploration of how Tina perceived her grief in comparison to others, questions emerged not about the sincerity of her grief but about the nature of her loss. Tina recognized that others were grieving the loss of "what was and might have been." She also realized that her grief was for the loss of "what never was and now could never be." When she realized that the meaning of her loss was not the same as that of others, she no longer felt guilty about not grieving like others. Tina was then able to refocus and reinvest energy into the relationship with her mother.

The cases we have cited have focused upon death-related concerns perpetuated by the death of a significant person in the life of an adolescent and the accompanying functional losses.

To concentrate on functional role loss can provide a way to focus upon changes in social structure. Awareness of anyone's death may stimulate some death-related concerns simply by reminding us of mortality. Death of a significant other, in particular, usually brings about immediate life style changes. The counselor's role is to help adolescents identify those effects and determine options for adjusting to such changes.

A CAUTION CONCERNING PERSONAL BIASES

Counselors must guard against letting their personal biases and prejudices discount the loss experienced by counselees. Counselors must acknowledge the meaning of the functional loss to the survivor. The counseling process is in jeopardy when counselors project their values rather than acknowledge the value attributed by the survivor. Consider Jake's description of his relationship with his father:

> Ever since I can remember my dad drank too much. Sometimes somebody from the bar would call and I'd have to go walk home with him. I can't tell

you how many times I'd help him up from the living room floor and take him to his bed. He'd always thank me for looking out for him. He always looked out for us too. He always made sure that mom got the rent and grocery money. I guess my taking care of him when he was drunk was a way I could show him that I cared about him. I know he cared about us. He'd tell me how sorry he was that he couldn't give us more and buy us nicer things.

Jake's description of his relationship with his father recounts aspects of nurture, intimacy, and maintenance. However, the conditions under which those functions were fulfilled were hardly ideal. Jake may well exemplify the tendency to bronze clay feet. His situation is typical of those in which counselors might be tempted to fall into cliché judgments, such as "he's better off without him," or "no great loss."

For counselors even to imply or suggest that such situations might have been unhealthy or less than ideal jeopardizes the counseling process by discounting the meaning for the counselees. This is not to say that in some cases of long-term counseling it might not be appropriate for counselors to assist adolescents in exploring situations and patterns of functional role fulfillment.

GUIDELINES SUMMARIZED

While we consider the death of a significant other to be the most crucial death-related concern, we contend that other death-related concerns can also be effectively addressed by the guidelines that we have suggested. We would summarize those guidelines as follows:

Keep in mind the developmental tasks of teenagers;

Be sensitive to the individual variables that adolescents bring to these tasks;

Listen for losses and acknowledge grief even when you have conflicting values;

Inquire about and acknowledge family, ethnic, and cultural rituals;

Explore the losses with regard to relational needs by inviting reminiscences;

Define existing support systems;

Identify functions those support persons provide;

Explore and, if necessary, rehearse contacting and expressing needs to support persons;

Recognize the functions and limits of those functions you as a counselor can provide;

Offer opportunity for peer sharing with other individuals or groups dealing with similar concerns.

While these guidelines can clarify the death-related counseling process, no guidelines can simplify it. Death-related concerns remain complex because they are distinctively individual and personal.

Counseling interaction will never be a means of replacing who and what was lost. At best, counseling can facilitate the movement from "Why?" to "What now?"

REFERENCE

Putney, R. S. Impact of marital loss on support systems. *Personnel and Guidance Journal*, 1981, *59*, 351–354.

BIBLIOGRAPHY

Bascue, L. O., & Krieger, G. W. Death as a counseling concern. *Personnel and Guidance Journal*, 1974, *52*, 587–592.

Bernstein, J. E. *Loss and how to cope with it.* New York: Seabury, 1977.

Elkind, D. *All grown up and no place to go: Teenagers in crisis.* New York: Addison-Wesley, 1984.

Frears, L. H., & Schneider, J. M. Exploring loss and grief within a wholistic framework. *Personnel and Guidance Journal*, 1981, *59*, 341–345.

Hare-Mustin, R. T. Family therapy following the death of a child. *Journal of Marital and Family Therapy*, 1979, *5*, 51–59.

Harper, J. Helping teenagers confront their fears and feelings about death: A workshop approach. In R. A. Pacholski & C. A. Corr (Eds.), *Priorities in death education and counseling* (pp. 27–42). Arlington, VA: Forum for Death Education and Counseling, 1982.

Hartley, M. P. Coping with life after death: The counselor's response ability. *Personnel and Guidance Journal*, 1980, *59*, 251–252.

Jackson, E. N. *Telling a child about death.* New York: Hawthorn, 1965.

Klagsbrun, F. *Too young to die: Youth and suicide.* New York: Houghton, Mifflin, 1976.

Krell, R., & Rabkin, L. The effects of sibling death on the surviving child: A family perspective. *Family Process*, 1979, *18*, 471–477.

Krementz, J. *How it feels when a parent dies.* New York: Knopf, 1981.

Landau, E. *Death: Everyone's heritage.* New York: Messner, 1976.

LeShan, E. *Learning to say good-by: When a parent dies.* New York: Macmillan, 1976.

McCoy, K. *Coping with teenage depression.* New York: New American Library, 1982.

Nelson, R. C. Counselors, teachers, and death education. *The School Guidance Journal,* 1974, *24,* 322–329.

Nelson, R. C., & Peterson, W. D. Challenging the last great taboo: Death. *The School Counselor,* 1975, *22,* 353–358.

Pendleton, E. (Ed.), *Too old to cry, too young to die.* Nashville, TN: Thomas Nelson, 1980.

Rosenthal, N. R. Attitudes toward death education and grief counseling. *Counselor Education and Supervision,* 1981, *20,* 203–210.

Rosenthal, N. R., & Terkelson, C. Death education and counseling: A survey. *Counselor Education and Supervision,* 1978, *18,* 109–114.

Stuecher, U. Supporting chronically and terminally ill children in hospitals: A challenge for educators. *Education Unlimited,* 1980, *2,* 22–27.

Watts, R. G. *Straight talk about death with young people.* Philadelphia: Westminster, 1975.

PART V

Annotated Resources

We hope that henceforth the present volume will be the first book to which readers will turn when they seek to understand or to help adolescents coping with problems of death, dying, and bereavement. At the same time, this book is designed as a place to begin—not a blind alley in which to end. Many other resources are also available—books, audiovisuals, and organizations—from which additional assistance can be obtained. In Part V, we have undertaken to identify a representative sample of such resources. In each case, contributors provide informative annotations to guide readers and to enable them to judge for themselves which entries to pursue for their own needs and purposes.

Chapters 14 and 15 begin with printed resources in the form of a careful selection of useful books. In Chapter 14, Elizabeth Lamers describes 44 books and discusses how they might be used with adolescent readers, while Charles Corr identifies an additional 41 books for adults in Chapter 15. The dividing line between these two groupings is a bit arbitrary, since adolescent and adult readers can obviously share many books with good results. It might therefore be worthwhile for any reader to look briefly at both listings before settling on titles that appear to serve his or her particular interests. Taken together, we believe that the annotated bibliographies in these two chapters will help to save time for those who wish to go forward from the present volume into other book-length literature that is somehow connected with adolescence and death.

In Chapters 16 and 17, Richard Pacholski balances what previously has been said about books with an extensive survey of audiovisuals and a shorter list of relevant organizations. Pacholski is the most competent mediagrapher working in the field of death and dying today, and an indefatigable student of other community resources. The scope, detail, and clarity of his compilation here are unparalleled. In Chapter 16, Pacholski identifies, catalogues under topical headings, and describes 155 audiovisuals for or about adolescents that have some connection with death-related issues—35 related to nuclearism alone. In Chapter 17, he adds a very useful list of helping organizations. These two chapters together constitute a rich resource for those in need, as well as for educators, counselors, caregivers, church groups, professional organizations, public action projects, and many others.

14

Books for Adolescents

Elizabeth P. Lamers

One hundred years ago, it was fairly common for children to die. In fact, most of the deaths in any year occurred to children under the age of 15. Perhaps that is why books available to children and adolescents then contained many references to death. Today the reverse is true. Death is unexpected in the years of childhood and adolescence. Correspondingly, until very recently, books for young people were unlikely to contain references to death (Estes, 1985). In our society, many parents are uncomfortable about discussing matters related to death with their children, and many teachers are equally inhibited with their students. As a result, adolescents who learn of the recent or impending death of a relative or friend may need assistance in developing perspective on issues relating to dying and death. Adults who are aware of some of the excellent books that have become available in the past few years can be of significant help to adolescents who have questions about death.

To be of most benefit to young people, adults should be familiar with a wide range of different types of books. Some are mainly intended for younger children, others for adolescents and adults. Some will deal with death in a direct manner; others will mention death only obliquely. Some will be helpful in promoting group discussions; others may be of more benefit to the solitary reader.

There is no single book that will serve all purposes and no book that will meet all the needs of a group at the same time. The adult will also recognize that questions about death—and material about death in books—may trigger the release of strong emotions. Discussions about death can produce strong feelings in both the adolescent and the adult.

The adult who is familiar with the resource literature described below and who manages to overcome the natural reluctance to become involved in discussions about death can prove to be of great benefit to adolescents wanting to learn more about death. The natural inquisitiveness of these young people can be turned to advantage, since exposure to books about death can lead them to explore books they would not have otherwise read. And the knowledge gained through reading about death can give them a broader perspective on many important issues of life.

Different books can be used in different situations. An adult mainly interested in eliciting ideas and feelings on death will want to use one set of books, while another set would be more appropriate if the adult wants to communicate certain ideas.

If there is a desire to create a dialogue with adolescents, then the adult needs to create a safe atmosphere. One way to do this is to ask adolescents to review and comment upon fiction and nonfiction books that are written for younger children. In this way, several things can be accomplished: adolescents with low reading ability can pick books they can easily read without embarrassment, and, at the same time, they can participate fully with the group. Also, by using children's books with adolescents, the adult helps to develop a safe distance between the sensitive adolescent and a difficult subject. In addition, this method allows the adolescent to become an "expert" on books for children by asking him or her to comment on the appropriateness of certain books for younger children. This sort of "distancing" may be necessary at the beginning of a discussion on dying and death. Answering questions such as "What do young children need to know about death?" makes adolescents realize that their opinions are respected. Once the adult/adolescent dialogue has been developed, it is fairly easy to move adolescents to related books designed for their own age group.

It may also be of value for adolescents to look at the different ways in which death has been handled in children's books over the last hundred years. For example, in *McGuffey's Readers*, the basal reader in schools from 1879 until the 1920s, over half the poems in the fifth level were about death, many the death of a child. Fairy tales have become much less violent in the last hundred years. Adolescent readers can look at books written in the late 1800s and note the treatment of death in these books. They can determine whether or not death was presented across a wide spectrum of literature or restricted only to a certain type of book. They might also investigate reviews of books in which a death is described. For example, a book that is now very popular, *Charlotte's Web* by E. B. White (1952), was criticized when it first appeared because Charlotte the spider dies at the end of the book, and, at that time, some thought it inappropriate to expose children to death, even in books.

What follows is a list of 44 books, including a brief description of each book, that are usually accessible. Included, also, are comments on ways in which each book might be used with adolescents. Naturally, adults will want to read the books they plan to use with adolescents so that there will be no surprises in the theories put forth by the book. The reader will note that there are not many books listed as appropriate for the middle grades. This is because adolescents are usually more comfortable with books definitely not intended for their age range. Some, particularly poor readers, assume they are being patronized when books close to but obviously below their age level are used. Those middle grade books listed are ones that are of value because they include information not usually given in books for adolescents or because they are particularly well written.

PRIMARY LEVEL BOOKS THAT CAN BE USED WITH ADOLESCENTS

Aliki. *The two of them.* New York: Greenwillow Books, 1979. In short poems, this beautiful picture book tells of the love between a grandfather and his granddaughter, starting with her birth and ending with his death. It depicts the grandfather helping the granddaughter as she grows and learns to do things, and later shows the granddaughter helping the grandfather after he has had a stroke. Finally, it describes the young girl grieving her grandfather's death and beginning to resolve her feelings.

Bartoli, J. *Nonna.* New York: Harvey House, 1975. A little boy narrates the story of his grandmother's death. It is very well done and includes the death, the funeral, the next day, and the first Christmas after his grandmother's death. This book covers a longer time span after a death than most primary books do.

Bernstein, J. E., & Gullo, S. V. *When people die.* New York: Dutton, 1977. This is a nonfiction book for young children on the subject of death and dying. Death is approached in a very matter-of-fact manner. Health, disease, accidents, disasters, murders, suicides, and war are discussed, as well as old age. Burial and mourning customs in different parts of the world are shown in the numerous black and white photographs accompanying the text. The authors also briefly discuss the grief and bereavement occuring after the death of a loved one.

Brown, M. W. *The Dead Bird.* Reading, MA: Addison-Wesley, 1958. This book is unusual in that it was written in the 1950s when death was thought to be an inappropriate subject for children. In this story, some children find a dead bird and bury it without adult help or intervention. It provides an accurate depiction of children's untutored inclination to treat death and burial in a natural way.

Carrick, C. *The accident.* New York: Seabury Press, 1976. In this book, Christopher calls to his dog. The dog hesitates and then dashes across the road in front of a pickup truck. The dog is hit and killed. Christopher's parents decide that it would be easier for him if they bury the dog without Christopher present. The story shows some of the problems that can occur because of this decision; it therefore serves as an excellent starting point for discussing the value of funerals.

De Paola, T. *Nana upstairs and Nana downstairs.* New York: Putnam, 1973. Tommy, the little boy in this story, has a great-grandmother and a grandmother living in his house. The great-grandmother dies while he is a young child. There are two events in this book on which adolescent comment might be invited. The first is the fact that Nana Upstairs (great-grandmother) is shown tied in her chair to keep her from falling. The second is when Tommy is grown and thinks of falling stars as kisses from his Nanas, an idea found in some ancient myths.

Graeber, C. *Mustard.* New York: Mcmillan, 1982. This story is about Mustard, a cat with a heart ailment, and his owner, Alex, who is eight. Alex has to learn to live with the cat's increasing infirmities. Alex must also recognize that he can't always shield Mustard from the harsh realities of life. Eventually, he learns to cope with Mustard's death. The book deals very nicely with the "if only" questions Alex raises after Mustard has died.

Kantrowitz, M. *When Violet died.* New York: Parent's Magazine Press, 1973. The family bird, Violet, has died of old age. Eva and Amy decide to hold a funeral for Violet and have their friends attend. This story provides a beautiful illustration of the creative ways in which children tend to deal with death.

Kennedy, R. *Come again in the spring.* New York: Harper & Row, 1976. The personification of death in this book makes it different from most of the other primary level books dealing with death. The book tells of Old Hark and his birds. Death comes for Old Hark in the winter, but Old Hark declares he can't leave until spring because his birds have not migrated south and they would starve. Death does not want to reschedule Old Hark. A series of wagers determines which of them will have his way.

Lee, V. *The magic moth.* New York: Seabury Press, 1972. This is the story of Mark-O who is six and has to learn to cope first with the dying and then the death of his older sister, Maryanne. The mother and father in this story are very direct in telling the other four children that Maryanne's heart problem cannot be corrected by the doctors and that she will not live much longer. Mark-O has a very difficult time understanding what is happening. The night Maryanne dies, a white moth hatches out of a cocoon Mark-O had given her. Mark-O, in trying to understand Maryanne's death and burial, likens it to the change of a caterpillar into a moth.

Miles, M. *Annie and the old one.* Boston: Little, Brown, 1971. This beautiful book is set on a Navajo Indian reservation. Annie's grandmother announces that she will "return to the earth" when mother completes the rug she is weaving. Annie understands this to mean that her grandmother will die and cannot understand why her mother continues weaving. This book deals most sensitively with children's magical beliefs about death. Annie tries several maneuvers to disrupt the weaving to prevent her grandmother's death. Grandmother talks about the natural cycles of life and death with Annie.

Stein, S. B. *About dying*. New York: Walker, 1974. This is one of the series of "Open Family Books for Parents and Children Together." It is a nonfiction book for children, including the very young. An unusual layout presents each page of text in two type sizes: very large for the young child, and smaller for parents and older children. The book is illustrated with black and white photographs, and is divided into two sections. The first deals with the death of a pet bird, the second with the death of a grandfather. Both sections include the funeral and some of the feelings that death can evoke. Although intended for primary level students, this book is also appropriate for use with younger children.

Stevens, C. *Stories from a snowy meadow*. New York: Seabury, 1976. This book contains a series of stories in which the animals are personified. One of the animals dies of natural causes (old age). The burial is carefully planned after much discussion by the other animals.

Tobias, T. *Petey*. New York: Putnam, 1978. Petey is a gerbil who is very important in Emily's life. Petey is dying. This is the story of Emily's love for her pet, her loss, and the beginning of her understanding that life is always changing and yet continuing. The story also faces the question of denying loss or death by quickly replacing the pet after death.

Viorst, J. *The tenth good thing about Barney*. New York: Atheneum, 1971. Barney was a pet cat. This is a story about grief as told by the little boy who owned Barney. The narration is very realistic and covers a wide range of the emotions encountered in grief. It also shows one way to approach the question of heaven when the little boy and the little girl from next door get in an argument after Barney's funeral over whether Barney is in the ground or in heaven.

Warburg, S. S. *Growing time*. Boston: Houghton Mifflin, 1969. Jamie's old dog, King, dies early in this story. Different members of the family help Jamie with his grief and anger in this sensitively written book. Adolescents have an opportunity to look at the problems that arise when parents do not share the facts of death with their children (King is buried before Jamie is told of his death) and when a substitute dog is immediately offered.

MIDDLE GRADE BOOKS

Coburn, J. B. *Anne and the sand dobbies*. New York: Seabury, 1967. Dan experiences both the death of his little sister, Anne, and that of his first dog in this story. Dan's questions are very adequately answered by his father and a neighbor, Mr. Field. This book is unusual in that it includes a complete funeral service. Coburn, perhaps because of his experience as the Episcopal Bishop of Massachusetts, includes the funeral service in a very natural way.

Paterson, K. *Bridge to Terabithia*. New York: Thomas Y. Crowell Company, 1977. Jess, a country boy, and his new friend from the city, Leslie, develop a special friendship despite their differing backgrounds. They come to share a secret place in the woods that they name Terabithia. The story takes a tragic turn when Leslie accidentally drowns while trying to go alone to Terabithia.

Leslie's death and its impact on Jess are realistically and sensitively handled.

Smith, D. B. *A taste of blackberries.* New York: Crowell, 1973. This story begins with a young boy describing what his best friend, Jamie, is like, and goes on to tell how Jamie died as the result of an allergic reaction to a bee sting. The narrator feels both grief and guilt: grief that his friend is dead, guilt because he left Jamie after he was stung and now wonders if he couldn't have saved him. All his fears and wonderings are dealt with reasonably either by his mother or by one of the other adults in the story. This book is excellent both in content and style.

White, E. B. *Charlotte's web.* New York: Harper & Row, 1952. This well-known story involves a pig and a spider. Wilbur, the pig, is the one in danger of dying in the beginning of the book, while it is Charlotte who dies a natural death in the end. Despite the fact that literary critics criticized this book, it received the Newbery Honor Award for 1953 and has remained a favorite of children ever since.

Zim, H., & Bleeker, S. *Life and death.* New York: William Morrow, 1970. This factual book explains life and death in very understandable terms. It not only covers the physical facts, but also a variety of funeral customs, past and present. While it was intended for the young reader, many adults would find it informative.

BOOKS FOR AGE 12 AND OVER

Alcott, L. M. *Little women.* New York: Grosset & Dunlap, 1947. (Originally published 1869.) This is probably the oldest regularly read book in which a main character dies. Unlike most of the novels written in the last half of the 19th century, Beth does not die with great show and memorable last words. Alcott makes the point in the book that dramatic deathbed scenes happen only in books. This book has value in showing how a person may be cared for at home, a situation that is again becoming more prevalent through the hospice movement.

Angell, J. *Ronnie and Rosie.* Scarsdale, NY: Bradbury Press, 1977. Ronnie is a new student at a large junior high school. Thus, this is a story of making new friends and adjusting to a new place. However, when Ronnie's father is killed in a traffic accident on Halloween night, it becomes the story of Ronnie and her mother adjusting not only to a new place, but also to a new life with just the two of them. With a little help from their friends and a lot of very real struggles, they sort out their feelings.

Blume, J. *Tiger eyes.* Scarsdale, NY: Bardbury Press, 1981. Davey's father has been murdered in his store during a robbery. This is the story of how Davey learns to cope with her father's death, and, incidentally, how her mother and little brother also learn to cope. The characters in the story are clearly drawn, making this a realistic tale of some of the possible consequences of a violent death.

Buck, P. S. *The big wave.* New York: Harper & Row, 1979. (Originally published

1948.) This is the story of a Japanese child who was orphaned when a tidal wave wiped out the fishing village in which he lived. Kino is deeply disturbed by what he has seen. Through gentle talks with his stepfather, Kino learns the oriental philosophy that life and death are interrelated. While this book is usually considered a middle grade book, when used to illustrate the differences between occidental and oriental views of life and death, it also has value for the adolescent.

Cleaver, V., & Cleaver, B. *Where the lilies bloom.* Philadelphia: Lippincott, 1969.

Cleaver, V., & Cleaver, B. *Grover.* Philadelphia: Lippincott, 1970. The Cleavers have written two books containing aspects of death and illness that have not been found previously in literature for young adults. In *Where the Lilies Bloom*, the death of the father means the children will become orphans and wards of the state. Not wanting to be separated in different foster homes, the children and their father work out a plan to keep his death a secret. They even bury their father in a grave he had dug many months before. In the second book, the mother is terminally ill with cancer. She decides she does not want her family to watch her suffer through a long illness and commits suicide. The story tells of her son and husband putting their lives back together after her death. Both books are successful in handling difficult subjects. And both books are popular with adolescents.

Coerr, E. *Sadako and the thousand paper cranes.* New York: Putnam, 1977. This story was researched by its American writer after she saw the statue of Sadako in the Peace Park in Hiroshima, Japan. Sadako was two when the atomic bomb was dropped. As a result of exposure to radiation from the bomb, she developed leukemia when she was 12. In Japan, children are told that if you fold 1,000 oragami paper cranes and make the same wish with each one, your wish will come true. Sadako began to fold paper cranes, wishing to get well, but she died before she reached her goal. After her death, her classmates completed the 1,000 paper cranes in her memory. Even today, children from all over the world still fold paper cranes and send them to be placed on Sadako's statue. This book shows another type of death that can result from war. It is all the more powerful because it is true.

Collier, J. L., & Collier, C. *My brother Sam is dead.* New York: Four Winds Press, 1974. This easily readable book presents a human facet of the American Revolutionary War. The story is narrated by 14-year-old Tim. His 16-year-old brother, Sam, a student at Yale, left school despite his parents' wishes and joined the Continental Army. Later, when his regiment was stationed near his home, Sam left camp to help with the family chores. Eventually he was caught, charged with desertion, and shot. This story is based on an actual family. The unexpected death of Sam for what may seem like a minor infraction can help students look at the "unfairness" of war.

Craven, M. *I heard the owl call my name.* New York: Doubleday, 1973. Mark is a young priest who is terminally ill. His bishop does not tell Mark the doctor's diagnosis, but instead sends him to a remote Indian village to serve the most difficult parish. The bishop hopes Mark will "learn enough of the meaning of life to be ready to die." Marta, the Indian "wise-woman," understands that Mark is dying, and, when Mark himself finally realizes it, does not deny to him that he has indeed "heard the owl call his name." This is an excellent book, made even better by its accurate portrayal of the life of the Coastal Indians of British Columbia.

De Saint Exupery, A. *The little prince* (Katherine Woods, Trans.) New York: Harcourt, Brace & World, 1943. This book can be read on many levels and therefore is suitable for a wide age range. Ideas such as how "the land of tears is a secret place," how one establishes ties with others, how that which is essential is invisible to the eye, and that "the body is just a shell" are ideas that could stimulate much reflection and many interesting discussions. The vocabulary is elementary, but the issues raised are profound.

Dodge, J. *Fup.* New York: Simon & Schuster, 1983. This is a simple story about ducks and people, about life and death. It is also the wonderfully written tale of the relationship between grandfather and grandson, and their individual beliefs about life and death. (Caution: contains explicit language.)

Farley, C. *The garden is doing fine.* New York: Atheneum, 1975. This story is set at the end of World War II (1945). Corrie, a high school freshman, has the same wishes and dreams as her best friend, but Corrie also has a father who is dying in a hospital. This book offers very good examples of the way children try to use magic to control events in their lives. Corrie eventually realizes that her father will die, but that he also will live on through the memories of those who knew him.

Fast, H. *April morning.* New York: Crown, 1961. On April 19, 1775, Adam Cooper became a man. On that day he finally realized his father loved him: he also saw his father shot down by British soldiers. It was the beginning of many changes for Adam and also the beginning of the Revolutionary War. This is a sensitive telling of a familiar story.

Frank, A. *Anne Frank: The diary of a young girl* (B. M. Mooyaart-Doubleday, Trans.). New York: Doubleday, 1952. Although the diary ends before Anne's death in a Nazi concentration camp, the "afterword" chronicles the events from the family's capture to the end of the war, including a brief history of the events leading up to World War II. This excellent book depicts an important historical time from the point of view of a young person who was there.

Gunther, J. *Death be not proud.* New York: Harper & Row, 1949. This is a nonfiction book written by a father about his teenage son's illness and death. It raises the questions: How is death faced? How do those who survive face the death of a loved one? How can the death of one so young and bright be justified? After his son's death, John Gunther is able to see death as part of the process of life.

Hughes, M. *Hunter in the dark.* Toronto: Clark, Irwin & Co., 1982. This Canadian book has won several awards. It tells the story of a very successful 17-year-old, Mike Rankin, who suddenly becomes seriously ill. The illness turns out to be leukemia, and Mike's parents decide to keep the truth from him. We see how Mike discovers the truth about his illness and how he learns to cope with all the attendant implications of the disease. The book ends before the reader is told whether or not Mike will survive his illness.

Hunter, M. *A sound of chariots.* New York: Harper & Row, 1972. This is an excellent book. The story covers Bridie's life from the death of her father when she is eight until she is 18 and finally has sorted out most of her feelings about her father's death. There are no magical solutions to problems in this book.

Klein, S. *The final mystery.* New York: Doubleday, 1974. This factual book explores the meaning of death and how people of different times, different religions, and different parts of the world have coped with it. The book also discusses "the war on death" by researchers and doctors, and what the world would be like if death were virtually eliminated.

Lund, D. *Eric.* Philadelphia: Lippincott, 1974. This book was written by a mother about her teenage son's terminal illness. Eric had acute leukemia, but he lived life to the fullest until the day he died.

Mann, P. *There are two kinds of terrible.* New York: Doubleday, 1977. Robbie breaks his arm on the last day of school and has to spend his whole summer vacation in a cast. That is one kind of terrible. But he finds out about another kind of terrible, a terrible that doesn't end, when his mother goes to the hospital for tests and never returns. He is left with a father he barely knows and without the mother he loved most in the world. This is the story of how he and his father start to build a relationship when they both miss a person they loved very much.

Moe, B. *Pickles and prunes.* New York: McGraw-Hill, 1976. There are actually two stories of death being told in this book. One tells of the concerns 12-year-old Anne has about her widowed mother's new, serious manfriend, while the other tells of the serious illness and death of Anne's new friend. A well written and realistic book.

Rosenthal, T. *How could I not be among you?* New York: Braziller, 1973. A dying poet writes about his illness in a direct fashion that has great meaning for young adults. A beautiful short book in verse form.

Segerberg, O., Jr. *Living with death.* New York: Dutton, 1976. This is a very well written factual book. Segerberg starts with the mythology of why human beings must face certain death. He covers beliefs and practices having to do with death from classical times to the present. His book is the most complete analysis of this subject written for young people. The last chapter discusses what individuals can do to have control over their lives, while acknowledging that we all die in the end.

CONCLUSION

The books that have been mentioned here are only a few of the many that might have been included, but they do give an indication of the rich variety of books that are available and can be used with adolescents in different situations. Adults can find other books on death for all ages by checking standard reference sources in this field (for example Bernstein, 1983; Wass, 1984), as well as the card catalogues in school and/or public libraries. It is surprising how many books for young people are listed under the subject "Death." Of course, adults must read these and any other books to make sure they are appropriate for the individual adolescents or groups in question.

At all times, adults should be sensitive to the fact that adolescents who ask tentative opening questions about death may have fears and fantasies that can be released and relieved through reading and talking. For a young person, one of the most supportive side effects of reading books about death can be the realization that he or she is not unique or alone in having questions about death. The perspective gained through reading books about death and dying may lay the groundwork for effective communication between adolescents and adults in this often-avoided, but important, subject area.

REFERENCES

Bernstein, J. E. *Books to help children cope with separation and loss.* (2d ed.). New York: R. W. Bowker, 1983.
Estes, S. Death and dying in teenage fiction. *Booklist*, 1985, *81*, 839–841.
Wass, H. Books for children: An annotated bibliography. In H. Wass & C. A. Corr (Eds.), *Helping children cope with death: Guidelines and resources* (2nd ed.). Washington, DC: Hemisphere, 1984.

15

Books for Adults

Charles A. Corr

This chapter is an annotated guide to 41 nonfiction books that are concerned either with the topics of dying, death, and bereavement, or with issues of adolescents and their development. We believe the present volume provides the best overall treatment of the conjunction of these two areas. Nevertheless, specific questions may be taken up more fully or in a different way in another book that would be valuable for many readers. Because we judge that book-length titles are more likely to be of substantial and enduring value, this chapter does not survey the journal literature. Those with specialized interests can gain access to that literature by consulting journals in appropriate fields, standard guides to periodicals, or the resource guides prepared by Wass and colleagues that are described in the bibliography that follows.

In the subsequent listing, titles have been selected for a variety of reasons:

1. because we believe the book is the best in its field;
2. because it is the sole or the major extended discussion of its subject;
3. because it is a good representative example of similar titles; or
4. because it is likely to be encountered by those searching out printed resources in these topical areas.

In each case, a brief annotation describing the contents of the particular book enables the reader to make an individual judgment as to whether or not it would be worth looking at the volume itself to determine its usefulness in the light of a specific set of interests. We note that many books are designed to be read or could be appreciated both by adults and by adolescents themselves. When that is the case, the title is included in this chapter. Other titles—fiction and biographical or autobiographical works—geared more to an adolescent audience have been listed in Chapter 14.

ANNOTATED GUIDE TO BOOKS FOR ADULTS

Adams, D. W. *Childhood malignancy: The psychosocial care of the child and his family.* Springfield, IL: Charles C Thomas, 1979.

Adams, D. W., & Deveau, E. J. *Coping with childhood cancer: Where do we go from here?* Reston, VA: Reston Publishing Co., 1984. Quite different approaches can be seen in these two books. The first is a text and resource for professionals; the second is a guide for parents and family members. David Adams is a social worker and Eleanor Deveau a nurse in the pediatric oncology service at McMaster University Medical Centre in Canada. Their work addresses the full range of psychosocial issues that have to do with children and cancer, stressing the value of honesty and realism throughout. Several pages in each book (especially in the latter one) develop themes that are of special importance for adolescents.

Bernstein, J. E. *Loss and how to cope with it.* New York: Seabury, 1977. Writing primarily for young readers, Bernstein seeks to explore the nature of loss, the impact of death, and the responses that frequently ensue. It is a useful practical guidebook, with information about books, films, and organizations that might provide additional assistance.

Bernstein, J. E. *Books to help children cope with separation and loss* (2nd ed.). New York: Bowker, 1983. This is an impressive guide to bibliographical resources —what they are and how to use them—in the field of separation and loss. It includes an annotated bibliography of 633 books; the section on death alone fills 72 pages and offers paragraph-length summaries and assessments of 139 titles. There are extensive indexes, a directory of helpful organizations, and additional unannotated lists of selected readings for adults. Those who are interested in books that overlap and go beyond both the age range and the topical scope of the present volume will find Bernstein's work to be an indispensable aid.

Conger, J. J. *Adolescence: Generation under pressure.* New York: Harper & Row, 1979. Part of The Life Cycle Series, this little book is a lavishly illustrated introduction intended for a popular audience. It is only a beginning and that only for lay readers. It is recommended within those limits and on the strength of its author's expertise.

Conger, J. J., & Petersen, A. C. *Adolescence and youth: Psychological development in a changing world* (3rd ed.). New York: Harper & Row, 1984. This large volume of over 700 pages is one of the most respected and influential of the numerous textbooks in developmental psychology that focus on adolescence. It surveys the field and provides a sound overall introduction to its subject. As is typical of most books of this sort, there are no entries in the subject index for "dying," "death," or "bereavement," although "suicide" is mentioned.

Eddy, J. M., & Alles, W. F. *Death education*. St. Louis: Mosby, 1983. Written by two health educators, this book is apparently intended to serve as a handbook for teachers, a textbook for students, and a collection of resources for reference. It contains three chapters on "modalities of death education" (how death education has evolved in the United States, how it can be offered across the life span, and different ways in which it can be taught), five chapters on "course content" (bereavement, grief, and mourning; euthanasia; suicide; consumer aspects in relation to the funeral industry; and the hospital/hospice scene), and ten appendixes ranging from educational activities and an annotated bibliography (only through 1981) to living will legislation and eye banks.

Friedenberg, E. Z. *The vanishing adolescent*. Boston: Beacon Press, 1959. Friedenberg's thesis in this early monograph, now a classic in the field, is "that adolescence, as a developmental process, is becoming obsolete" (p. 133). He means that the concerns of adults, the impact of the schools, and other manipulative social pressures favoring conformity and group adjustment are undermining adolescence as an explicit period between childhood and adulthood in which the central task is dialectical self-definition, in which values such as tenderness and respect for competence are confirmed, and in which integrity and self-esteem are established. Does this have relevance 25 years later, either as a prediction come true or as an enduring danger?

Giovacchini, P. *The urge to die: Why young people commit suicide*. New York: Macmillan, 1981. Giovacchini is a psychoanalyst who has done extensive work with adolescents. His book "is especially intended for those who are most immediately immersed in the daily lives of teenagers: parents, guidance counselors, and other concerned adults" (p. 8). Writing in a clear, literate, and thoughtful style, Giovacchini emphasizes the ability to identify with the problems of suicidal adolescents in our society. Multiple examples trace the development of typical problems and suggest practical ways to be of help. In terms of its reading level, we might place Giovacchini's work somewhere between Klagsbrun's book (q.v.) and the volumes edited by Hatton and Valente, or Peck, Farberow, and Litman (q.v.).

Gordon, A. K., & Klass, D. *They need to know: How to teach children about death*. Englewood Cliffs, NJ: Prentice-Hall, 1979. Gordon and Klass offer concrete guidance for parents and teachers concerning death education for children. In the light of four primary goals for death education, the authors outline suggested curricula by grade and goal, with specific resource and activity suggestions in each case. Pages 181–209 deal with grades 8 through 12. Health care and funeral services are taken up as consumer issues. When it was first published, this book was far better than anything else available in its field, and it remains in the first rank in its topical area.

Hatton, C. L., & Valente, S. M. (Eds.). *Suicide: Assessment and intervention* (2nd ed.). Norwalk, CT: Appleton-Century-Crofts, 1984. As Edwin Shneidman says in his "Foreword to the Second Edition," this is "an eminently useful handbook for the assessment of suicidal risk and for effective intervention with potentially suicidal persons—and, if necessary, for comforting counseling of survivors of suicidal death of a loved one" (p. xi). In Shneidman's words, the second edition "contains substantial changes relating to the history, to theoretical development, and to ethnic issues of suicide" (p. xi). This book might be described as a serious text for professional practitioners, a kind of everyday desk reference with numerous case examples. The scope is broader than our area of concern, but the book does contain separate discussions (pp. 195–230) of suicide in children, young adolescents, and late adolescents or young adults.

Jewett, C. L. *Helping children cope with separation and loss.* Harvard, MA: Harvard Common Press, 1982. Adults who wish to help children cope with separation and loss of whatever sort will find here a good outline of the principal issues in question and a set of sensible suggestions as to what they might say or do.

Kastenbaum, R. *Humans developing: A lifespan perspective.* Boston: Allyn & Bacon, 1979. This textbook on lifespan human development is distinguished from many others in the field by its author's sensitivity and willingness to include death-related issues throughout its scope. In Kastenbaum's own words: "Death is not merely tacked onto the last few pages of a chapter on old age" (p. xi). Chapters 12 through 14 (pp. 416–509) address issues of adolescence.

Klagsbrun, R. *Too young to die: Youth and suicide.* Boston: Houghton Mifflin, 1976. We have recommended this book to adolescents, college students, parents, teachers, and counselors with good response. Klagsbrun has the ability to present a difficult subject in a readable and helpful way. She surveys the realities of suicide among young people, suggestions for those who wish to help either in crisis situations or in the aftermath of a suicide, and the larger social and cultural situation within which youth suicide has recently become such a problem. It is a useful introductory account.

Knott, J. E., Ribar, M. C., Duson, B. M., & King, M. R. *Thanatopics: A manual of structured learning experiences for death education.* Kingston, RI: SLE Publications, 1982. This supplementary workbook for educators and learners offers 50 exercises or structured learning experiences, and discusses how they might be best used in death education. Most of the exercises are suitable for adolescents or college students.

Krementz, J. *How it feels when a parent dies.* New York: Knopf, 1981. Krementz' idea was to photograph 18 children (half of whom are teenagers) who have experienced the death of a parent, and to invite each to provide a brief essay (averaging about four pages in length) describing or commenting upon his or her situation. The concept is unusual and may help to humanize this sort of loss, especially for others in similar situations.

Langone, J. *Death is a noun: A view of the end of life.* Boston: Little, Brown, 1972.

Langone, J. *Vital signs: The way we die in America.* Boston: Little, Brown, 1974. These two books by a medical journalist offer popular accounts of death and its social implications. They are widely read by adolescents and would also be useful for adults seeking nontechnical introductions to these subjects.

LeShan, E. *Learning to say good-by: When a parent dies.* New York: Macmillan, 1978. LeShan's concern is to help young people understand and accept their feelings following the loss of a parent through death. Her book conveys sensitivity to the difficulties of the grieving situation, together with confidence that coping is not beyond the capacities of one who is permitted to share feelings in open communication with sympathetic and concerned adults.

Lifton, R. J., & Olson, E. *Living and dying.* New York: Praeger, 1974. This little book manages to achieve a popular presentation of the very serious themes of holocaust and transformation. It sketches themes that are elsewhere developed more fully in Lifton's writings: the place of death in the life cycle; the impact of the nuclear era and the threat of meaninglessness; problems of historical continuity, significance, and symbolic immortality.

Meagher, D. K., & Shapiro, R. D., *Death: The Experience.* Minneapolis: Burgess Publishing Company, 1984. This spiral-bound booklet of nearly 200 pages contains a wide range of readings, references, and 32 death-related exercises—mainly of the paper-and-pencil type—for use in connection with a death and dying course. It is intended as a kind of supplementary laboratory manual, and would be especially appropriate for adolescents and college students.

Offer, D., Ostrov, E., & Howard, K. I. *The adolescent: A psychological self-portrait.* New York: Basic Books, 1981. This book is essentially the report of an extensive, empirical study of over 20,000 normal, disturbed, and physically ill adolescents conducted over a period of nearly two decades. Data from Australian, Israeli, and Irish adolescents are also included. The topical focus is on five aspects of the self: psychological, social, sexual, familial, and coping. The authors conclude that the most dramatic of their findings "are those that permit us to characterize the modal American teenager as feeling confident, happy, and self-satisfied—a portrait of the American adolescent that contrasts sharply with that drawn by many theorists of adolescent development who contend that adolescence is pervaded with turmoil, dramatic mood swings, and rebellion" (pp. 83–84). It is an important book, especially for scholars and researchers.

Offer, D., Ostrov, E., & Howard, K. I. *Patterns of adolescent self-image.* San Francisco: Jossey-Bass, Inc., 1984. Like its predecessor, this book is based on studies using the Offer Self-Image Questionnaire to determine what adolescents think of themselves and of their world. In this case, Offer and his colleagues extend their work through particularized studies of both normal and disturbed adolescents. Once again, they contrast common misunderstandings of mental health professionals with the adolescents' own self-image. It is dependent upon and somewhat more specialized than the previously mentioned volume coauthored by Offer, Ostrov, and Howard.

Peck, M. L., Farberow, N. L., & Litman, R. E. (Eds.). *Youth suicide.* New York: Springer Publishing, 1985. In this volume, 15 of the best-known clinicians and scholars in the field take up psychodynamic, treatment, and prevention issues in suicide among children, adolescents, and youth. It is an important new resource for professionals, with two substantial chapters on the role of the schools in this area.

Pendleton, E. (Ed.). *Too old to cry, too young to die.* Nashville, TN: Thomas Nelson, 1980. Under a variety of topical headings, this book records the experiences of 35 teenagers and young adults who have cancer. It thereby serves as a forum from which others can learn.

Rice, F. P. *The adolescent: Development, relationships, and culture* (3rd ed.). Boston: Allyn & Bacon, 1981. This textbook brings together adolescent development and behavior with group life and culture. Cross-cultural comparisons and subcultural data are features not ordinarily found in general books of this kind.

Sahler, O. J. Z. (Ed.) *The child and death.* St. Louis: Mosby, 1978. This is a standard anthology of 23 papers that grew out of a professional conference in the field. It looks at families, caregivers, survivors, and ethical or educational issues. Although now a bit dated, it contains some good pieces, especially for professional readers.

Santrock, J. W. *Adolescence* (2nd ed.). Dubuque, IA: Wm. C. Brown, 1984. A knowledgeable colleague describes this book as the best introductory textbook for a course in adolescent psychology. We mention it here as another good example of its type.

Satir, V. *Peoplemaking*. Palo Alto, CA: Science & Behavior Books, 1972. *Peoplemaking* is a family therapist's book for family members that deals with family processes and communications. It is witty, innovative, and stimulating. It is a kind of guidebook for families that would be especially useful as preparation for dealing with adolescents.

Schowalter, J. E., & Anyan, W. R. *The family handbook of adolescence*. New York: Knopf, 1979. Writing primarily for parents, two physician-authors explore common health, psychological, and social issues faced during adolescence. Although not specific to our issues, it is useful nevertheless.

Schowalter, J. E., Patterson, P. R., Tallmer, M., Kutscher, A. H., Gullo, S. V., & Peretz, D. *The child and death*. New York: Columbia University Press, 1983. Apart from a variety of scattered references, there is no sustained discussion of adolescents and death in this book. Nevertheless, it is a useful resource in the more general field of children and death. Twenty-nine selections from a good group of contributors take up the following general topics: the child's perception of death; children's reactions to parental death; caring for the life-threatened child; staff, parents, and the dying child; the sudden death of a child; and parental bereavement and grief. Dominant perspectives are medical and psychological.

Spinetta, J. J., & Deasy-Spinetta, P. (Eds.). *Living with childhood cancer*. St. Louis: Mosby, 1981. Based upon a conference in San Diego, this book is concerned with adjustment and adaptation to childhood cancer in the context of the increased likelihood of long-term survival. The editors review past work in this field (among which their own studies are highly regarded) and introduce discussions of such topics as: changing patterns of care in pediatric oncology; stress; denial; ethical and religious issues; use of the Kinetic Family Drawing; nonmedical costs of illness; siblings; hypnosis; implications for schooling; and key issues in long-term living (visible physical impairment, marriage, employment, and insurance). Parents, adolescent and other young patients, and caregivers also have their own say. A valuable contribution to the field of psychosocial oncology.

Stanford, G., & Perry D. *Death out of the closet: A curriculum guide to living with dying*. New York: Bantam, 1976. As its title might suggest, this is an early book in the field for teachers and counselors at the secondary school level. Stanford and Perry offer a rationale for this sort of death education, suggest ways to deal with problems that are likely to arise, show how to organize content (for example, as an elective course, a minicourse, or a unit integrated within the existing curriculum), and survey materials and teaching strategies. Perhaps the most useful portion of the book, occupying almost half of its length, provides synopses and discussion/study questions for 19 books that are related to this subject and that are particularly suited for or popular with young readers.

Sternberg, F., & Sternberg, B. *If I die and when I do: Exploring death with young people*. Englewood Cliffs, NJ: Prentice-Hall, 1980. This book is at its best in reproducing poems, drawings, and statements from middle school students (aged 11 to 13) in a 9-week death and dying class. The narrative text describes the structure of the course and uses its major topics as themes around which to group the students' work.

Stevens-Long, J., & Cobb, N. J. *Adolescence and early adulthood*. Palo Alto, CA: Mayfield, 1983. The insistent and distinguishing point of view in this textbook is that of a developmental perspective that seeks to depict adolescence not as a special period but as part of the normal overall life cycle. The authors look at each aspect of adolescent development in relation to their underlying theme of identity achievement. To that end, they treat early (and middle) and late adolescence as distinct periods of development and group topics accordingly.

Van Ornum, W., & Van Ornum, M. W. *Talking to children about nuclear war*. New York: Continuum, 1984. Essentially a handbook for parents, this slim monograph seeks to help adults create opportunities for discussion with children about nuclear war. Without adopting a political or moral position, the authors seek to foster dialogue about this very important issue of our time. Their premise is that children are distressed about the possibility of nuclear war and its implications, and that such distress is a family issue that needs to be shared with parents and other informed adults.

Wass, H., & Corr, C. A. (Eds.). *Childhood and death*. Washington, DC: Hemisphere, 1984.

Wass, H., & Corr, C. A. (Eds.). *Helping children cope with death: Guidelines and resources* (2nd ed.). Washington, DC: Hemisphere, 1984. These two contributing authors' volumes set the standard for comprehensive, up to date, and practical treatment of the full range of issues in which children and death are linked. *Helping Children Cope with Death* offers four chapters of guidelines for parents, counselors, and teachers, and three chapters of resources (annotated bibliographies of 44 books for adults, 156 books for children, and 136 audiovisuals). *Childhood and Death* adds to these perspectives a clinical viewpoint in its survey of five major topics: death-related thoughts and fears; dying (patterns of coping and ways to be of help); bereavement; suicide; and death education (at home and in the schools). Together, these books are an indispensable resource in their field

Wass, H., Corr, C. A., Pacholski, R. A., & Forfar, C. S. *Death education II: An annotated resource guide*. Washington, DC: Hemisphere, 1985. These two annotated resource guides bring together books and articles on death education at all levels: selected text and reference works, bibliographies, periodicals, audiovisuals, organizations, research instruments in the field, and many other useful resources. In addition to updating coverage of categories in Volume I, Volume II adds a hospice training bibliography, a discussion of thanatological topics in literature, and an appendix of selected documents. Both volumes are especially recommended for educators and scholars.

Wass, H., Corr, C. A., Pacholski, R. A., & Sanders, C. M. *Death education: An annotated resource guide*. Washington, DC: Hemisphere, 1980.

Watts, R. G. *Straight talk about death with young people*. Philadelphia: Westminster, 1975. The significant feature of this book is its origin in discussion groups with a Presbyterian minister and junior high school students. Topics covered include death, dying, grief, funerals, and beliefs about life after death.

16
Audiovisual Resources

Richard A. Pacholski

DEATH EDUCATION

Each of these audiovisual packages provides the basis for more or less extensive instructional units on death and dying, introducing a number of basic subjects as the descriptions indicate. While there is content variation among the different programs, all address themselves effectively to adolescent audiences and cover the material in some depth. Teacher's guides are provided. Each entry states the distributor for that particular audiovisual package, but all addresses for distributors are listed separately on pages 275–277.

General Surveys of
Thanatological Topics for
Middle School Students

Death—Facing a Loss focuses on death in the family and the loss of a pet. The nature and the effects of grief and bereavement are covered; emphasized is the fact that grief is *natural*. The titles of the four programs in the series are: "Facing the First Goodbye"; "I'll Miss Gram a Lot"; "My Turn to Mourn"; and "Why Did Duffy Have to Die?" Society for Visual Education; four color filmstrips and audiocassettes, approximately 12 minutes each, 1978.

The Life Cycle approaches life, change, loss, and death from a developmental standpoint. The topics of the six filmstrips in this program are adolescence, young adulthood, marriage, separation and divorce, aging, and death. Educational Record Sales; 40 frames each, 1978.

Understanding Death: A Basic Program in Death and Dying is composed of six filmstrips and three accompanying audiocassettes. "Thinking About

Death" gives general background and encourages students to examine their own experiences with and attitudes toward death. "Mourning" discusses grief as a normal human emotion, one not exclusively associated with death. "Practical Guidelines" examines death certificates, wills, and organ bequests. "Death's Moment and the Time that Follows" explains why "death" is difficult to define, and why scientific advances constantly force changes in society's conception of death and of life. The fifth program, "Dying Occurs in Stages," presents the theories of Dr. Elizabeth Kübler-Ross. Finally, "The Gift of Life" examines various types of "symbolic immortality" and argues that a well-spent life can rob death of some of its sting. Eye Gate Media; approximately 10 minutes each, 1976. Available as a set or singly.

Understanding Death Series. Included in this series are four programs especially designed for middle school students and an accompanying program for parents and teachers. In "Life-Death," death is presented as a natural part of the life cycle; natural, too, are feelings of grief. In both "Exploring the Cemetery" and "Facts About Funerals," a boy visits and gets information from a cemeterian and a funeral director, respectively. The fourth program, "A Taste of Blackberries," is adapted from a book by Doris Buchanan Smith. A boy loses his best friend, then works through his grief to an awareness of death as a natural part of the human experience. Finally, "Children and Death: A Guide for Parents and Teachers" offers advice on truth telling, death education, and the changing stages and levels of children's understandings of death. Educational Perspectives Associates; five filmstrips and audiocassettes, approximately 20 minutes each, 1974. Individual programs are available separately.

General Surveys of Thanatological Topics for High School Students

The first of the two filmstrips in *Living with Dying* presents death as part of the natural cycle of life and discusses various ways to achieve symbolic immortality. Fear and denial are natural but can be overcome. The second filmstrip demonstrates how our culture encourages a denial of death in children and offers positive suggestions. Tbe program, which won an award in 1973 from the National Council on Family Relations, ends by dramatizing the five "stages" of dying and explaining how a caregiver can be most helpful. Sunburst Communications; two color filmstrips and audiocassettes or records, 14 minutes each, 1973.

Widely used in secondary schools, *Perspectives on Death: A Thematic*

Teaching Unit is the only program available that treats death in the arts. "Death Through the Eyes of the Artist" illustrates—on filmstrip and audiocassette—the work of such masters as Michelangelo, Rembrandt, Bosch, and Picasso, and explains how style, color, and symbolism can "capture the face and mood of death" (22 minutes). In "Death Themes in Literature," narrators read from Shakespeare, Poe, London, Wilder, and others (audiocassette, 20 minutes). Musical selections like "Danse Macabre," Mozart's "Requiem," Schubert's "Der ErlKönig," "Taps," and "Deep River" are presented in "Death Themes in Music" (audiocassette, 18 minutes). A fourth filmstrip-audiocassette program (28 minutes) illustrates funeral customs around the world. Educational Perspectives Associates 1972. Available as a set or singly.

Perspectives on Death surveys various bioethical issues in the filmstrip entitled "The Right to Die," as well as issues like active and passive euthanasia, and those slippery concepts, "quality of life" and "the right to die." Varying definitions of death and related problems are examined also. Modes of immortality are studied in the second filmstrip, "Toward an Acceptance." Is death simply annihilation? What are the promises of various religious faiths? Can death be outlived through family, work, and creativity? Sunburst Communications; 11–12 minutes each, 1976.

Another well-made filmstrip program from Sunburst, *When Disaster Strikes: Coping with Loss, Grief, and Rejection*, studies in depth the effects of many life crises—illness, accident, broken romance, natural disaster, property loss, military combat, as well as death. The connections between physical illness and emotional stress are explained, but major emphasis is on psychological responses to crisis: the "stages of crisis"— shock, anger, acceptance; attendant feelings like despair, guilt, "feeling crazy," isolation; and the nature of "grief work." Sunburst Communications; three color filmstrips and audiocassettes, approximately 15 minutes each, 1980.

General Surveys of Thanatological Topics for Advanced Students, Parents, and Teachers

The *Dimensions of Death Series*, a collection of 10 filmstrip-audiocassette programs, is the only available introductory resource of such ambitious scope. To illustrate the wide range of topics covered, here are the titles of the 10 units and the subject matter of each:

1. "Death and the Creative Imagination"—painting, sculpture, music, poetry, and prose fiction;

2. "Cross-cultural Aspects of Death"—history and anthropology;
3. "Religious Viewpoints on Death"—Judaism, Catholicism, and Protestantism;
4. "Death as a Moral and Ethical Issue"—philosophy, particularly ethics;
5. "Man's Attitudes to Death"—sociology and psychology;
6. "Developmental Concepts of Death"—psychology;
7. "Death, Grief and Mourning"—the psychology of grief;
8. "Coping with Fatal Illness"— psychosocial counseling;
9. "The Funeral in American Culture"—U. S. history; and
10. "Death as a Practical Matter"—consumer education.

The best organized and most detailed programs are 5, 6, and 7, those dealing with death and dying from sociological and psychological perspectives. While 1 and 4 are comparatively weak, the others are useful for general audiences. Educational Perspectives Associates; approximately 20 minutes each, 1977. Available as a set or individually.

Of interest to advanced students as well as to teachers and others embarking on death and dying instructional units in the classroom, *Death and Dying: A Teenage Class* employs an unusual approach. Filmed in documentary style, the program traces the growth and development of a Washington, DC, high school death and dying course. We watch the instructors develop their rationale, experiment with teaching methods, and design discussion strategies. Then the camera goes along with the students on field trips to a funeral home, crematory, and cemetery to film student reactions. McGraw-Hill Training Systems; color film or videotape, 10 minutes, 1980.

Understanding Grief

Several fine audiovisuals can help facilitate classroom discussion of grief resulting from the deaths of significant others, whether family members or friends. What is it like to lose a parent or grandparent, a sibling or a classmate? What does it mean to grieve? How does it *feel*—emotionally, spiritually, physically? How can a young person work through those bad times and come to terms with reality? These programs explore such questions, demonstrating how growth and positive change can result from even very painful losses.

But He Was Only Seventeen—The Death of a Friend. Six months after Steve is killed in an automobile accident, his friends and high school classmates try to sort out their feelings. Guided by an understanding teacher, they begin to face up to their feelings, to understand the complex nature and effects of grief. Each person's grief is unique, they learn, and in the process deepen their understanding of themselves and others. Grief teaches them the difference that their friend Steve has made in their lives. Sunburst Communications; three filmstrips and audiocassettes, approximately 15 minutes each, 1981.

"But Mr. Wilson . . . Why Did It Have to Be Melissa?" explores similar themes in an audiocassette format. A high school senior has recently died of cancer, and her classmates discuss their shock, their fears, and their grief with their teacher. In the discussion, insights are offered into both normal and pathological grief reactions, the "stages" of dying, and the effects of human mortality on religion and culture. Developed by Steven P. Lindenberg, this program is designed both for use in high school classrooms and for counseling purposes. Professional Associates; audiocassette, 21 minutes, 1982.

Death of a Gandy Dancer explores how the dying of Grandfather Ben affects other members of the Matthews family. Ben's daughter and son-in-law are concerned and loving, but both want to hide the truth from Grandson Josh, the focal point of Ben's last days. Casting and acting are superb, and the story is rich in insight for students of death education. Family dynamics in the dying trajectory, the importance of memory and progeny, truth telling, and the advantages of choosing one's manner of dying are just a few topics that discussion can explore. Learning Corporation of America; color film, 26 minutes, 1977.

Footsteps on the Ceiling is a tender story of a girl's love for her grandmother, told without words. Kept away from her grandmother's deathbed, the girl goes to the attic where she and grandmother have spent much happy time amidst old family "treasures." She returns with one special gift to the now empty bedroom—for grandmother has died—to show her love once more. Phoenix Films; color film or videotape, 8 minutes, 1981.

Last Rites—A Child's Reaction to Death focuses on a boy who, at his mother's funeral, cannot grasp the meaning and the reality of his loss. He retreats into fantasy until a stranger is able to get through and help the boy accept the death. This film on "the mystery of death and its incomprehensibility to a child" is an excellent teaching tool. Filmakers Library; color film, 30 minutes, 1979.

A similar set of topics is dramatized in *A Matter of Time*. When her mother is diagnosed as terminally ill with cancer, Lisl, a high school senior, becomes depressed, angry, and withdrawn by turns. She gets no help from her father, sunk in his own quiet grieving. Her classmates won't talk about it. So Lisl is counseled by a perceptive social worker who reminds her, "you still have *now*," and, as the mother's death approaches, "you can choose the things you like to remember." In the end, Lisl can verbalize positive, loving feelings for her mother and grow from the experience. This is a moving story sensitively told, based on the novel by Roni Schotter. Learning Coporation of America; color film or videotape, 30 minutes, 1981.

Ojiisan is a fine miniature portrait of a relationship: as he maintains a vigil at the bedside, a young man reacts to the dying of his grandfather. University of Southern California; black-and-white film, 10 minutes, 1980.

This One for Dad presents a more complex family situation. David is diligent, perhaps obsessively so, in looking after his terminally ill father. But David is a loner. He cares for no one, and no one, apparently, cares for him. He wants one thing only—to be the number-one runner in his high school. When his father dies, David runs aimlessly into the countryside until he meets a man who discusses with him the meaning of running and winning. Moved by the man's questions, David wins the track meet "for Dad" and opens himself to the friendship of others. While this well-made film effectively portrays a death in the family from a teenager's perspective, it also offers valuable lessons for young people and counselors about the dangers of internalizing negative feelings. Paulist Productions; color film or videotape, 18 minutes, 1981.

Finally, *Very Good Friends* explores grief resulting from the death of a sibling. When her 11-year-old sister dies, a 13-year-old is tortured by grief, anger, and guilt. Her parents help her sort through her feelings, accept the loss, and rest more comfortably with her memories. This fine dramatization of a death in the family can effectively stimulate classroom discussion. Learning Corporation of America; color film, 20 minutes, 1977.

NUCLEAR WEAPONS AND NUCLEAR WAR

For many years, nations have had in place the means of wiping all human civilization off the face of the globe. Yet nations persist to this day in expending billions of dollars developing the wherewithal to perform that global scouring many more times over. The nuclear weapons race thus adversely affects the global quality of life in its massive diversion of material wealth and human energy from perennial human problems of poverty, hunger, and disease. And in individual lives all over the globe, growing fears of annihilation of both the self and of humankind are having as yet untold effects.

Sourcebooks

Teachers, discussion leaders, counselors, and others wanting to explore the history and the impact of the nuclear arms race, the effects of nuclear war, and the means—if there are any—of securing the future for generations to come, may choose from hundreds of audiovisual programs. Basic sourcebooks to guide such choices are the following:

> *Nuclear War Film List* reviews and describes over 100 films, and is updated monthly. Available for $2.00 from John Dowling, Physics Department, Mansfield State College, Mansfield, PA 16933.

> *War. Peace. Film Guide* (188 pages, 1980) describes and evaluates over 285 films, program aids, and other materials. Available for $5.75 from World Without War Publications, 67 East Madison, Suite 1417, Chicago, IL 60603.

> *1984 National Directory of A-V Resources on Nuclear War and the Arms Race* (57 pages), edited by Karen Sayer and John Dowling, is available for $4.00 from University of Michigan Media Resources Center, 400 Fourth St., Ann Arbor, MI 48103.

> *Guide to Disarmament Media* (May, 1982) describes 26 films, videotapes, and slideshows especially appropriate for educational purposes, lists guidebooks and other sources of information, and offers advice on program planning. An *Update* (October, 1983) lists 50 additional titles. Available for $1.00 each from Media Network, 208 West 13th St., New York, NY 10011.

For brief reviews, descriptions, and availability information on what the writer calls "the eleven best" or classic films on these topics produced from 1965 to 1982, see the "How to Run a Film Series on the Nuclear Arms Race and Nuclear War," by John Dowling in *The Bulletin of the Atomic Scientists*, 1982, *38* (6), 51–52. *Landers Film Reviews*, a periodical, is the best ongoing source of information and ideas about new audiovisual releases.

The diversity of these materials and the broad range of issues explored in audiovisuals relating to nuclearism suggest the value of dividing our discussion in this section according to the following six topical headings: general introductions; detailed explorations; consciousness raisers; calls to action; feature films; and impact upon children and adolescents. In each case, entries include the best (award-winning) and most recent (since 1982) audiovisual programs especially appropriate for school and general audiences.

General Introductions

For a balanced introduction to both sides of the "nuclear freeze" issue and an analysis of its implications, teachers should consider *Issue: The Nuclear Freeze Controversy*. Produced by the *New York Times*, this filmstrip-audiocassette program covers the history of the debate, outlines the roles played by government agencies on the one hand, and freeze proponents (chiefly grassroots movements) on the other, and gives a chronology of key events shaping the debate over the years. The growing importance of the issue in public opinion and its possible impact on political development in the next few years in the United States and elsewhere are also explained. Social Studies School Service; color, 17 minutes, 1984.

Nuclear Strategy for Beginners, originally presented on the PBS's "NOVA" series, also surveys the historical background of present-day nuclear policies, and provides helpful definitions and explanations of key concepts ("strategic bombing," "counterforce and countervalue targets," "flexible response," "mutual assured destruction" [MAD], and so on). Informative film clips, illlustrations, and interviews with various authorities make this a very fine introductory survey. Time-Life Video; color videotape, 60 minutes, 1983.

Another filmstrip-audiocassette program attempting to survey both sides of the issue is *Arms Control: Contemporary Issues.* The divergent views of many authorities are presented: Roger Mollander of the antinuclear group Ground Zero; David Trachtenburg of the Committee on the Present Danger; and Ronald Lehman of the U.S. Department of Defense, among others. Topics discussed include the effects of nuclear war, nuclear arms proliferation, recent arms control efforts, and the implications of growing public concern about these issues. Produced by the *Encyclopedia Britannica.* Social Studies School Service; color, approximately 20 minutes, 1984.

The arms race and what to do about it is also the topic of *The Freeze,* a film that presents the differing views of many people—private citizens, political and military leaders, workers in nuclear weapons facilities, scientists. Intercut with these interviews are scenes of the Hiroshima-Nagasaki bombings, clips from several other award-winning nuclear issues films, diagrams of patterns of destruction were a nuclear bomb to be exploded over San Francisco, and arguments that there can be no such things as "civil defense" or "surviving" all-out nuclear war. The only thing to do, the film concludes, is to freeze nuclear weapons production. It is a well-made film, suitable for intermediate grades through adult audiences. Direct Cinema Limited; color film or videotape, 25 minutes, 1983.

A fifth program giving an overview of nuclear issues is *What About the Russians?* The approach here is to examine current U.S. military/nuclear policies in light of how we interpret Russian attitudes, motives, and plans. Are they really "ahead"? Can they be trusted? How are they responding to NATO deployment of Pershing II missles? And why? Authorities like Robert McNamara, Paul Warnke, Mark Hatfield, and George Kennan offer penetrating insights into the nature of American thinking—and "misthinking"—about our major world adversary, and suggest ways out of the present nuclear impasse. Educational Film and Video Project; color film or videotape, 26 minutes, 1983.

Detailed Explorations

Several film programs explore the historical and political backgrounds of contemporary nuclear realities in great detail. These films, therefore, are best shown to audiences prepared to benefit fully from them.

Prophecy describes the effects of the Hiroshima-Nagasaki atomic blasts from the *Japanese* perspective. Using clips of film taken by Japanese cameramen (released here for the first time in the United States), *Prophecy* records the immediate destruction in the two cities and documents the thousands upon thousands of deaths both from the blast itself and from subsequent radiation poisoning. Highlights from "nuclear history"— weapons tests around the world, for example, and "improvements" in the nuclear arsenals of the superpowers—are intercut with scenes showing the disabilities, the scars, and the continuing medical treatment of many Hiroshima-Nagasaki survivors. In summary, the Japanese say to us: "It's your future. It's your choice." Red Ribbon Award winner, 1983 American Film Festival. Films, Incorporated; color film or videotape, 45 minutes, 1983.

No Place to Hide draws some particularly disturbing insights from the early history of the atomic age in the United States. It reviews some of the propaganda films of the 1950s (for example, *Self-Preservation in an Atomic Attack, You Can Beat the A-Bomb,* and *Duck and Cover*) designed to reassure Americans that they could survive atomic attack by ducking under furniture and then soaping off the radiation. The community fallout shelter projects of the 1960s, proffered by the government with a bit more subtlety are then recalled, juxtaposed with telling commentary that reminds us we have no such "civil defense" plans in place today; those 1960s shelters and their carefully stockpiled food are rotting away. Questions are forcefully raised: Who has been lying to us? Why? Can anyone survive? What can one know about nuclear weapons and the realities of nuclear war? An award-winning film (American Film Festival, 1982), it is an excellent stimulus for class discussion. Direct Cinema Limited; color film or videotape, 29 minutes, 1982.

Also carefully focused in its approach to nuclear issues, *No First Use: Preventing Nuclear War* raises questions about the nuclear arms race and current policies by examining a particular aspect of the present-day standoff between the two superpowers: the "defense" of Western Europe. The United States, its NATO allies, and Russia are perhaps closest to a nuclear exchange in Europe. This film explains why, examining the postwar history of the area and the gradual build-up of armed forces on both sides in response to one another's growing arsenals. Because of Russian superiority in manpower and conventional weaponry, NATO depends heavily on its nuclear strength. Plans are in place for the use of "tactical" nuclear weapons to respond to a Russian invasion, and President Reagan and his NATO allies are unwilling to adopt a "no-first-use" policy. Thus the tension, thus the danger. The film presents interviews with military and national leaders responsible for current policies. An alternative proposal offered by the Union of Concerned Scientists (the producers of this film)—building up NATO's conventional forces so that both sides would be less likely to resort to the nuclear option—is then presented and analyzed. A balanced yet moving presentation of crucial issues, this film was a finalist at the 1983 American Film Festival. University of California Extension Media Center; color film or videotape, 30 minutes, 1983.

The purpose of the final film in this group, *How Much Is Enough: Decision Making in the Nuclear Age*, is to explain in some detail just how and why key nuclear arms decisions in the past 20 years were made. Some of these decisions, simply arbitrary or crassly political, are both surprising and disturbing. For example, John Kennedy campaigned for the presidency claiming that he would counter Russian superiority in nuclear missiles. Not only were the Russians *not* ahead in the numbers game, but Kennedy, once elected, approved deployment of 1000 missiles (Eisenhower had budgeted but 200) for no other reason than that "1000 is a good, round number in our culture," in the words of one advisor. The film also backgrounds our triadic nuclear structure—bombs on land and on sea and in the air—and its growth from turf struggles of the three military services. Also discussed are the development of MIRV's, the effects of the Salt I treaty, and the impact of French and British nuclear capability on Russian policies. The thinking of The Committee on the Present Danger, a strong advocate of continued nuclear arms build-up to counter what it sees as the Russian threat, is covered at some length (significantly so, for Ronald Reagan and many of his advisors and arms control negotiators are members of that committee). Interviews with policymakers past and present, and stimulating graphics to illustrate complex information make this film an excellent tool for understanding our present nuclear situation. It is a winner of several awards, including first prize at the United States Film and Video Festival. Documerica Films; color film or videotape, 59 minutes, 1982.

Consciousness Raisers

Attempting to raise audience consciousness of the real nature of nuclear weapons, three films emphasize the horrible, utter totality of destruction following upon a nuclear war. *If You Love This Planet: Dr. Helen*

Caldicott on Nuclear War is the famous Canadian film the U.S. government called "propaganda" and tried to censor upon its release in 1982; it subsequently won an Academy Award for its quality. Basically a filmed lecture by Dr. Caldicott, the film outlines the consequences of a single 20-megaton bomb explosion. Caldicott's analyses are supplemented with film clips and photographs of the damage done to the cities of Hiroshima and Nagasaki, and the sufferings of survivors. As is well known, Dr. Caldicott is an activist in the antinuclear movement; she urges her audience to direct action (protest marches, civil disobedience, and the like). Whether or not we agree with her methods, we must come to grips with the frightening data and insights Caldicott gives us. Direct Cinema Limited; color film or videotape, 26 minutes, 1982.

Nuclear War: A Guide to Armageddon takes a similar approach to documenting the effects of a nuclear blast, in this instance in a primarily British context. The narrator postulates the detonation of a one-megaton bomb over St. Paul's Cathedral in central London, and then describes the death and destruction to follow. Effective animation and film clips of the Hiroshima bombing illustrate the presentation. The narrator concludes by questioning the value of fallout shelters, arguing that "survivors" of atomic warfare would have no civilization to return to. Our only hope is to reduce the likelihood of nuclear conflict *now*. It was a finalist at the 1983 American Film Festival. Films, Incorporated; color film or videotape, 25 minutes, 1983.

In 1982, 150 residents of Stafford, Vermont, produced a "pageant" about nuclear destruction in their town. *Button, Button: A Dream of Nuclear War* is a 14-minute film outline of that event. Employing the costumes and conventions of mime, theater, and dance, and with background music ranging from Verdi's "Requiem" to folk, the people present scenes from daily life intercut with gathering armies and growing arsenals. Politicians exchange their blather, generals posture, and the red phones are brought out. Finally, buttons are pushed and nuclear holocaust occurs. People "dance" wildly in panic and pain as the film —now in slow motion and overexposed—records the barrenness of the aftermath. This highly recommended film can both stimulate discussion of nuclear issues and demonstrate, under a discussion leader's guidance, the great evocative power of the theater. Cantomedia; color film or videotape, 14 minutes, 1982.

Calls to Action

Several other films might be grouped under the heading of "calls to action." Reaffirming that the consequences of nuclear war are simply unacceptable, these films argue that steps must be taken to nullify the nuclear war-making capabilities of the nations.

A particularly effective film to stimulate classroom discussion, *One Million Hiroshimas* highlights the presentations made by a number of physicians, scientists, military people, and others at the Second Congress of International Physicians for the Prevention of Nuclear War in Cambridge, England, 1982. The overall thesis is that the nuclear arms race threatens humankind with extinction, but that much can still be done to lessen the risks. Among the participants are Carl Sagan, Helen Caldicott, Jonas Salk, Bernard Lown, and two retired military leaders —a Russian general and an American admiral—who agree in a conversation that nuclear arsenals on both sides must be reduced. This film was a finalist at the 1983 American Film Festival. Resource Center for Nonviolence; color film or videotape, 28 minutes, 1982.

Sponsored by another activist physicians group, Physicians for Social Responsibility, *Race to Oblivion* carefully combines an interview with a badly disfigured survivor of the Hiroshima bomb with footage of nuclear explosions, scenes of devastation, and statements of arms control activists calling for a freeze in weapons production. This meaningful combination of the "theoretical," the actual, and the personal, together with moving scenes of children singing "If there's ever to be peace on earth, it's up to you and me," results in a powerful film, especially recommended for general audiences. Physicians for Social Responsibility; color film or videotape, 49 minutes, 1982.

Two films focus on various antinuclear activists and activities, emphasizing that much is being done, much *can be done* to halt the spread of nuclear weapons. *Gods of Metal* comments at length on current budget priorities that allocate billions for weapons and precious little to alleviate hunger and disease. People are interviewed who have protested against militarism in various ways—refusing to pay the "defense" share of their taxes, and protesting at munitions plants, for example. The film ends with scenes of mass antinuclear protest marches and calls on its audience to act in similar fashion. It was nominated for an Academy Award (Best Short Documentary) in 1982. Icarus Films, Incorporated; color, 27 minutes, 1982.

The Time Has Come stresses the international character of growing activism against nuclear weapons, presenting footage of protest marches in Europe and in Japan, as well as in many cities in the United States. Individuals representing many religious, ethnic, and national groups are interviewed and filmed as they work together in various antinuclear activities. A well-made film, suitable for all school and general adult audiences (intermediate grades and up), it was a finalist at the American Film Festival, 1983. Available from NARMIC/American Friends Service Committee; color film or videotape, 27 minutes, 1983.

A man who has seen the globe in its entirety, Apollo 9 astronaut

Russell Schweikart, said that "there are no frames. There are no bound-aries." Beginning with Schweikart's insights, the film *No Frames, No Boundaries* reminds us that nuclear weapons and nuclear war *will* reach across national and indeed continental boundaries to wreak their havoc. Historically, the film explains, nations could go to war with some assurance that their walls would protect them, and that their efforts at destruction would have a self-contained result. The folly behind today's nuclear build-up is that people still believe they can go on warring as they always have and still live on as a state and a race. Better, the film argues, to work toward disarmament, toward the breaking down of frames and boundaries, building a new world upon the commonalities of human experience and ideals as revealed, for example, in all religious faiths. Some may see such ideas as simplistic, but this well-made film (a finalist at the 1983 American Film Festival) will, in any case, stimulate thought and discussion. Creative Initiative Foundation; color film or videotape, 21 minutes, 1982.

Feature Films

Many feature films over the years have turned nuclear themes into theatrical entertainment for the masses. While pressure to turn a profit at the box office often results in complex issues being oversimplified or trivialized, feature films, because of their entertainment value, can be powerful teaching tools. Their length, of course, may make scheduling difficult, and their artistic complexity will challenge the conscientious teacher. But for those willing and able to make the effort, here are a few fine films from which to choose, films praised for their artistic value and for their stimulating presentations of nuclear issues.

On the Beach, based on the novel by Nevil Shute, portrays a group of Australians awaiting the aftereffects of a nuclear war that has destroyed the rest of the world. Directed by Stanley Kramer, starring Gregory Peck, Ava Gardner, and Fred Astaire. Available for rental from United Artists 16 or for purchase on videotape from Direct Cinema Limited; color, 133 minutes, 1959.

Dr. Strangelove: Or How I Learned to Stop Worrying and Love the Bomb is a very funny and very frightening look at the dangers of nuclear war, focusing on the sort of very imperfect human beings likely to be in charge. Fine performances by Peter Sellers, George C. Scott, and Slim Pickens. Available for rental from Swank Motion Pictures or for purchase on videotape from Social Studies School Service; black and white, 93 minutes, 1964.

Fail Safe demonstrates the inevitable, and fatal, flaws in our vaunted technology. A computer error launches a nuclear attack on Moscow that cannot be called back. The harrowing conclusion depicts the fruitless efforts of world leaders to forestall retaliation and universal annihilation. Henry Fonda and Walter Matthau give brilliant performances. Available for rental from Budget Films or for purchase on videotape from Direct Cinema Limited; color, 111 minutes, 1964.

In *Seven Days in May*, a five-star general plans a military coup against a U. S. president who has signed a nuclear disarmament pact with Russia. The film makes one wonder about who, in our democracy, really runs things. Directed by John Frankenheimer, with fine performances by Burt Lancaster, Kirk Douglas, Fredric March, and Ava Gardner. Film version available (for rental or purchase) from Films, Incorporated; videotape may be purchased from Social Studies School Service; black and white, 118 minutes, 1964.

Three more recent feature-length films worth considering are *The Day After, Testament*, and *Wargames*. Broadcast on ABC-TV in 1983, *The Day After* depicts the horrible, destructive aftermath of nuclear bombs dropped on Kansas City and, by suggestion, elsewhere around the globe. Thus, the film questions the wisdom of nuclear "deterrence," mutual assured destruction (MAD), and other moral issues of the arms race. Social Studies School Service; color videotape (purchase only), 150 minutes, 1983.

Testament begins with a similar premise, that a major city (San Francisco) has been bombed, but concentrates on the human responses within a surviving but dying family. This focus on the personal—in a very understated manner at that—proves ultimately more moving and more convincing than many films that recreate fireballs, crushed buildings, and mass death. *Testament* can affect one at deeper levels than *The Day After*, and is in every other way a superior work of film art. Social Studies School Service; color videotape (purchase only), 90 minutes, 1983.

Wargames modernizes the premise of the 1964 film *Fail Safe*, reminding us of the continuing fallibility of our "superior" technology. In this story, a precocious young computer hacker unwittingly breaks into super-secret Defense Department files and, thinking he's playing a war game, sets in motion the irreversible countdown to World War III. Social Studies School Service; color videotape (purchase only), 114 minutes, 1983.

Impact Upon Children and Adolescents

The psychological and emotional effects of present-day nuclear realities upon people—and in particular upon children—are just now being explored. Several audiovisuals deal with these topics. Of special interest to classroom teachers is *Growing Up with the Bomb*, a 17-minute videotaped interview (a segment of ABC's news program "20/20") with two Harvard child psychiatrists, William Beardslee and John E. Mack. Focusing on children aged 10 to 18, these authorities argue that fear of nuclear holocaust is widespread and significant. Children typically have fewer defenses against such fears than do adults, so parents, teachers, and counselors must try to channel and alleviate those fears. Beardslee and Mack explain what can be done. Social Studies School Service; color videotape, 17 minutes, 1982.

Professor Mack is also featured on a more recent program, *In the Nuclear Shadow: What Can the Children Tell Us?* He and psychiatrist-author Robert Jay Lifton open the film with background commentary. Mack introduces a questionnaire on nuclear issues he devised for children, and then children themselves—ranging in age from 7 to 17—tell their feelings. Their comments are both very moving and thoughtful. As they describe their fears and their nightmares, their frustrations and anger at what adults have done, they argue the necessity of immediate action. The world is worth saving, and the children believe there is hope. Film consultant Karen Sayer says that, "if you could show only one film about the impact on children of the threat of nuclear war, *In the Nuclear Shadow* should be it." Educational Film and Video Project; color film or videotape, 26 minutes, 1983.

Similar insights into the fears—and the great wisdom—of children as they attempt to deal with nuclear realities is offered in another recent film, *Bombs Will Make the Rainbow Break*. Children are interviewed as they play. They tell about their drawings of explosions and fireballs and horrible dying. The film concludes with footage of a recent children's march on the White House protesting the arms race; letters from children all over the country were read aloud during the Washington rally. The point is that much *can* be done. A very polished, carefully produced film, it is the winner of the 1983 CINE Golden Eagle Award. Films, Incorporated; color film or videotape, 17 minutes, 1983.

A group called The International Physicians for the Prevention of Nuclear War has been conducting classroom discussions at various grade levels, exploring the thoughts and opinions children have about nuclear weapons and nuclear war. Conducted by "nondirective" leaders, these discussions have been videotaped and edited into several separate programs. A 21-minute overview of the whole project, *There's A Nuclear War Going On Inside Me*, includes an introduction and rationale presented by discussion leaders Dr. Eric Chivian, and Roberta Snow; it then offers selections from student comments recorded in first-, third-, fifth-, seventh-, and ninth-grade classrooms. Separate *edited* tapes made at grade levels three (35 minutes), five (13 minutes), and nine (24 minutes) —*(Third, Fifth, Ninth) Graders Discuss Nuclear Issues*—are available, as are *unedited* tapes (60 minutes long) of discussions in grades one, three, five, and nine. Intersection Associates; color videotapes, 1983.

CARING FOR DYING ADOLESCENTS: AUDIOVISUALS FOR MEDICAL STAFF, COUNSELORS, PARENTS, AND WELL-PREPARED YOUNGSTERS

An Adolescent Copes with Death: Debbie. In an interview, Debbie explains the course of her disease (Ewing's sarcoma), her reactions to treatment, and her attitude to her prognosis. This videotape is recommended for health professionals by the Association of American Medical Colleges. St. Louis University Medical Center; color videotape, 27 minutes, 1979.

Can't It Be Anyone Else? Three youngsters (ages 10 and 12) dangerously ill with leukemia share their experiences, feelings, and fears with one another, with their family members, and with the filmmaker. Typically, children have much wisdom, courage, and hope to offer the rest of us; this film provides insight and inspiration to parents of seriously ill children and to professional caregivers. It is an excellent film for parent and caregiver training sessions. Pyramid Films; color film or videotape, 54 minutes, 1980.

In *Care of Dying Children*, Dr. Bill Bartholomew, Professor of Pediatrics at the University of Texas, lectures on the dying child's sense of self, and awareness and definition of time; then he explains how the child passes through the "stages" of dying. Suggestions are offered to improve institutional and home caregiving. National Public Radio; audiocassette, 60 minutes, 1978.

Death Be Not Proud is a feature-film version of John Gunther's classic 1949 memoir of the same name, recounting the dying and death of the author's son, victim of a brain tumor. The emphasis is on the parents' responses. Learning Corporation of America; color film, 99 minutes, 1976.

A Different Kind of Life presents interviews with three cancer patients, one of whom is a young adolescent named Missy. The program examines how they react to changes in their daily lives, especially to the changed attitudes, of relatives, friends, and coworkers toward them, now that their disease is being managed. Within themselves, these cancer patients experience heightened levels of guilt (cancer must be "punishment"), physical vulnerability (cancer is some alien force that "eats your bones"), and fear of death (maintaining "hope" on the brink of mortality is burdensome). Trying to lead "normal" lives in their communities, each must suffer the silence, fear, and evasions of others. Such responses are particularly painful to Missy. Returning to high school with an amputation and hair loss from chemotherapy, she "feels like a freak." This well-made program is a good introduction to some of the spiritual and psychosocial difficulties experienced by the cancer patient; parents, teachers, and caregivers will find it informative. PBS Video; color videotape, 29 minutes, 1980.

Fighting Back. This moving and uncompromising documentary film records the cases of four children, ages 9 to 16, stricken with leukemia, at the War Memorial Children's Hospital in London, Ontario. Their treatments, their reactions, their remissions, their relapses, as well as the reactions of their parents, are presented realistically. It is a superlative, award-winning program for caregiver education and, indeed, for properly prepared student and patient audiences. Documentary Films; color film, 90 minutes, 1981.

Two films demonstrate the power of religious faith to sustain cancer victims and their families. *Jill* documents the last months of a young adult who comes to terms with her condition through strong faith in God. This film thus emphasizes the positive side of coping, and is especially useful for audiences with a Christian commitment. Quadrus Media Ministry; call toll-free: 800/435–4489; color film, 26 minutes, 1978.

Jocelyn tells a similar story. The protagonist is 17 and dying of cancer. What sustains her is her tremendous—and authentic—spiritual strength. Yes, she is blessed with good family and good friends, but her faith and her poise come from inside her. Perhaps the best use for this film is to share it with seriously ill patients who need encouragement and motivation. Jocelyn has so much to share. Filmakers Library; color film or videotape, 28 minutes, 1980.

Old Friends, New Friends—Gerald Jampolsky, M.D. This film brings together some very special people in a very special way, spotlighting the special approaches to dying children taken by Dr. Jampolsky. Also featured is a visit to Jampolsky's Center for Attitudinal Healing by Mr. (Fred) Rogers. Family Communications; color film or videotape, 29 minutes, 1980.

Time to Come Home. The risks and the rewards of caring for a dying child *at home* instead of in the hospital are discussed, chiefly through interviews with parents. Parents are conceived of as the primary caregivers, but nurses and the physician are essential members of the team in these situations. The "team" approach can work well. University of Minnesota; color film, 24 minutes, 1979.

We Can Help. Ongoing care and rehabilitation of pediatric cancer patients are the topics of this film. Several patients and their families describe their participation in a comprehensive treatment program combining physical therapy, vocational rehabilitation, counseling, and medical care. Polymorph Films; color film, 20 minutes, 1981.

Winning Battles: A Film About Children with Cancer highlights a pediatric cancer program at Stanford University Children's Hospital in which all caregiving staff are specially trained to provide a warm, supportive atmosphere for the children and their families. Filmakers Library; color film or videotape, 8 minutes, 1979.

You See—I've Had a Life is an older film but, in our opinion, a classic. At 13, Paul Hendricks is diagnosed as having leukemia. The whole family shares the experience with him, working to enhance the quality of his life in the time remaining. The film records Paul's continuing school and athletic activities, treatments by medical staff, and the personal reactions of the parents and of Paul himself. The words of the title accurately suggest the essence of Paul's character and the quality of his response to death; *he* says them to reassure a friend who came to offer sympathy. Viewfinders, Inc.; black-and-white film, 32 minutes, 1973.

UNDERSTANDING AND COUNSELING GRIEVING ADOLESCENTS

Two videotape programs explore the difficulties adolescents and other family members experience when a parent becomes ill with cancer. *Cancer: A Family Journal* documents a 6-month period in the life of the Silva family: the father, age 43, is suffering the final stages of his disease; his wife and his children, ages 9 to 15, are caring for him at home. The family is close and loving. They value communication and sharing. But the difficulties each family member experiences in this situation are painful nonetheless. The parents are concerned about how much, and when, to tell the children. The children all help with the chores and the caregiving, but struggle to maintain, as they must, their own "space." Inevitable disruptions of family routines give rise to resentments and anger as the father's condition worsens and his need for care intensifies. Finally, the camera returns to the household 6 weeks after the father's death to record the reactions of the survivors. *Cancer: A Family Journal* depicts in exceptional detail the intrafamilial dynamics of chronic illness and grief. It also portrays the effective roles of the competent professionals who worked with the Silva family in those last days. It is a well-produced, informative program. Sidney Farber Cancer Institute; color film or videotape, 57 minutes, 1982, with study guide.

Teenagers are the special concern of *Helping Children Understand Cancer in the Family*. Designed for both professional and patient education, this program introduces the viewer to the special needs and problems of the cancer family. Topics covered include:

1. cancer's effects on the body;
2. the importance of talking about the disease;
3. the roles of medical staff;
4. changes in family activities; and
5. coming to terms with death.

Hospice House; slides and audiocassettes, or videotape, 21 minutes, 1983.

Hey Mark! The Fox Is Dead! This videotape program presents and analyzes a dialogue involving three teenagers responding to the sudden accidental death of a friend. This audiocassette is "designed to enrich the practitioner's repertoire of skills in making clinical interventions with bereaved adolescents." Concepts covered include unconscious feelings, trade-off, normal grief work, active and recollective mourning, and poor grief reactions. Steve P. Lindenberg narrates. Professional Associates; audiocassette, 17 minutes, 1982.

THE DEATH OF ONE'S CHILD: PROGRAMS FOR GRIEVING PARENTS AND THEIR COUNSELORS

Fathers and sons—the generations and death—is the topic of *Good-bye*. As a father experiences the dying of his 12-year-old son of cancer, he is moved to remember and rethink his relationship with *his* father. Grieving for others is, among other things, part of one's *own* "death work." Paulist Productions; color film or videotape, 27 minutes, 1980.

In *Parents' Responses to Their Children's Illness*, parents of severely ill children as well as parents of children who have died are interviewed in various contexts—alone, with other family members, and with outsiders—so that a wide range of intellectual and emotional responses is revealed. The program is described by the Association of American Medical Colleges as the best available introductory audiovisual on this topic. University of Michigan, Medical Center; color videotape, 27 minutes, 1977.

To Die with Dignity: To Live with Grief. The topic is *coping* with dying and death. In conversation, a minister-counselor, a doctor, a terminally ill cancer patient, and a couple whose son has recently died exchange their views and experiences. University of Michigan; color videotape, 29 minutes, 1978.

Valley of the Shadow . . . A Journey Through Grief is a deeply sensitive study of the grief of a father who has lost two children, ages 5 and 8, in an auto-train accident. The father's grief initially was mismanaged, resulting in adverse physical effects and illnesses. The film explores the biochemistry of grief, and explains how this situation was resolved. National Funeral Directors Association; color film or videotape, 38 minutes, 1980.

When a Child Dies. Three bereaved couples, each of whom lost their child in different circumstances, offer their insights into grief. The particularly destructive nature of parental grief is explained, as well as the attendant rage and frequent loss of religious faith. Reasons for the high rate of divorce following the death of a child are highlighted. Recalling their experiences, these parents provide much useful information for caregivers. This prize-winning film (Mental Health Film Festival; American Film Festival) was funded by, and is available from, the National Funeral Directors Association; color film, 24 minutes, 1979.

The Compassionate Friends, a self-help organization for bereaved parents with over 400 chapters nationwide, is an important source of both printed information (books, booklets, and pamphlets) and audiocassette programs on all parental and sibling bereavement topics (see p. 283). Fourteen presentations by professionals and bereaved parents (each 15–18 minutes long) are offered back to back on seven audiocassettes as follows:

Siblings and How They Grieve by Karol Wood Wendt, M.S.W.
Questions Most Frequently Asked About Sibling Grief by Karol Wood Wendt

Impact of Grief on Marriage by Nancy Hogan, R.N.
The Bereaved Single Parent by Erma Beck, Ph.D.

Fathers and Grief by Bill Goveia, Dr. Edgar Jackson, and Jim Kunsman
A Bereaved Father Shares by Bill Schatz, Bereaved Father

Thanksgiving and Christmas Holidays, by Shirley Melin, Chapter Leader
Handling Birthdays and Other Special Days by Shirley Melin

Anger and the Grieving Process by Leroy Joesten
Guilt in Bereaved Parents by Margaret S. Miles, Ph.D.

The Sexual Adjustment of a Bereaved Couple (Part I)
The Sexual Adjustment of a Bereaved Couple (Part II), both by Clarice Schultz, R.N., B.S.N.

Reinvestment—Reorganization—Recovery by Dorothy Greiner, Bereaved Parent
Writing as Therapy by Marie Butler, Photojournalist and Bereaved Parent

Also available are cassette recordings of 11 Compassionate Friends Conference Workshops, featuring the presentations of nationally recognized authorities on these topics (each is 90 minutes long): *Mourning* by Glen Davidson, Ph.D. (1980); *Emotional Healing* by Father Ken Czillinger (1979); *When Is Professional Help Needed* by Glen Davidson, Ph.D. (1983); *Sudden/Accidental Death* by Colleen Murray, M.A. (1983); *Understanding Sibling Grief* by Dr. Kenneth Klein (1983); *Where Is God in All of This?* by Rev. Joseph Bayly (1983); *Dreams and Unusual Happenings* by Paula M. Reeves, M.A. (1983); *Surviving a Suicide* by Iris Bolton, M.A. (1980); *Anger, God and You* by Father Ken Czillinger (1980); *Siblings 1–12 Years* by Jody Gyulay (1979); *Writing When It Hurts* by Marie Butler (1980). Available from The Compassionate Friends; audiocassettes, $5.00 each (purchase only).

SUICIDE AND ADOLESCENTS

Audiovisuals for
High School Students, Teachers,
and Counselors

For a straightforward, informative overview of the topic of teenage suicide we recommend *Adolescent Suicide: A Matter of Life and Death*. Dr. Seymour Perlin is featured in this survey of suicide causes and preventative measures. Several vignettes demonstrate pressures operating on suicidal adolescents: quarreling parents, death of a loved one, trouble in school, loss of a love, pregnancy, and so on. Myths are dispelled and intervention techniques are demonstrated. A teacher's manual is included. American Association for Counseling and Development; color film (order #75122 C), 39 minutes, 1979.

Several other audiovisuals introduce these issues very effectively. *Did Jenny Have to Die? Preventing Teen Suicide* is a prizewinning (American Personnel and Guidance Association), well-reviewed (*Media and Methods, Booklist, School Library Journal*) filmstrip-cassette program specially designed for high school audiences. It presents basic information in a very attractive format. Part I introduces Jenny as a popular, attractive, talented student—and a suicide. Close friends and family members then tell of the problems in the life of this "normal" girl: her parents' divorce, her breakup with her boyfriend, her rejection by the college of her choice. Part II shows Jenny's teachers and friends, with the benefit of hindsight, discovering warning signals of Jenny's state of mind. Part III generalizes from the insights and information presented in Jenny's case. Why is suicide such a problem in the teenage population? What can parents, teachers, and friends do to anticipate and prevent it? Sunburst Communications; approximately 15 minutes each, 1980.

Another filmstrip-audiocassette program, *Suicide: Who Will Cry for Me?* presents similar information: a survey of myths surrounding the problem of teenage suicide, risk factors among the teenage population, and warning signs for which friends, teachers, and counselors need to be alert. Audio Visual Narrative Arts; three filmstrips and audiocassettes, approximately nine minutes each, 1979.

Several fine *films* present basic information on suicide for a high school audience, each from slightly different perspectives. In *Childhood's End: Adolescent Suicide*, two girls, now healthy and happy after counseling and treatment, recall their suicide attempts and their states of mind at the time. In contrast, the parents and friends of a "successful" suicide victim describe their failed attempts to "get through," and their difficulties in living with their grief. Filmakers Library; color film, 28 minutes, 1981.

A Family of Winners focuses on a typical American family and some of the problems created by our "success" orientation. A teenage boy, feeling he cannot live up to his father's expectations for him—attending a name college and being an athletic champion—commits suicide. His survivors, and we, are left to wonder why. Paulist Productions; color film or videotape, 28 minutes, 1981.

In recent years, the city of Loveland, Colorado, has lost an unusually large number of its teenagers to suicide. In an effort to stem the tide, several Loveland pastors, teachers, police officers, parents, and teenagers became involved in the film, *In Loveland: Study of a Teenage Suicide*. In interviews, these people share their experience and insights into the causes of suicide, and stress the importance of open communication systems—in the home, church, and school—to identify troubled teens. The suicide death of one 15-year-old, Mark Cada, is analyzed in detail. It is a well-produced film, especially recommended for teachers, counselors, and parents. ABC Wide World of Learning; color film or videotape, 28 minutes, 1982.

Inside I Ache is a brief but well-made story that would be an effective stimulus to class discussion. As a newspaper reporter covers a drug overdose case, he mentally prepares his reply to a troubled teenage girl who, considering suicide, had written to him for help. A film-discussion guide for teachers is included. Mass Media Ministries; color film, 17 minutes, 1981.

Help Me: The Story of a Teenage Suicide presents Sandy as a troubled school student similar to Jenny (see pp. 271–272). After her suicide, a psychiatrist consults with grieving family members and friends, and explains what must have happened. Lessons in recognizing suicidal tendencies and in offering help are presented in conclusion. S-L Film Productions; color film or videotape, 25 minutes, 1978.

A Last Cry for Help in contrast, is open-ended in its approach. Here the protagonist, again an apparently normal high school girl, is unsuccessful in her suicide attempt. Furthermore, the psychologist counseling the shocked family members is only partly successful in correcting family interrelationships. The filmmaker's purpose is thus to encourage discussion rather than to present prepackaged lessons. The fine acting in the dramatization together with a solid body of factual content make this a superlative film. Learning Corporation of America; color film, 32 minutes, 1980. A four-part color filmstrip-audiocassette version of this film, with script and teacher's guide, is available from Educational Dimensions Group.

Ronnie's Tune is a dramatization of complex family reactions following the death of a teenage son. Ronnie's mother finally reveals to a visiting niece, Julie, that Ronnie committed suicide and that Ronnie's father has walked out on her as a result. Only with great effort is the mother now willing to talk about these events and to share her grief. After tears, grieving, and much thought of her own, Julie decides to learn to play Ronnie's banjo. Wombat Productions; color film, 18 minutes, 1978.

Suicide—Teenage Crisis reports how one California community is working together to stem the tide of suicide by offering counseling to teenagers, parents, and teachers. McGraw-Hill Training Systems; color film, 10 minutes, 1981.

Originally produced by CBS as a segment of "60 Minutes," *A Teenage Suicide* is an information-packed film especially useful for parents and counselors. Reemphasizing the extent of the problem of teenage suicides in the United States, this program examines major causes of suicidal tendencies (loneliness, depression, lack of communication, failed or unrealistic expectations, etc.) by focusing on several case studies. MTI Teleprograms; color film, 16 minutes, 1979.

Similarly, *Teenage Suicide—Is Anyone Listening?* examines in depth the problem of depression in adolescence, focusing on two teenagers who have repeatedly attempted suicide. Barr Films; color film, 22 minutes, 1980.

Audiovisuals for the College Level

Two films deal with suicide as a problem for college-age young people. *College Can Be Killing* describes the operation of the suicide prevention programs at Northwestern University and the University of Wisconsin. Students, deans, and counselors explain the relationships between the pressures of college life and suicidal tendencies. Methods of counseling college students who are at risk are explored in great detail. This program is highly recommended for teacher and counselor training. Indiana University; color film, two parts, 30 minutes each, 1978.

The second film, *I Want to Die,* may be useful for showing to general audiences to stimulate discussion, as well as for counselor training programs. A family situation is dramatized: Bill, a college student, shatters the calm of the Thanksgiving dinner table to announce that he's not going back to school, that he feels "empty and alone," and that he's thinking of killing himself. The film then traces family interrelationships up to this point, and we discover that in this family, there is a long history of failures to communicate. As a conclusion, actor Kirk Douglas suggests means of identifying and helping suicidal young people. University of Illinois Film Center; film, 25 minutes, 1977.

DRUG ABUSE AND DEATH: THREE FILMS FOR HIGH SCHOOL STUDENTS, PARENTS, TEACHERS, AND COUNSELORS

A Day in the Death of Donnie B. Donnie B. is an inner-city drug addict, his death a foregone conclusion. Voice-over commentary on the drug problem by mothers, doctors, police officers, ex-addicts, and clergymen adds chilling irony to the reality of Donnie's dying when, inevitably, it comes. National Institute of Mental Health; black-and-white film, 18 minutes, 1970.

Death, Drugs, and Walter. The short and unhappy career of Walter, a 12-year-old heroin addict, is followed to its end, in the toilet of a Harlem tenement where, wearing a Snoopy T-shirt, he finally overdosed. Interviews with Walter's grieving aunt and his friends raise many points for discussion about the dangers of drugs, the unmet needs of children, and the kind of society in which this sort of thing can happen. Viewfinders, Inc.; color film, 13 minutes, 1969.

Richie is about teenage drug addiction and its impact on a family. Richie's parents cannot understand his increasing dependency on drugs and his resulting behavior changes. Disintegrating communication and hostile confrontations climax in the father's shooting of Richie. This film is based on the book by Thomas Thompson. Learning Corporation of America; color film, 31 minutes, 1978.

DISTRIBUTORS

ABC Wide World of Learning
1330 Avenue of the Americas
New York, NY 10019

American Association for Counseling
and Development
5999 Development Ave.
Alexandria, VA 22304

Audio Visual Narrative Arts
P. O. Box 9
Pleasantville, NY 10570

Barr Films
3490 E. Foothill Blvd.
Pasadena, CA 91107

Budget Films
4590 Santa Monica Blvd.
Los Angeles, CA 90029

Cantomedia
P. O. Box 315
Franklin Lakes, NJ 07417

The Compassionate Friends
P. O. Box 1347
Oak Brook, IL 60521

Creative Initiative Foundation
222 High St.
Palo Alto, CA 94301

Direct Cinema Limited
P. O. Box 69589
Los Angeles, CA 90069

Documentary Films
159 W. 53rd St.
New York, NY 10019

Documerica Films
P. O. Box 985
Vallejo, CA 94590

Educational Dimensions Group
P. O. Box 126
Stamford, CT 06904

Educational Film and Video Project
1725 B Seabright Ave.
Santa Cruz, CA 95062

Educational Perspectives Associates
P. O. Box 213
DeKalb, IL 60115

Educational Record Sales
157 Chambers St.
New York, NY 10007

Eye Gate Media
14601 Archer Ave.
Jamaica, NY 11435

Family Communications
4802 Fifth Ave.
Pittsburgh, PA 15213

Filmakers Library
133 East 58th St.
Suite 703A
New York, NY 10022

Films Incorporated
1144 Wilmette Ave.
Wilmette, IL 60091

Hospice House
6171 S.W. Capitol Hwy.
Portland, OR 97201

Icarus Films, Inc.
200 Park Avenue South
Room 1319
New York, NY 10003

Indiana University
Audiovisual Center
Bloomington, IN 47401

Intersection Associates
56 Chestnut St.
Cambridge, MA 02139

Learning Corporation of America
1350 Avenue of the Americas
New York, NY 10019

Mass Media Ministries
2116 N. Charles St.
Baltimore, MD 21218

McGraw-Hill Training Systems
P. O. Box 641
Del Mar, CA 92014

MTI Teleprograms
4825 N. Scott St.
Schiller Park, IL 60176

NARMIC/American Friends Service
Committee
1501 Cherry St.
Philadelphia, PA 19012

National Funeral Directors Association
135 West Wells St.
Milwaukee, WI 53203

National Institute of Mental Health
Drug Abuse Film Collection
National Audiovisual Center
General Services Administration
Washington, DC 20409

National Public Radio
Customer Service Department
P. O. Box 237
Niles, MI 49120

Paulist Productions
P. O. Box 1057
Pacific Palisades, CA 90272

PBS Video
475 L'Enfant Plaza, S. W.
Washington, DC 20024

Phoenix Films
470 Park Avenue South
New York, NY 10016

Physicians for Social Responsibility
P. O. Box 35385
Los Angeles, CA 90035

Polymorph Films
118 South St.
Boston, MA 02111

Professional Associates
P. O. Box 6254
Harrisburg, PA 17112

Pyramid Films
P. O. Box 1048
Santa Monica, CA 90406

Quadrus Media Ministry
610 E. State St.
Rockford, IL 61104

Resource Center for Nonviolence
P. O. Box 2324
Santa Cruz, CA 95060

S-L Film Productions
P. O. Box 41108
Los Angeles, CA 90041

Sidney Farber Cancer Institute
35 Binney St.
Boston, MA 02115

Social Studies School Service
10,000 Culver Blvd.
Dept. A4
P. O. Box 802
Culver City, CA 90232

Society for Visual Education
Division of Singer Company
1345 Diversey Parkway
Chicago, IL 60614

St. Louis University Medical Center
Audiovisual Department
1402 South Grand Blvd.
St. Louis, MO 63104

Sunburst Communications
39 Washington Ave.
Pleasantville, NY 10570

Swank Motion Pictures
201 S. Jefferson Ave.
St. Louis, MO 63166

Time-Life Video
100 Eisenhower Dr.
Paramus, NJ 07652

United Artists 16
729 Seventh Ave.
New York, NY 10019

University of California
Extension Media Center
Film Distribution
2223 Fulton St.
Berkeley, CA 94720

University of Illinois Film Center
1325 S. Oak St.
Champaign, IL 61820

University of Michigan
Media Resources Center
400 Fourth St.
Ann Arbor, MI 48109

University of Michigan Medical Center
Media Library
Towsley Center for Continuing Medical
   Education
P. O. Box 57
Ann Arbor, MI 48109

University of Minnesota
Department of Physical Medicine and
   Rehabilitation
University Hospital
860 Mayo, Box 2197
420 Delaware St., S. E.
Minneapolis, MN 55455

University of Southern California
Film Distribution Center
Division of Cinema/Television
University Park
Los Angeles, CA 90007

Viewfinders, Inc.
P. O. Box 1665
Evanston, IL 60204

Wombat Productions
Little Lake, Glendale Road
P. O. Box 70
Ossining, NY 10562

17

Organizational Resources

Richard A. Pacholski

CARING FOR CHRONICALLY ILL ADOLESCENTS

The **Association for the Care of Children's Health** (3615 Wisconsin Ave., N.W., Washington, DC 20016; tel. 202/244–1801) was founded in 1965 "to foster and promote the health and well-being of children and families in health care settings by education, interdisciplinary interaction and planning, and research." Members are chiefly medical and administrative professionals, but interested parents are joining in increasing numbers. The Association's publications (a quarterly journal, a newsletter, various bibliographies, and other books) as well as its yearly conventions and study sections address themselves to a whole range of child-care issues including, for example, the seriously ill child, the dying child, the child with cancer, and children in hospice settings.

Focusing all of its efforts on improving the care of seriously ill and dying children, **Children's Hospice International** (501 Slater's Lane #207, Alexandria, VA 22314; tel. 703/556–0421) was founded recently to meet a real need: of the 1300 hospices now operating in the United States, no more than a couple of dozen accept children. CHI works to encourage the inclusion of children in existing and developing hospices and home care programs. In addition, it both promotes and facilitates hospice approaches to caregiving—when needed—in *all* pediatric care facilities as well as in the public arena. CHI helps interdisciplinary hospice teams by serving as a clearing house for information about caregiving for both patient and family members, by conducting training programs for pediatric hospice professionals and volunteers, and by sponsoring and facilitating research. Available for purchase are manuals on home care of dying children and audiocassettes of presentations at a recent symposium on pediatric hospice care. Membership includes a quarterly newsletter.

The activities of the **American Cancer Society** are typical of those of many national, regional, and local organizations concerned with people suffering from particular diseases. The Society (national headquarters: 777 Third Avenue, New York, NY 10017; tel. 212/599–8200) publishes and distributes a variety of printed and audiovisual educational materials for the general public as well as for health professionals and educators. Staff members, associated professionals, and volunteers provide many types of medical, counseling, and educational services to and for cancer patients and their families. The Society has divisional offices in every state and regional offices in many cities.

Similarly, through its state affiliates, the **Leukemia Society of America** (800 Second Avenue, New York, NY 10017; tel. 212/573–8484) provides help for needy leukemia patients, sponsors research, raises funds, and educates the public about the disease through a variety of publications and audiovisual materials. It is also involved in professional education, sponsoring symposia and providing scholarships and awards for medical professionals.

The Boston chapter sponsors a supportive program called OUTREACH for patients and family members that is typical of approaches used by other local affiliates:

O = Open Doors of friendship
U = Unite patients and families
T = Trust one another
R = Reach out to understand others and oneself
E = Educate oneself to new ways of life
A = Approach life with new Awareness through sharing
C = Comfort one another at Crucial, Critical times in life
H = Hearing others talk about good days and bad days is how OUT-REACH helps families to cope

Organizations providing similar services for people with other diseases, their families, counselors, and caregivers are as follows:

American Heart Association
7320 Greenville Ave.
Dallas, TX 75231
tel. 214/750–5300

Cystic Fibrosis Foundation
6000 Executive Blvd.
Suite 309
Rockville, MD 20852
tel. 301/881–9130

Parents Campaign for Handicapped Children and Youth
Closer Look
Box 1492
Washington, DC 20013
tel. 202/822–7900

American Lung Association
1740 Broadway
New York, NY 10019
tel. 212/245–8000

National Multiple Sclerosis Society
205 E. 42nd St.
New York, NY 10017
tel. 212/986–3240

Muscular Dystrophy Association of America
810 Seventh Avenue
New York, NY 10019
tel. 212/586–0808

In caring for terminally ill children and adults and their parents, **The Center for Attitudinal Healing** (19 Main St., Tiburon, CA 94920; tel. 415/435–5022) supplements traditional medical care with an environment based upon these principles: "health is inner peace; healing is the process of letting go of fear." Thus, the emphasis in caregiving is upon the easing of stress and tension through supportive programs and activities involving sharing and loving. For example, participatory art and music activities are offered for adolescent patients. Their siblings participate in rap sessions designed to let them air *their* difficulties and fears within their families. Telephone and pen-pal programs let patients, siblings, and parents communicate with others in similar situations. The parents are brought together with one another in many contexts (workshops, discussion groups, social activities, on the telephone) for mutual help and sharing. The Tiburon Center is involved in local and national educational programs, and will assist in forming centers elsewhere in the country. Dr. Gerald Jampolsky explains his "principles of attitudinal healing" in his recent book, *Teach Only Love* (New York: Bantam, 1983).

Parents of children hospitalized with serious illnesses undergo grievous sufferings of their own. Their pain and fear are aggravated if their child is being treated in a hospital in a distant city for long periods of time. In such circumstances, being with one's child may mean long nights sleeping in cots or chairs, or in expensive and impersonal motels. It may mean missed meals or lonely meals on the run. It may mean the disruption of normal home life for one's other children, as well as growing tensions about one's job or other responsibilities. Often such a parent does not have the companionship of spouse, other family members, or friends.

Ronald McDonald Houses®, springing up in increasing numbers in the United States, Canada, and other countries, alleviate these problems for parents by providing an inexpensive place—a home away from home—to stay near the hospital while the child is being treated. A homelike atmosphere is fostered, with parent-guests sharing upkeep responsibilities and, more importantly, serving as family for one another —sharing advice and information, offering hope and a friendly shoulder. Each house has a trained resident manager and a staff of volunteers working in close cooperation with the medical and counseling staffs of the nearby hospital.

Each Ronald McDonald House operates independently, and is developed to meet local community needs. Some 83 Houses have now been established, with over 20 more set to open in 1985. Nearly 100,000 family members are "guests" in Ronald McDonald Houses each year. McDonald's Corporation assists in increasing public awareness and in providing start-up funding for new Houses. Individual restaurant franchises run promotions for their local Houses; Philadelphia-area franchises, working with the Philadelphia Eagles football team, helped establish the first Ronald McDonald House there in 1974.

For further information, contact Mr. Bud Jones, International Ronald McDonald House Coordinator, Children's Oncology Services, Inc., International Advisory Board, 500 N. Michigan Ave., Chicago, IL 60611; tel. 312/836–7129.

SUMMER CAMPS FOR CHRONICALLY ILL AND BEREAVED ADOLESCENTS

Many summer camps nationwide serve children and adolescents with special physical and psychological handicaps, diseases, and conditions: cerebral palsy; diabetes; epilepsy; muscular dystrophy; cystic fibrosis; visual, speech, and hearing impairments; respiratory problems; physical handicaps; brain damage; mental retardation; and emotional disturbances. **The National Easter Seal Society for Crippled Children and Adults** (2023 W. Ogden Ave., Chicago, IL 60612; tel. 312/243–8400) publishes descriptive directories of such camps.

For adolescents aged 12 to 17 the United Ostomy Association (2001 W. Beverly Blvd., Los Angeles, CA 90057; tel. 213/413–5510) sponsors a five-day **U.O.A. Youth Rally.** Meeting in a different location each summer, young people who have had enterostomal surgery gather, under the guidance of professional medical staff and counselors, for typical "vacation" activities, socializing, and sharing with one another, as well as medical education and professional counseling about their conditions. Rallies in recent years have taken place in Washington, DC; Boulder, Colorado; and San Diego, California. Admission is open to all interested young people at minimal cost. Scholarships are available. Contact the national office of U.O.A. for further information.

Camp Sunburst (Columbia Pacific University Foundation, 150 Shoreline Highway, Mill Valley, CA 94941; tel. 415/924–6084 or 415/332–7832; or contact Geri Brooks, Director, 672 Orange Avenue, Novato, CA 94947; tel. 415/892–1794) may be unique in that it serves terminally ill children as well as those with chronic but not necessarily life-threatening illnesses. Offerings include typical summer camp activities as well as a variety of supportive services and programs for parents and siblings. 24-hour medical care is available; staff members are specially trained and experienced.

In recent years, over 60 summer camps in the United States, Canada, and Europe have been established for young people suffering from and being treated for cancer. Staffed by medical and counseling professionals, these camps provide for the treatment needs of the children; the emphasis, however, is on the usual summer camp activities like boating, fishing, swimming, arts and crafts, and socializing, giving children with cancer the opportunity to share, to help one another, and to be accepted by peers. **Children's Oncology Camps of America** (Edward S. Baum, M.D., President; c/o The Children's Memorial Hospital, 2300 Children's Plaza, Chicago, IL 60614; tel. 312/880–4564) serves as the umbrella organization for these camps. It publishes a newsletter and a directory, and assists in the establishment of new camps. Dr. Baum stresses the increasing need for such activities and programs for children with cancer since, in ever larger numbers today, children are being cured of their diseases. (A number of camps also offer special programs for *siblings* of cancer children.)

Finally, one camp providing a unique service for children and adolescents deserves special mention. **Camp Amanda** (JoAnn Zimmerman, Director, 4116 65th Street, Des Moines, IA 50322; tel. 515/276–2634 or 515/244–3761) offers four weekend camping experiences yearly for children who have had a death in their family, whether of sibling, parent, grandparent, or other close relative. The purpose of Camp Amanda is twofold: to provide campers an opportunity "to run and play and laugh and make noise again—to really have a good time," and to meet other children their own age who are grieving as they are. In this way, children discover "they all share the same feelings . . . and that those feelings are normal, and they are OK for having them." Professional staff foster an atmosphere of love and acceptance. Camp Amanda charges no fee but serves only residents of Iowa. Wouldn't it be pretty to think that here is the beginning of a movement? In the summer of 1984, a week-long camp for children living with cancer, **Camp-A-Panda**, was offered for the first time by these same sponsors.

CARING FOR GRIEVING PARENTS

Formed in 1970, **The Candlelighters Foundation** (2025 I St., N. W., Washington, DC 20006; tel. 202/659–5136) is a loosely structured international federation of over 155 regional and local groups of parents of children suffering from or lost to cancer. The member groups have a variety of names and activities, but all are essentially self-help support groups, providing mutual aid, sympathy, listening, counseling, companionship, socializing—as needed. Many operate 24-hour telephone lines; some sponsor "junior auxiliaries" for teenage cancer patients or siblings.

The national organization assumes larger responsibilities. It serves as an educational and communications link among affiliated groups through newsletters, bibliographies, and other materials; helps in the formation of new local groups; sponsors regular gatherings of affiliates, many on the subject of new developments in research and treatment; conducts a parent-to-parent letter-writing program; and lobbies for increased federal funds for cancer research projects.

Parents, teachers, counselors, and other professionals may contact the national headquarters of Candlelighters or a local parents' group. These people are most happy to share, and are invaluable sources of information and insight. As noted above, group names may vary locally: for example, **LODAT** (Living One Day at a Time), **IMPACT** (Interested, Motivated Parents Against Cancer Today), **CURE** (Children's United Research Effort—St. Louis), **COPE** (Cincinnati Oncology Parents' Endeavor), **PALMS** (Parents Against Leukemia and Malignancies Society —Kansas), **Living with Cancer, Inc.** (Grand Rapids), **Parents Who've Lost Children** (Tucson), **First Sunday** (Detroit).

While The Candlelighters Foundation focuses its activities on parents of children with cancer, **The Compassionate Friends** (P. O. Box 1347, Oak Brook, IL 60521; tel. 312/323–5010) provides self-help, counseling, and communication to grieving parents no matter what the cause of their children's deaths. The rapid growth of this organization in recent years attests to the effectiveness of its operational philosophy and its programs. Over 400 local chapters nationwide provide support, friendship, listening, and caring, whether in meetings, social events, in letters, or on the telephone. Formal conferences are held periodically. This group publishes a nationally distributed newsletter and a number of audiovisual programs.

Similar in purpose to The Compassionate Friends, **Parents of Murdered Children** (1739 Bella Vista, Cincinnati, OH 45237; tel. 513/242–8025) works to meet the special needs of parents and family members of murdered children—needs arising from the sudden horror of the event, and the attendant intrusions from the law enforcement and criminal justice systems, from the media, and so on. Volunteers will contact—in writing or by phone—any parent of a murdered child and attempt to link that parent to other such parents or survivors in their area (chapters have been established in 15 states and Canada). Members of the group will also consult, on request, with professionals in medical, legal, social service, mental health, and funeral service fields, with police, with ministers, and with educators. They provide advice on forming local chapters of POMC, and have available a variety of informational pamphlets and a newsletter.

SUICIDE

Research and Education

Professionals in many specialties devoted to the study of suicide and suicide prevention are members of the **American Association of Suicidology** (2459 S. Ash, Denver, CO 80222; tel. 303/692–0985), the preeminent national group in the field. Its many educational programs and publications can also benefit general audiences. Tbe Association publishes a quarterly journal, *Suicide and Life-Threatening Behavior*; a triennial newsletter, "Newslink"; "Proceedings" of the annual meetings; a number of informative, low-cost booklets and pamphlets; a national directory of suicide prevention and crisis intervention agencies; and a directory of over 100 support groups in 32 states and Canada for bereaved *survivors* of suicide victims.

Prevention, Intervention, and Postvention

Since 1906 the **National Save-a-Life League** (815 Second Ave., Suite 409, New York, NY 10017) has provided counseling services for suicidal people and for family members. With over 100 affiliated groups nationwide, the League maintains a 24-hour hotline (212/736–6191), and offers financial assistance and a referral service to its clients.

The activities of the **Suicide Prevention Center of Los Angeles** (1041 South Menlo Ave., Los Angeles, CA 90006; tel. 213/386–5111) are typical of those performed by such centers elsewhere in the country. In addition to offering counseling and other services to clients and their families in Southern California, the Center conducts and publishes research (on drug addiction and alcoholism as well as on suicide), offers training workshops for professionals, runs a speaker service, and has available a variety of literature for professionals and general audiences.

A Boston organization with seven regional affiliates, **The Samaritans** (802 Boylston St., Boston, MA 02199) operates somewhat differently. Members of this group are trained volunteers who *befriend* suicidal, depressed, and lonely people. A unique outreach effort, "Lifeline," uses volunteer *prisoners* to counsel suicidal fellow prisoners in Boston-area jails. The Samaritans also provide a 24-hour walk-in counseling service and a hotline (617/247–0220), and conduct workshops for professionals and interested lay people.

Local offices (there are over 900 nationwide) of the **National Mental Health Association** (1800 North Kent St., Rosslyn, VA 22209; tel. 703/528–6405) may be consulted for information and help on suicide and indeed any mental/emotional health topic. While the Association does not provide direct services, it functions as a community referral center. In addition, it produces and distributes readings and audiovisual programs on a full range of topics including, for example, coping with divorce, death, and other losses, alcoholism and drug abuse, and depression, as well as suicide prevention and intervention.

INDEX